Senior Assailants

Scott Parry

ISBN:

Contents

Dedication

Years ago, I was out with my Mom and Dad when it became clear to me that absolutely nobody paid any attention to the two of them as they went about their day. Passersby would look directly at them without seeing them at all. They were both over eighty years old and they were invisible. We put this theory to the test immediately and I asked the two of them to walk into a restricted area at a local event to see if anyone would stop them from going past the "Employees Only" sign hanging on the closed door but not a soul said a word to them. They went into a restricted area and came back out ten minutes later without a word of warning from any employees. Over the next few months we tested the results at a variety of venues and the results were always the same…seniors are invisible. This is what lead me to the idea of Senior Assailants.

Chapter One

A few of the women had gathered in the waiting area of a posh downtown Toronto office. One by one they would arrive and take a seat in the multitude of available seats in the lounge. They would smile and nod in a congenial manner to each other, but they had actually never met the other ladies before in their lives. The entire group were strangers to each other, so they did not begin to socialize until they were given the directive to do so, and, they had not yet been given that instruction. An exceptionally well-dressed woman in her mid-thirties entered the waiting area and made an announcement, "Good morning, ladies. My name is Scarlet Larson, and I will be your liaison for the day. No matter what pops into your head today please let me know and we will acquire it at once. I am truly here to make your time with us go smoothly and for all of you to be as comfortable as possible. You will hear us referring to your comfort today and that is what we want to achieve so that you are all at ease with any decisions you may make today or in the future."

"Where are the bathrooms please?" One woman queried.

"Are you going to be serving coffee or will we get a break at some time?" said another.

Scarlet responded, "Once all of our invited guests have arrived, we can go into the presentation room and get started. It shouldn't be too much longer."

She left the area and headed to a closed door that seemed to house some offices for staff members, but they couldn't be exactly sure. The space was modern in style, and everything there seemed like it was bought and installed three days ago. Everything looked and smelled new. Floor to ceiling glass windows throughout with brushed aluminum window frames made the room feel boundless. White was the colour surrounding you, with the walls painted in a flat finish, and the doors contrasting in a high gloss. It looked like a room you would find yourself in at an art gallery. The ladies all looked away from one another for most of the time in an attempt to remain anonymous. A couple of them ventured over to the windows to take in the view from the fortieth floor overlooking Lake Ontario. It was quite breathtaking. Two more women came into the lobby and found seats and sat and waited for further instruction. There was now a total of ten women. Moments later the ten were addressed by Scarlet when she said, "Hello everyone, my name is Scarlet Larson, and I am here to assist you all through our scheduled day that we have planned out for you. If you could all follow me into the boardroom." She turned around and headed for the boardroom door, opened it, and held it open for the guests to make their way in. When they entered the room there was a twenty-foot-long boardroom table made from some exotic wood that had a shine in which you could see your own reflection. One end of the room was all glass and metal like the lobby area and the other three walls had no artwork at all. The room was sterile looking. Along one wall there was a ridiculously long buffet sporting copious amounts of coffee and tea supplies and soft drinks and bottled water set out for the guests. Scarlet still remained at the door waiting for one straggler, who had fallen asleep in her chair while she was waiting to get started. Scarlet whisked across the room and delicately roused her guest with a subtle nudge on her shoulder.

"Oh, my goodness," she piped up, "I must have drifted off for a moment. Is it time to go?" She asked.

"No. We are just going into the room now and we will be commencing in a few minutes." Scarlet said.

Scarlet now had all of the new guests corralled into the boardroom. She helped them get off unnecessary coats and other unwanted accessories. When that task was organized with coats into a closet, it was on to the coffee and tea. Scarlet whizzed around the room asking for coffee and tea preferences and saw to it that all guests now had a beverage and one of the treats from the sideboard. Minutes later the group was settled and sitting down facing towards a blank screen on the wall. The room was now silent.

"Good morning to all of you. My name is Scarlet Larson, and I will be your liaison for today's special meeting. We are part of the Ministry of Defense in a new team referred to as the "Special Projects Branch" which handles extremely sensitive international matters. We will be joined today by a variety of government experts in their fields to assess your skills and capabilities. There will be no physical exertion by anybody during our session, I promise. We are now waiting for the Director of Special Projects Branch who will begin your time here today with a full overview of what they have in mind for this dynamic group. At any given time today if you do not wish to continue for the entire day, please just let me know and we will make arrangements to get you home. A full hot lunch will be served at 12:30 to keep up everyone's energy. This is really a fact-finding mission for the Ministry, and we are convinced that this carefully selected group of people will be able to help the Canadian Government carry out some really spectacular assignments. I will go get the director now and be back with him momentarily, if that is okay with the group?" Scarlet looked around the room and didn't see any hands waving or people leaving so she took the opportunity to go alert the director.

She lightly rapped on the tall wooden door, rap, rap, rap. "Please enter," a voice from behind the desk said.

"Hello Mr. Smits. The group is assembled, and they have been given the opening brief. They all have no idea at all as to why they are here." Scarlet said.

"Fantastic Miss Larson. I will be there in just a minute." Jimmy said.

Scarlet reappeared in the board room and announced that the Director would be joining them momentarily. Then she sat at a desk in the corner, pulled out a lap-top and began getting ready to take minutes from the meetings. There was a similarity to the group of women assembled, they were all over seventy years old. It was clear that they all could walk and had some degree of mobility, but this group of seniors wasn't going to run a 10K run in the future. So far, they had two things in common with each other, their age, and their gender. At no time did any of the participants notice this fact at all. As of yet. They all sat quietly and continued to drink their beverages and eat some light pastries when the door swung open, and a rather large man entered the room. He was a towering six feet seven inches tall and weighed about three hundred pounds. He could have easily passed for a BC Lion's football team lineman. His head was shaved perfectly without a mark or blemish anywhere. It was practically shiny. He sported a dark navy-blue suit fastened in the three-button style,

which added to his height, and a crisp white shirt with a Merrick tie and matching pocket square. He looked like he was about to host the Juno Awards, but such was not the case. He had other things on his agenda that day.

"Hello," his deep bass voice pressed out. "My name is Jim Smits. I am the current Director of Special Projects, and we operate under the Ministry of Defense which means we report our findings to the Ministry directly and they provide the financial aid for our operations. This is a new directive for the Ministry, and we are delighted that all of you were able to attend our brainstorming mission. There are many things we have to discuss with all of you but for today we will all stay together and work as a group. During our time together please let me know if you, for even one second, do not feel comfortable with our vision or any topic that may come up. We need your valuable feedback but, if you ever feel intimidated or scared, merely let us know and we will give you a ride right to your door, wherever that might be. We have chosen you all from different cities throughout Canada to provide us with the broadest view of the country through your eyes. I am sure that most of you have realized that everyone in this group is over seventy years old and represents the senior demographic of the country. This day is a fact-finding mission to see if we can stop the forces of evil entering this great country that we call home. Please let us know if you need any breaks throughout the day. We do not want you feeling uncomfortable for any reason. With that being said, I want to begin with a short video to get things moving along." He aimed the small black controller in his hand towards the wall and suddenly a screen appeared, and a video began loading. While the video was buffering all of the windows at the end of the room had black out screens dropping down to block out the daylight, which by the time the blinds hit the bottom, was completely blacked out and the room was pitch dark. The blank screen flickered to life and the video presentation began. The group all stared intently at the TV and the video commanded their complete attention.

The narrative of the video was a simple message, family is everything. The film showed families doing several different types of events together and talked about how great planning leads to great rewards as people get older and try to decide who and what to do with family legacies. The message was clear, love thy family. Pass on your successes to your family because you can't take it with you. It was beautifully filmed, and they had used a multitude of different locations, so it was clear that money had been spent on the production of this video, which also meant there was a good chance that the Special Projects was going to be well funded. The big question was -why were they there today? How could this group of seniors help a government agency? Maybe it was a tax survey and all they would have to tell the Ministry was to charge less taxes. That would definitely be a repeating theme. The video presentation played out to its end, and the screen went black. The lights in the room did not turn back on instantly which made a few of the ladies slightly uncomfortable but they all stayed perfectly still having no idea what was coming next. Mr. Smits voice came over the speakers and said, "Please do not be alarmed ladies.

Our research has shown us that if you eliminate some of your senses the others can become heightened in their sensitivity. I would like to speak to all of you when you are at ease with no disruptions going on around you. I am aware that you have never met or seen each other until today. You all come from different cities from across the country and all of you are over sixty-five years of age. You all come from well-educated families and have never been divorced. Most of you have had children, different quantities, and different genders. Your amassed family incomes are all terribly similar to each other and you all grew up, and currently live in a middle, middle class neighbourhood with two cars and one vacation per year. I assume that all of you here today would describe your lives as great. Well, what we are proposing to you today is to make your lives even better."

The lights remained off for a few minutes of silence and then Mr. Smits said, "There is one more thing that none of you know but it is part of the reason why we have brought you all here to chat with us about you and your family's future. Our job, simply put, is to make life for you and your families better. It's that simple. So now we are going to have the real talk about all of your futures…they are not going to last much longer. I mentioned that you do not know each other or your back stories so I will bring all of you up to speed. You have all been diagnosed with at least stage two cancer and from my conversations with your primary physicians, none of you are scheduled to survive more than one year from today. These are not odds. These are facts. Each one of you has some form of incurable cancer and what we are proposing to you all is to make the rest of your time on earth be taken to an extreme level of care. The Kennedy's would blush when they see what we have prepared for all of you. We are offering for the balance of you and your families' lives be taken to a level of care you did not know even existed in Canada. Your every need attended to by the highest quality professionals in their fields. We are also telling you that, even after you have left this world and your body, the agency will continue to take care of your entire families for the rest of their lives. No more financial worries for the rest of your days. Seems too good to be true, right?"

The lights in the room came halfway back on so the room wasn't bright but still they could see each other's faces again. The white walls, that looked blank, sprang to life and began showing family pictures of children playing and shots of Christmases gone by and birthdays and reunions when suddenly one of the woman recognized her own children in one of the pictures. As the minutes went by and the women kept gazing around the room at all of the photos it became clear that all of the portrayed photos were of the women in the room and just their families. Within a short time, there was not a dry eye in the house. They saw that the Ministry had somehow obtained these private family photos and put them on display for all to see. Enough minutes had passed that the women were seeing they had all been brought to this office for something awfully specific and not just a random chance. One of the attendees said, “And so how do we attain this utopia for our families Mr. Smits?”

“That is the question that I have been waiting for one of you to ask me. You know that we are aware of your medical conditions, and we have all of your financial information since you were born, but in order to get to the promised land of zero financial burdens the Government of Canada would like to ask you a couple of questions. Please do not feel that you have to answer any of these questions today, but they are serious questions that you will need to answer before we finish our sessions here with you over the next couple of days. So, our proposal is this, we will give each of you one million dollars for yourselves if anything should happen to you as a life insurance policy, AND we will also give one million dollars to every living family member to absorb the burden of your families’ losing their Matriarch. No matter what. No questions asked. All of your surviving family will all receive one million dollars to assist in moving ahead with their lives once you are gone. This is a bizarre thing to hear from anybody at any time in one’s life, but we have been given a new initiative from the Federal Government to help eliminate some serious problems around the world.” Jimmy walked over to the control panel and aimed his pointer towards it and the room lights came back up and all could see one another clearly again. Mr. Smits then said, “I want everyone to have a little break to get up and stretch your legs before we start back up. I will have some snacks brought in for you all to nosh on before we start up again. Is everybody doing okay so far?” he asked the group. No words were spoken and just some nodding and a couple of the ladies went down the hall to visit the lavatories.

Jimmy whisked himself into the back control room which was just down the corridor through a clandestine door. Inside the room the boardroom was wired from front to back. They had cameras and listening devices in every inch of the room to hear the feedback from their unknowing guests. The information gathered from these meeting was always valuable and would often help lead groups through some of the difficult transitions the common folk would have to go through. There were ten cameras and twenty microphones so there was no way that they were not going to hear the feedback from the women attendees that day. “Everything set Tim?” Jimmy askes one of the technicians.

“Everything is a go boss. We are ready for round two. How about you, how are you holding out?” Tim said.

“I am absolutely ready for round two. I can’t wait to hear the reaction from this group of people. Should be extremely interesting.” Jim stated.

Within a few minutes, Scarlet was walking to each member of the group, addressing them all individually and guiding them back towards to the room with the boardroom table. Presently she had completed her task of getting all ten of the women back into their seats at the table.

Shortly after, Mr. Smits returned to the room. He was smiling in a polite way, but it was clear that he was moving on to a new topic and he was looking for the group's undivided attention.

"Ladies, we cannot thank you enough for being here today. Some of you had to travel many miles and had to be separated from loved ones for a while but now is the time that I will start to introduce you to the Government of Canada's new plan. We would like to implement this immediately to be managed by the Special Projects group. I want to speak frankly so we can get on with our presentation, so I will not dance around facts. They can cloud things so quickly and keep us from hitting our main objective. So, on that, all of you know that within twelve months you will get sick and die from your disease. This is a fact. Some of you may live longer through prayer or surgery but we have looked at thousands of case studies and we do not believe that there is any chance that any of you will survive your cancer. For this unfortunate demise, I am deeply sorry. On the other hand, this is where we come in. As I started with, we are proposing that we will make your family thrive for the rest of their lives and they will never know it was all your doing. If you choose to follow our proposed path you must keep this a secret inside of yourself for life, simple. We encourage you to discuss this with your significant other but then they will be asked to participate with whatever it is we have in store you. They too would have to maintain the covert status of the operation for life. Is everyone following along so far? How about a show of hands. Does the group get everything so far?" Jimmy asked the group.

No show of hands but some nodding. One women shot her hand up and asked, "So what do we have to do to get free lifelong Medicare. Who do you want us to sanction." She giggled out loud.

"Funny you would ask that because I'm going to tell you. Currently one of the world's largest kingpins in the human trafficking rings of children under the age of ten lives in the Philippines. We know where, we know how many, we know when, but our hands are tied. We cannot just waltz into someone else's country and shoot all of the bad men because we want to. There are laws protecting these people and it makes them all ridiculously hard to find and bring to justice. Virtually impossible, however; imagine an elderly couple on holidays in a foreign country not knowing where they are or what they are doing. These are the types of people that could easily move around a city without even being noticed. Once mom breaks out the walker and dad stumbles along behind saying "What's that dear, I can't hear you," other countries security systems fail miserably because they never assume that some old couple is there to plant an explosive device under the chair of the current ruler. They would never see it coming." Mr. Smits finished.

"And just how are we to get away once we plant that bomb under the chair?" One of the ladies queried.

"You don't. The price you will pay to make every member of your family a millionaire is that you surrender your life. There is no getaway car or a massive shootout. This is you making sure the bomb is in the correct spot and goes off at the correct time. There is no second act, no encore. You must make sure that the sanction is completed correctly or the deal's off. Once you try and put a hit on these type of people, they will disappear for years yet still run their operations from overseas. These kind of criminals are the most dangerous men alive, and they will do anything to keep themselves at the top of the heap." Jimmy said. "You do not reason with these people."

"So, you want us to be murderers, killers?" One women added.

"We are proposing that you become problem eliminators for the Federal Government of Canada. You already know what will become of yourselves within a year, all we are proposing is that maybe your sacrifice is worth something to the Canadian people that they would be happy to give you themselves if they had the means. Some of these tasks are situations that are no longer issues that we as a country can keep overlooking year after year. Can you even imagine the heartbreak of having one of your granddaughters kidnapped and sold into slavery and prostitution. It would be devastating. If we were able to nip this in the bud before some of these violent offenders can disappear back into the landscape of the world and have them answer to the call of justice. It is rare because these criminals are well insulated from the real world and their abundance of funding makes it virtually impossible." Jim said.

"There is no way I could pull off what you are proposing. It is utterly ridiculous. A guest added.

"You are wrong. Old people are invisible. Put a pink and yellow track suit on anyone over seventy and nobody's going to notice you at all. Over the next couple of days, we have some exercises that we had planned out for you to put our theory to the test. Can an old person walk into a bank and accidently walk into the vault? Yes. It is going to happen to you, and you will be astounded. You can go anywhere, and no one will question it. If you get asked a direct questions you fall back on the "I don't know where I am...have you seen my husband?" routine. It works every time. What I would like to propose to all of you right now is that we call it a day and reconvene tomorrow. I know that this will give you a chance to relax and think of any further questions you may have for me or my team. The last thing we want to do is to overwhelm you on the first day. We have arranged for limousines to return you to the hotel so you can have something to eat and drink and take in the information that you heard today. When we meet again tomorrow all of your questions and concerns will be addressed. The final piece of information is a simple one, you speak to no one. Do not share this chat today with any family, friend, co-worker, at any time or there will be consequences. For all of your sake's, please follow our rules for the next couple of days and if you decide this is not for you, we will send you back home like it never took place. Okay everyone, have a wonderful evening and we will continue here in the morning. Again, thank you all for your time and patience with us. It is really appreciated." Mr. Smits said.

The women all stood and began gathering their things so they could catch the elevator down to the lobby. Jimmy watched the women on the monitors in the security office to see what reactions he could spot, and any comments being exchanged between the participants. This was the first time that all the women had revealed that they each had terminal cancer at different stages. They didn't even know each other's names as of yet, but that was still part of the plan. How resourceful were these ladies. Could they think independently or were they too old and worn out to even wear a vest bomb into an office tower full of slave traders and press the kaboom button. Time would tell.

The ladies all made their way to the lobby where the cars were waiting to take them back to the hotel. Five women went to one hotel and the other five went to a different hotel. Jimmy wanted to see if the women even noticed that the group had been separated from each other. They made their way through the rotating door onto the street and into the cars. Surprisingly, five of the women that were all staying at the Royal York went in one car together and the other five all went to the same hotel in different cars, so you never know how certain information is going to hit you. Jimmy was fascinated by these small minute details, but all mattered to him. This was a new position and he wanted everything to go right. He was given the task to help Canada to start cleaning up some of the deadwood floating around his country and he wanted to help cleanse his homeland from these polluted villains. He was also eager to listen in on the conversation of the women on their drive back to the hotel. Then Jimmy looked at his phone screen and could see that Scarlet was calling. He took the call.

"Hello Scarlet, how can I help you?" He asked.

"Small problem sir, one of your test subjects was trying to reach her husband." Scarlet said.

"And…did she?" Jimmy asked.

"Yes, she did. She immediately began to talk about the clandestine operation, so we canceled the phone call before she was able to tell her husband anything of value. She thought she had dropped the phone line, but she will attempt to make contact when she is back at the hotel, I think. Her hotel room has been bugged so let's monitor her progress throughout the evening and see if she says anything that she shouldn't be passing along." Scarlet responded.

"All right then. Monitor her calls closely and if she attempts anything again let me know and I will have the Doctor pay her a visit. They were all told to keep a secret and failing that there would be consequences for those actions. They just don't realize how serious yet." Mr. Smits said.

Three hours later Jimmy got another message from Scarlet. It seems that one of the participants could not stop herself from trying to contact her husband, but the call wouldn't go through. She picked up the house phone on the nightstand and called her husband. One ring, two rings, three rings and then it went dead. That was odd. It also wouldn't ring through. Maybe the cell service was having a bad day. She heard a quiet knocking at her room door and went over to answer. She peeked through the eye hole and saw handsome young man standing outside of her door. "Can I help you sir?" she asked.

"Hi there, I am Dr. Thomas Cook from the Special Projects agency to check up on you. We take all of your vitals every day to make sure we are not working you too hard if you have a few minutes to spare. Or if you wish I can come back later tonight." He said.

"Alright then. We might as well get this done now so I don't have to be disturbed later." She said as she opened the door to her room.

He stepped inside the room, closed the door behind himself, and said, "This will only take a minute, I promise."

Ten minutes later Dr. Thomas Cook vacated her room.

Chapter Two

The following morning the group reconvened at ten o'clock in the lobby area outside of the boardroom. A few of the ladies had chatted together the previous night but they really did not know each other at all. They would have a difficult time recognizing each other on the street, with the exception of the few ladies that had mingled a little bit. When Scarlet arrived to open the boardroom doors one of the women asked, "What happened to the other lady that was here? I don't see her amongst us this morning."

"Not to worry ladies. Mr. Smits will bring you all up to speed once we get started. You all know the routine, please grab a coffee or tea, and collect a treat before you take your seats. He will be with you momentarily to get things under way. Thank you." Scarlet said in her sweetest voice.

Fifteen minutes later Mr. Smits entered the room smiling and beaming like a new contestant on a game show. However, when he walked to the head of the table and faced the audience his countenance blackened and with a sober look upon his face, he addressed the group. "I have some rather disturbing news to share with you this morning but there is no easy way for me to deliver this to you. Mrs. Forsham, the missing member of our little group, will not be attending any further meetings. Last evening, she suffered a major stroke event and, in spite of the excellent care in the ICU at the hospital, she has died due to complications with her heart. This is one of the factors that the Ministry has been concerned about when adding mental stress to elderly people but there is no easy way to help save your country. It takes all of us Canadians to band together to crush evil and tyranny. That is what this group's sole purpose is, to weed out some of society's deadliest people to make our country a better place where we can remain free from oppression. My staff and I feel just terrible about the loss of a genuinely great Canadian citizen that came to the call of duty for her country when they needed her the most. She will be survived by her husband and family and will be deeply missed by this Ministry and her friends."

Jimmy walked across the room and dramatically poured himself a cup of coffee and pressed one hand to his forehead with a "I cannot believe this awful thing has happened," look for the effect on the others in the room. He managed to squeeze one tiny tear drop that rolled down his cheek at the perfect time as he arrived at the edge of the boardroom table and began to review some notes on a page. A couple of the other women noticed the teardrop and saw him wipe it away, but they now knew the truth. This man really cares about these people. He is a man we can trust.

"We cannot allow this tragedy to slow us down or impede our progress. We have to pick ourselves up and keep moving forward in the spirit of justice." Mr. Smits announced. He leaned forward and put his two hands on the edge of the table, applied his body weight and looked at all of the women one by one. He made eye contact with each person before he said, "Your country needs you now like it never has before. There are too many shady characters about for just our police and military forces to fend them all off. These loathsome sods are watching for us to push back using the same legal methods that have been effective over the years, but slowly they have learned our processes. The criminals know who we are and how we will attack. They are ready for us at all times. We need to find new sources, new ways to infiltrate the enemy and bring them down. That is where this new task force comes into play. You can be our front line while they are busy looking in the wrong direction. If we are able to hit these organizations and take out some of their key leaders, although we won't stop them from being criminals, we can slow them down by fragmenting their organizations and causing chaos. This would give our police forces a chance to tip the balance of good and evil. We know we will never eliminate all of the heinous crimes that happen but if we could remove some of their top brass, it would be amazing for our troops and officers. Some of these illegal operations could take months before they could get back on track or even more perfect is that they can't recover from legal action, or a raid and we can focus our efforts in other areas and hopefully continue our success against this tyranny."

He stood back up and straightened out his back and continued to look around the room from face to face to see if he could tell yet which ones will have what it takes, and which ones would fade into oblivion. Time would tell. He had never worked with civilians in this type of operation, but his ego told him that he could manage to get some seniors to see his way of thinking. Jimmy's goal was simple, protect his country against scumbags, whatever it took.

He pressed a button on his remote control and the screen illuminated. He kept the content paused as he looked at the group and said, "I would like to show you a video of some of the worldwide operations that we would like to slow down or possibly eliminate, for good. These videos are not a movie made for your entertainment, these are videos of innocent people who live in and around this tyranny every day. You may find that this is disturbing content, but we want to make sure that you all understand the magnitude of this situation. There are a lot of wicked people out there and unfortunately you are about to see first-hand what they do, and, in some circumstances, how they do it. Once you have seen these images you can't unsee them, so I am asking this group right now for the last time, are you up to the task? If not, you are free to walk out that door and go back to your life and families to live out what time you have left. As you know, there will be no compensation paid to you for a job that you did not complete. In order to qualify for the money, you've got to help your fellow citizens irradicate these black souls of society. So, who doesn't feel up for a video?" Jimmy asked.

There was silence in the room, so absolute that the air was heavy with apprehension. He was not beating around the bush. He had asked for the group to make their final decision today. He could not take the chance of having a member of the group expose them for what they were aiming to accomplish, like going out and killing some bad people. The group sat silently for a couple of full minutes. Finally, Mrs. Maria Coleman asked, "What if something happens to us before we can accomplish the task you have selected for us? What if we pass on or die before we can get it done, do our families still get the money?"

"That would be based on how much of the task you had completed, however; the Government of Canada is asking you to take a tremendous risk with the remainder of your life and for that they will pay everyone in full for whatever you do. The only way you would not be paid is if you exposed the operation to the general public because then there would be legal fights and public hearings to seek out the truth, which we do not have time for anymore. We need to act now, and you are the candidates that we believe can get the job done." Mr. Smits relayed to them.

"My doctor told me I have a year maximum to live. How soon do I need to do something for you in order to qualify for the money. If my health fails to the point that I am not able to move about what happens then?" One of the women asked.

"You will be paid in full. No matter what. You will have to take our secret information to the grave with you. Never an utterance to a soul for as long as you live." Mr. Smits said.

He stood in place and saw there was a hint of doubt creeping into the room. The "what ifs" had appeared and needed to be dealt with, quickly.

"Ladies, may I suggest that we take a short recess to allow all of you to clear your minds and make some final difficult decisions. The money is not an issue because you will all be financially rewarded for your sacrifices; the real issue is, can you do it. Can a senior pull off the sanctioning of a major syndicate crime boss? This is the only question in front of all of you at this moment." Mr. Smits said.

He vacated the room in a hasty manner. Before anybody could ask another question, he was out the door and down the hall. Scarlet appeared and double checked the coffee and tea supplies and then she too disappeared. Jimmy and Scarlet hurried back into the control room and watched the monitors to see the group's reactions. It took some time, but the women did start to interact with each other and began to tell their thoughts to one another. This is what Jimmy had been waiting for. A chance to see each person's mettle. Could they pull off this morally reprehensible act or were they just too politely Canadian of a housewife to imagine doing such a deed. Within a few minutes they were all smiling because some of the women were absolutely on a mission to garner as much money as they could from the Canadian Government. They had paid taxes all their lives and now this was a chance to get some of this money back, at least for their families. There would be some comfort in knowing that they had helped their loved ones live a financially healthier life. The astonishing thing taking place was that no one had walked out yet: just given up. They all had the choice to walk out the door, head to airport and fly home first class and be done with this nonsense, however; there was a current of curiosity to see where all this covert stuff was going. None of the women were trained spies but it sure would be an amazing finishing story. Jimmy, Scarlet, Tim, and Dr. Thomas all watched the group interacting with one another and beginning to weigh the pros and cons. So far, they felt there was a stronger yes vibe than no. Dr. Thomas glanced at his watch and said to Jimmy, "You had better get back in there and put them through the visuals of supreme violence. Let's see how many will be left after the lunch break. This is the first real test."

Jimmy left the room and headed back to the boardroom and reconvened with the guests. "I want to apologize for my delay. Prime Minister Trudeau wanted an update on our task force's position with regards to our potential recruits and their progress to date. I take complete responsibility for all of this dilly-dallying about when I should simply show you the video and let you make your own decision. Would that be alright with you all?" As he lowered his voice to a whisper and unpaused the frozen screen on the wall, the video began. Only one of the women was standing when the video started but quickly all of the women were in their seats, transfixed to the monitor with the surround sound system blaring away, making it feel like you were practically there with the people on the screen. The film only showed quick flashes of death and destruction, and then parks and waterfalls, and back to children enslaved by hooded abductors. It juxtaposed life and death, and good and evil, in way that made you want to get up and take a stand for the rights of all these tormented souls. There were many shots of happy, loving families eating amazing meals and sharing good times and long-lasting memories, and then back to disease victims in hospital wards clinging to life. It was like watching some parts of a Quentin Tarantino movie. Clever mixed with gruesome. Jimmy looked at his watch and knew there was only a few minutes left. He scoured the room with his eyes looking for any breaks or weaknesses in their selected candidates.

"We are in a crisis right now and your country needs your help. You are doing this for your country, and your family." The video announcer finished with.

"Was that the real Justin Trudeau? His hair looked terrific." One of the ladies said.

"That was really him. The Prime Minister has covert information on some of these notorious criminals and their whereabouts, which is part of what we do. You will get an opportunity to meet him right here once you have completed your orientation. What I would like to suggest is that we take a lunch break for a couple hours to relax and unwind and possibly meet back here to chat a bit more? Does that sound agreeable to everybody?" Mr. Smits proffered this as a suggestion.

All of the women looked around the room to see what each other's reaction was to the video. It was so much to take in; however, some of the heads were already nodding in positive agreement. Many of them had never seen videos of people being injured or killed on TV in their lives. It was a lot for a group of senior women to digest and in addition, the very thought of meeting the Prime Minister in person was like meeting Her Royal Highness the Queen. Something they just could not fathom would ever happen to them. It was clear that the women were definitely interested in meeting the Prime Minister of Canada because it would be the honour of a lifetime. The nine remaining participants all seemed to be looking back and forth at each other waiting for someone to make the first move. Scarlet stepped in immediately and said, "If all of you could please follow me down the hall we have a lunch set up for your enjoyment. We have every person's special requirements so if you do not see something suitable, please let me know."

The group followed quietly to the lunchroom area and began to peruse the lunch food selections. They all meandered about until they had filled their plates with lunch selections and started chatting with one another. The room had tables that sat four people each, so Mr. Smits and his team were curious to see who would sit with whom and about what they would talk. Every room in the building (including washrooms) was wired from top to bottom to be sure not to miss a single comment that may affect their plans. They knew all too well that many people get into detailed conversations in restrooms, and they couldn't afford to miss out on anything. They had to see and hear the effect they were having on the group in order to assess their abilities and what they may be willing to do to help their families and their country. Their compliance was also the sign Jimmy was looking for to be sure that he had selected the best possible candidates for doing some heroine-type activities. He would reveal more of their expectations later, but for now all the women needed to do was to eat lunch and relax. They continued to watch the monitors and listen intently so they could follow along with the groups' emotional state at this point in time. Only one woman made some negative comments about the video content, but she was also intrigued with the idea of actually meeting the Prime Minister. It was absolutely unanimous that meeting Justin Trudeau was the highlight of this adventure among all of the ladies. Jimmy knew that the attrition rate of these ladies following through with the entire orientation was going to be critical to their overall success, but the team knew that they had to push on and see who was still going to be in the room by the end of the day. Jimmy left the monitor room, went down the hallway and entered the lunchroom. He headed over to the foods displayed so beautifully and made a couple of selections and looked for an empty seat at an occupied table.

"Oh my goodness," he exclaimed, "This Shepherd's pie is delicious. I hate to say it may be better than my wife's recipe, but I will lie if you were to tell her that." He said to the table. The comment was met with a few giggles as Jimmy tried seeming very approachable and sincere. He started to ask general questions to the people sitting at his table so he could assess what their frame of mind was at the time. They had just gone through their "Clockwork Orange" video presentation and the true goal of the video was to see if the group could turn off their righteous ethics and consider the bigger picture that was being presented to them. The Ministry still needed these women to perform acts of cruelty, but it was against despicable men who did not deserve to ruin the lives of innocents. Jimmy had read all the data collected from these nine women and he was exceedingly confident that at least half of them would be capable of seeing their assignment through.

"How is the Royal York Hotel? Are you finding it comfortable? Please let me or my staff know if there is anything you are missing, and it will be brought to your room." Jimmy said.

"I had no idea that they had rooms so big in the hotel. I've never been to the top floors of the building, but it is spectacular. The view, the suite, the food is all just so fantastic. I feel like one of those children on Make A Wish when they get to go and do something incredible for their last hurrah. It is like a movie where somehow, I got to be a cast member." Mrs. Fletcher said.

"We are so glad that you are enjoying our hospitality. After lunch today once we all reassemble in the boardroom, we are going to move along rapidly. This is when we really lay it all out for you. Then you will be taken back to the hotel for the night and in the morning transportation to your next destination will take place. You will be given some reading from us to make certain that you clearly understand our vision and how everything will come together. It will be an easy pace and should connect all of the pieces together for you. Should be an interesting chat." Jimmy finished.

Mr. Smits stood and made his way to the exit door and turned back to face the group and said, "How about we all reconvene in one hour?" He looked at all of the faces to check for any heads nodding or shaking the wrong way. So far, so good. "Wonderful. I will see you all when you return to the boardroom." He left the room and returned to the monitoring room with Scarlet, Tim, and Dr. Thomas Cook to discuss the afternoon's presentation. Tim had noticed that one of the participants was showing signs of stress in her movements and her demeanour. Patricia Patterson from Calgary was tearing up and looking away from the screen during some of the parts of the video, mostly all of the violent segments. They would keep a watchful eye on her and see if there were any chinks in her personal mental armor. They needed to recruit people that could complete their tasks once they were assigned, without faltering. Failure was not an option.

"Let's keep a watch on her in the next session. This is where it gets intriguing. Who still has the moxie to commit a crime? We'll have a much better read on them by the end of the day." Jimmy said.

Scarlet swung open the glass doors leading into the boardroom and most of the women returned to the chairs that they had previously sat in. Patricia however, sat in the chair closest to the glass exit doors, which at least demonstrated that she had the ability to adapt and change on the fly. Most people would have instantly gone back to their previous spot so Patricia kind of surprised the leaders. Was she showing potential or fear? It was time to get engaged in the second half of the day, which was literally - would you, could you, should you - by giving a show of hands, however; all of their responses were being recorded so that the outcomes could be analyzed at a later time.

Jimmy entered the room and took his place at the front. He picked up his remote control, pointed it at the wall and seconds later a list of questions appeared.

"The purpose of this next exercise is to determine some of your basic character traits. Nothing more, nothing less. This is a simple show of hands as we go through the information. Does everyone comprehend? I need you to pick an answer for every question. There are no "I'm not sure" responses in this section. Is that perfectly clear to everyone? Good, let's get started." Jimmy said.

The screen came to life with these questions:

1. Would you lie?
2. Have you lied?
3. Are you skilled at lying?
4. Have you lied today?
5. Would you cheat?
6. Would you steal?

The list went on and on and the attendees followed along and raised their hands for yes or no until Mr. Smits got to the last question, would you kill? The moment the group had all been waiting for, how many hands would raise up in an affirmative vote? Instantly they had some strong candidates to work with. Jimmy was delighted to see four of women raise their hands. One of the women hovered in the maybe zone until Mr. Smits said to her, "Is that a yes or a no, Mrs. Winehouse?"

"It's a concerned yes. You are only referring to bad men, right? This is not women and children that you are asking this question about, is that correct?" Lexy Winehouse waited for a confirmation.

"Some people say abortion is killing. It is hard to find the line in the sand that makes everything okay to commit a crime. For our purposes, let us assume that all of the bad guys are grown-up men. Does that help you with your decision?" Mr. Smits asked.

"Then this is an absolute yes." Lexy said extending her arm into the air to demonstrate her "yes" vote.

Jimmy was completely floored. They had five yes votes after the basic orientation which couldn't have been more encouraging for the Ministry group. Their plan was underway and now they had something to work with. The key now was to not overwhelm the ladies with copious amounts of information but rather slow the mood down and get their minds off the idea of killing somebody. They switched the screen to a video package that was all bells ringing, flowers blooming, rainbows arcing, children laughing and several photos flashing by of happiness and people of all ages hugging and smiling. Every time Jimmy and the staff watched this video, they felt a bit pumped up about family and country. These are two things that they wanted to impress upon this group from the start. It is an amazing feat to help your family, but it's truly heroic to help your country. Jimmy knew he had five rock solid contenders that could help the Ministry weed out criminals and disrupt their operations. It was an exciting moment. Just as the video was ending Jimmy announced a champagne toast for all of the challenging work these ladies had done over the past two days and how invaluable their service to their country has been. Scarlet wheeled in a rolling cart with an ice bucket filled with bubbly and popped the cork and filled some glasses. The five "yes's" all said yes to a glass of champagne, and the no's turned it down. The Ministry group assumed they did not have anything to celebrate. Jimmy realized that he would need to take another approach with the four "no" votes. He smirked to himself and thought, "It's been a long time since I had to do the old song and dance to see if I could win someone over." He would have Scarlet arrange times for him to visit the Royal York Hotel that evening and see if he could influence any of them to be swayed to his way of thinking. If not, they would cross that bridge when they got to it.

The group actually felt at ease finally because they all knew they were going back to their respective homes tomorrow. They hadn't got to know the other women at all, but they were told that none of them should really try and make friendships when they are assisting the Government of Canada with an operation of this nature. The less they knew about each other, the better off they would be. However, all of that was about to change. Those five "yes's" had given the group a new hope. Could they get good Samaritans to kill?

The group dispersed and headed for the ground transportation back to the hotel. Scarlet pulled the four "no" votes aside and set up meetings with each of them in their suites with Mr. Smits, accompanied by Miss Larsen, which they all agreed to. Jimmy and Scarlet knew they had just one chance to convince the four negatives into four positives. They were up for the challenge.

Chapter Three

The car pulled up in front of the main entrance to the Royal York Hotel and the bellmen whisked open the door for Mr. Smits and Miss Larsen. They exited the car and made their way into the posh interiors of the iconic building. This hotel was a feast for the eyes and had every element that defines luxury. The rooms were all so exquisite that one just looked from area to area with mouths agape, however, you never let anyone see you showing any signs of awe. One had to pretend that they had seen all of this a million times before. They crossed the main lobby and found the elevator core and waited for an available lift. Moments later the elevator bell rang to identify its readiness, and they entered. Scarlet reached out her hand and selected the PH – Penthouse Units, and the doors quietly slid shut. Seconds later they had arrived at the top, they left the elevator and headed down the hall to Mrs. Ivy Miller's room.

"Well, you ready for this?" Jim asked her.

"I was born for this. Let's get four out of four Jimmy. If we close this tonight, we can get moving ahead on the strategies side rather than the recruitment aspect. I am looking forward to beginning the operation and getting down to the significant business of ending heinous criminals, for good." Scarlet said.

"Agreed. I do not believe that Ivy will be hard to break. The only major issue working against us is that she has Stage

3 cancer so we just don't know how much longer she will be able to move about or travel, if necessary. According to our files, she has got all of her affairs in order, so she is well prepped for the inevitable. Her husband is also quite ill so we don't know if she will be willing to leave him alone for any considerable lengths of time. I guess we will probably find out tonight." Jimmy said. He reached out one of his giant-sized hands and rapped on the door. Swiftly the door opened to reveal Ivy Miller standing in a white cotton Royal York housecoat from the closet and a large cocktail of some sort in her hand.

"Mr. Smits, Miss Larsen, please come in and join me for a cocktail." Ivy said.

She sauntered down the short hallway into the open living room area and found her way over to a large soft looking sofa and flopped herself onto the seat. "Please," she paused and waved her hand about at all the remaining furniture, "find a seat. I have tried them all and they are all exceptionally comfortable. How on earth did they find so many comfy, cozy objects to sit upon. I do not think that they purchased this furniture from the Brick." Ivy said.

Mr. Smits walked over to a large-scale, heavy looking chair and lowered his huge frame deftly into it and allowed the cushions to envelope him. Miss Larsen went over to the bar and offered, "May I pour any of you a drink?"

“I would love a gin and tonic with plenty of ice.” Jimmy said.

“Oh, that sounds refreshing, I want one of those too please.” Mrs. Miller agreed.

“No problem. Would you prefer a lime or lemon twist Mr. Smits?” She asked Jimmy.

“Lime please.” Jim said.

“And you Mrs. Miller? Lime or lemon?” Scarlet said.

“Hmm, good question. Make mine a lime please Miss Larsen.” Ivy responded.

Scarlet efficiently concocted the drinks and passed them out on a lovely silver serving tray provided at the bar. She meandered her way around the furniture and sat down in close proximity to Ivy.

“I sure am glad that you weren’t too shocked today from seeing some of the content of those Government video productions. I know they can be upsetting because they can give me nightmares if I look at them for too long. It is especially important that you know how grateful the Canadian people are to true humanitarians like yourself Ivy. Even the fact that you are considering our proposal shows us your mettle, and we appreciate your positivity and your valuable time. Thank you so much.” Jimmy said.

“You are such an honourable citizen. You make us all proud to be Canadian.” Scarlet added.

"This is the time when your country needs your help to squelch some of the tyranny that runs rampant throughout the nation. When we first contacted you for this special opportunity it was because we all knew your condition and how serious your situation would become for you and your family. The unfortunate reality is that you have incurable cancer, and it will take your life within the next twelve months. I am sorry, but it is that cut and dry. This Ministry is begging for your help to aid us in eradicating some of these bad eggs from our society and in return, the Government of Canada will improve the lives of your family long after you are gone. I know that I told you that you will not need to spend your last days on earth hiding in a bunker somewhere or hanging out with loathsome characters in a half-way house for recovering criminals. This task force will require you to do one thing for us and you will only do it once. When you have completed the assignment, you can go back to your family and live out the balance of your days with the best care that money can buy. This is your chance to make the rest of their lives be the best they can be with all of the spoils. Does this make any sense to you Ivy?" He said.

"I'm scared. I am afraid to die, and I am petrified to shoot a bad guy. I don't think I could do something like that even if you had given me years of training. Pulling the trigger of a gun when someone's back is towards me would be easier, but I still don't know if I have it in me. I want to help you so badly, and I know that the family would be forever grateful to know that they would all be looked after when I am gone, but, at this point, the thought of killing another human being is reprehensible." Ivy concluded.

"That makes perfect sense Ivy. We both know what a kind and decent person you are." Added Scarlet.

"I have something that may make you feel a bit less angst with this state of affairs. We are not asking you to shoot a fellow human being in the back. What we want from you is to simply enter a building through the front door, take a package to a person's place of business, and walk away without having anybody notice you come or go. You see Ivy, you are well aware at this stage in your life that no one pays any attention to the old. You can come and go as you please and people don't give you a second glance. Old people are invisible to the world and especially to the young. This isn't about you performing a clandestine caper, this is about you placing a package in a room that bad men and women meet in to conduct their business. Walk in the front door and walk back out the front door." Jimmy said.

"Human trafficking continues to grow in this country, and we need it to stop. A dear friend of mine had one of her daughters snatched away in broad daylight coming home from school, never to be seen again. The heartache and the not-knowing has destroyed her life to the point that she is barely a mother to her remaining son. Her husband is devastated because he often feels responsible for her kidnapping even though he had nothing to do with it. If there was a way that she could do what we are presenting to you she would drop everything to aid us in this endeavor. This is why we need you. We need to take control of our country again and abolish these unconscionable people, for good." Scarlet pleaded.

"You make it all sound so easy. Not one person would even notice me. It sounds a bit like of a sell job, you two. I don't want the last days of my life to be spent playing cloak and dagger. I'm too old to spend the last days of my life being scared shitless, as they say." Ivy remarked.

"And you shall have it all. We need a small portion of your time and one act of courage, and you will be done. Ivy, the Prime Minister is counting on you ladies to help redeem some decency into this country. He wants you to make this sacrifice for your country and the people in it. We need you, Ivy. This corruption will only continue to grow without your help. Can we count on you Ivy? Will you dedicate yourself to your country?" Jimmy said.

"Alright then, I'll do it. Originally you had mentioned that I could have Mr. Miller, my husband, join me in this quest. Is that still on the table?" Ivy pressed.

"Of course it is Ivy. Mr. Michael Miller would be a welcome participant, however; can he keep a secret?" Jim looked at her and winked.

"Oh Ivy, I envy your courage. You have what makes this country the best in the world - guts. Thank you, Ivy." Scarlet said.

"So, we will see you tomorrow morning at the office. The limo will bring the group over at 9:00 am. See you then Ivy." Jimmy said.

The two of them stood and made a hasty retreat for the door so as not to let Mrs. Miller have too much time to reconsider her answer. They slipped out the door and zipped down the hall before Ivy could even see them out. They popped into a stairwell and waited for a second just in case Ivy looked down the hallway and wanted to chat further. It's hard to talk when you are no longer there.

***

They quickly moved back into the corridor and made their way to Patricia Patterson's room. Scarlet lightly rapped on the door and the two waited to be received. A moment later Mrs. Patterson pulled open the door and invited her two guests to enter. The room was almost a duplicate of Mrs. Miller's suite and the two made their way over to the soft seating area and chose their positions. Patricia was not as friendly and open as Ivy had been. She was guarded and annoyed. It was clear that she was going to be difficult, but, no worries. This is what Jimmy and Scarlet specialized in: getting a yes. They all sat down but no words were exchanged. Jimmy was surprised that Patricia did not offer a beverage of any kind, which showed the pair that this meeting could be a short one. Patricia sat on the edge of a sofa and glared at the two guests and finally said, "I can't do it. I cannot be a murderer. I know you have explained and shown me in great detail, but it still does not change who I am as a person. These people need to be held responsible for their crimes but in a legal manner, the way a civilized society operates. The criminals need to be represented by a lawyer that can demonstrate their side of the story. I live by my own moral compass, and I just don't feel that what you are proposing fits into my personal ethics. I sorry Mr. Smits and Miss Larsen, but I will not be able to help the Prime Minister of this country sanction murder. It is just not right." Patricia said.

"I completely understand and so does the Prime Minister. We knew going into this venture that not everybody could deviate from their principles to do this task. We are forever in your debt for even considering carrying out this deed, but the Prime Minister wants to hit this corruption right on its ass. With that being said Mrs. Miller we will say goodnight and we hope you have a wonderful flight back home. Needless to say, we wish you the best of luck with your upcoming battle with cancer. If there is anything we can do to help you or your family during the process, please let us know. You have close friends in the Government now." Jimmy told. He rose from his chair and the two made their way to the door and said their goodbyes. Patricia surprised both of them by giving them each an enthusiastic hug. She stood in the open doorway with a look that said she had something else to say, but she simply said goodnight and let the door close.

"Oh well. That didn't go exactly as planned. Could you please contact Dr. Cook and let him know that Mrs. Patricia Miller is no longer part of the Special Projects Task Force. Thank you, Scarlet." Jim said.

"Of course, Mr. Smits. I will let him know at once." Scarlet answered.

***

Scarlet and Jimmy walked down the hallway to Mrs. June Spicer's suite and knocked on the door. Mrs. Spicer answered the door and the two guests entered. June was a happy and vivacious woman and loved talking to anyone that would listen or exchange conversation at all. Her husband, Gary Spicer, was what most people call a "stick in the mud" type person and was not an affectionate man so, whenever June could get some attention, she would gladly take it. Gary had been a hard-working, union man for forty years and kept to himself for most of his life. The best thing that ever happened to him was when June, for some unknown reason, took pity on him at a dance years ago, kissed him on the dance floor and the rest was history. He was a steady man that went to the same place every year for vacation and always sat at the same table when they would go out for dinner to the same restaurant. If the table was occupied, he would wait. If it was taking too long, he would inevitably give up and go home rather than trying a different restaurant, so while June had love in her life there was absolutely no excitement. She married a robot, but at least she always knew where he was and who he with and all she had to do was give him a little nooky here and there and he was in heaven. When she found out that she had been diagnosed with cancer Gary took it poorly. He knew there would be no chance of ever finding a perfect woman like June, so he had always kidded around by saying, "June, if you go then I go. This world will not need the likes of an old sod like me hanging around once you have passed on." The good news for the task force is that they would work together to complete a mission, whereas the others were still yet to be discovered. The other issue on Jimmy's mind was that June was Stage 3 and it seemed to be progressing fast and furious. When she was examined by the Special Projects medical team, she had just been identified with cancer, but it was ripping through her body at an alarming rate. With this in mind Jimmy was hoping that her and Gary would be their first trial run to help in eradicating some bad guys. He knew he had to work quickly but he never dreamt that June was going to hit them with a no vote right out of the gate. When he made all of his original selections, he was sure that all of them would agree to the terms, but such was not the case.

They made their way into the open area of the suite and June lead them to the dining table and asked them to have a seat.

"Can I offer you something to drink?" She offered. She looked Jimmy in the eye and waited for his response.

"I'll have a beer of any kind if you have one." Jimmy said.

"And what can I get you Scarlet?" She asked now looking directly at her.

"A beer sounds perfectly refreshing, thank you." She answered.

She made her way over to the bar and seemed to run out of energy halfway through the job. Her mind was directing but her body would not co-operate. She looked at the pair and in an embarrassed way said, "Do you mind at all helping get these beverages sorted out? I'm just have a hard time keeping that motor running these days."

"Of course, June," Scarlet pleasantly said and came over to the bar and helped Mrs. Spicer sit down at the dining table. She quickly went back to the bar and pulled three cans of Molson's, poured them into tall glasses and brought them back to the table. "Here we go June," Scarlet said as she passed out the glasses.

“I don’t regularly drink beer because it tends to make me gassy but I’m here on my own tonight, so, here’s to living,” she held up her glass in the air and made a cheers motion.

“Bravo to that June.” Jimmy agreed.

“To good fortune.” Scarlet held up her glass and announced.

“So how can I help the two of you this evening?” June queried.

“June, I was really counting on you. I thought that, of all the participants, you would be the first to say yes because of your condition and your family’s financial affairs are horrendous. I have access to everybody’s information, so I have already seen that your family is on the brink of financial ruin. This is your lifeline June. This can help your ten grandchildren have the life they deserve. The one I know you want them to have. We will look after your family for the rest of their lives with no questions or conditions. That is why I thought you originally signed up for this crazy scheme. Let us take on the money woes of your household and you can just stay calm and look after yourself. As I told you before June, we will supply the best medical care for you while you go through this experience. Your family will have the means to be by your side until the end.” Jimmy said. “You are worthy of this gift.”

“Where will we say all of this money has come from?” She asked coyly.

“You and Gary bought two hundred shares of Coca-Cola when you got married and you forgot all about it until the other day. People do not spend a lot of time wondering where the funds came from. It has been our experience that they are far more interested in spending the money.” Jimmy said.

“That is true Jimmy. Money is hard to get but so easy to spend. Has this worked in the past?” June asked.

“There has never been a past. You are the pilot project to help Canada take a bite out of crime, one gangster at a time.” Jimmy explained.

“I don’t know if I should be honoured or baffled.” She said.

“This is your chance to change the lives of everyone in your immediate family. How many people get the opportunity to do something as grand as that.” Jimmy said. “This is also the chance to work directly with the Prime Minister of Canada. There are few people that can say that about their country.”

“What about my condition? What if I can’t do what it is you need me to do? What if I’m too weak to perform the task?” June probed.

“If you agree to work with us June you will be our first assignment. The program will begin with you. This way you can get this done quickly and you can get back to Whistler with your family where you belong. I mentioned previously that you would never have to go shoot a person. We are not gun-wielding maniacs. You would have to drop off a package to the place where bad people hang out and then shuffle away and we look after the rest. Remember June, seniors are invisible to the world. That's why you can wear pink track suits and never be seen." Jimmy said.

"What a story for the end of your life June. You save countless lives in your country, and you bolstered the financial future of your family. What a glorious ending to a beautiful life." Scarlet added.

"I can see what you mean - you're right. I'll do it. How did his dad Pierre Trudeau say it, "Let it go with bang rather than a whimper." She spoke.

"Then we will both be seeing you tomorrow morning at the office. What a wonderful time we have shared with you this evening June. We are truly blessed to have you collaborating with us on this important work. Thank you." Jimmy said.

Jimmy and Scarlet stood up from the table and headed back towards the exit door. Jimmy reached for the handle and turned back and said goodbye again to June and then the two left the room while June was still sitting at the table, a bit too tired to make her way to the door. When she heard the door close; she stood up and made her way to the bedroom for a quick nap. She felt positive and charged up and knew she would have to recruit her husband to complete any task, but he would be perfectly fine with that. He would kill for her.

***

Jimmy and Scarlet strolled down the hall to their last holdout. Peggy Woodford was a tough read. She seemed to flip back and forth on the good and evil situation. They couldn't really get a read on her so this was a superb occasion to find out if she wanted to continue with the Special Projects group. They arrived at PH Ten and knocked on the door. A minute passed and there was no answer which seemed odd. Scarlet reached her hand forward and pounded hard to stir up the dead. The door swung open and there stood Peggy who was smiling and looking vibrant and happy. "Oh, my goodness," she exclaimed, "I wasn't expecting anybody tonight."

Jimmy was a little taken aback because he knew that Peggy had been told, and she confirmed, that they would be visiting her this evening. "Please, come in and take a load off." She said as she stepped aside for the two to enter. "Let's all sit down in the parlour, shall we?" Peggy led the pair down the short hall to the main salon. Jimmy headed for his favorite type of chair and Scarlet went to her trusty friend, the sofa. Peggy sat down on an empty chair and looked at the two and asked, "What do I owe the pleasure of this visit?"

"Well Peggy, after the presentation today you seemed to have decided to not participate in the task group, so we are here to see if there are any unanswered questions you may have or if there are further details that you require to help make this critical decision because the Prime Minister really wants you." Jimmy said.

"Oh, you big flatterer. Does that line work on all the ladies Mr. Smits? Well as I told you earlier, I would enjoy very much being part of your secret spy agency and I can't wait to get out there and find some bad boys and give them heck!" She exclaimed.

"Okay then. I was confused but I understand now. You want to be part of our group, is that right?" Jimmy asked.

"Absolutely true. I am so looking forward to doing something challenging I can't wait for my first assignment." Peggy responded.

"Well, that is great news and that is why we came by tonight, just to say thank you one more time and to say that we are looking forward to working with you." Jimmy said as he looked over at Scarlet not having a clue what was happening.

"I'm sorry you two, could please excuse me for a moment." Peggy said. She stood up and headed for the bathroom and closed the door.

Jimmy leaned forward and said in a whisper to Scarlet, "What the hell is happening here? You were there when she turned us down flat cold. Now she is all over this. I don't fully understand yet but at least it is a yes." Jimmy said.

A few minutes later Peggy walked into the salon and seemed to be taken aback. Her eyes opened wide, and she appeared to be frightened. She gazed at the two of them and cautiously asked them, "Hello there. Have we had the chance to meet yet? I am Peggy Martin, and this is my husband, Martin." She looked around the room briefly and stated, "I do not know where that man has gotten off to but I'm sure he'll be back." She paused for a heartbeat and said, "I'm sorry, I didn't catch your names?"

"Oh, how rude of me, I am Jimmy Smits, and this is my associate, Scarlet Larsen." Jimmy said.

"What a pleasure to meet you both. Your last name sounds so familiar to me, Smits. Maybe I know your mother. Nonetheless, how can help you two today? Are you friends of my husband?" She asked.

"Yes, I am. I was in the neighbourhood, and I thought we should stop by and see how he is doing." Jimmy said.

"Well, you just missed him. I don't know where he got off to, but he will be back soon. Do you want to wait till he comes home?" She asked them.

"No, we don't want to be any trouble. Could you let Martin know that we came by today." Jim said.

"Absolutely Johnny. I will let him know as soon as he gets home." Peggy said.

Jimmy and Scarlet both stood up and made their way over to the door and swung it open. They looked behind them, but Peggy was nowhere to be seen. Jimmy yelled out from the door, “Okay then Peggy, we’ll see you later.”

A few seconds later Peggy popped her head out from around the corner and said, “Oh, hello there, I wasn’t expecting any company. Please come in and have a drink.”

“Oh, my goodness. Will you look at the time? We have to get running along Peggy but it sure was nice to see you again.” Scarlet said.

The two stepped into the hallway and let the door close behind them. They looked at each other and Scarlet did her best twisted face and Jimmy burst out laughing. “Well, I guess that’s why we couldn’t get a read on her. Nobody could!” Jimmy finished.

Later that night Jimmy Smits made the call to Dr. Thomas Cook to discuss Patricia Patterson and her lethal nut allergy and her future in the program.

Chapter Four

Jimmy was sitting in the conference room chair at the end of the table sipping his morning coffee, waiting for the guests to arrive. This was an important day because this group of women represented the task force that his team had assembled to do their bidding. The critical issue in his mind today was - are they capable of following through with the undertaking that they were about to be given? None of these participants had ever even seen explosives, let alone touched them in their entire lives. The assignment was basic; carry a bag into a designated area, place it where instructed, set the detonator and then remove yourself as quickly as possible. Seemed so straight forward, however; amateurs make mistakes because they are not practiced, and it is not part of their personal routine, which creates a high likelihood for disaster. As Jimmy pondered these thoughts the telephone on the table chimed and a voice came on, "Mr. Smits, there is a call for you on line five," the voice intoned.

Jimmy walked over to the console and pressed line five, "Hello, this is Jimmy."

"Good day to you Jimmy," said the deep raspy voice, "How are our candidates coming along so far?"

"Oh, hello Mr. Bouchard. I wasn't expecting to hear from you today," he paused, took a calming breath, and said, "Everything is going as planned. We have rolled out the scenario to the group and we have eight positive responses out of the ten confirmed at this time. Two of the women have been referred to Dr. Cook for treatment and unfortunately one of the ladies seems to be in the onset of Alzheimer's, so her status will have to be monitored closely but other than that hiccup, all is going very well." Jimmy relayed.

"Jimmy, I do not pay you for pretty good. I pay you for perfection. Is this understood Jimmy?" Mr. Bouchard said.

"I misspoke sir. What I meant to say is everything is going exactly according to plan, and we will discuss assignments this afternoon before we send the group back to their homes while we work out the final details. By the end of day today we will have our group informed and ready to begin training for their specific tasks. They will all be briefed and ready for our target dates, as you expected sir. One of our candidates, June Spicer, has Stage 3 cancer and her health is deteriorating rapidly so I thought we might want to use her for our trial run next month. The good news is that she is married to a devout individual who will crawl over broken glass shards for her, so we wish to use the two of them together, and of course it can be our litmus test for future duo acts. He will not thrive in life without her, Mr. Bouchard, so we believe that he will implement the necessary deed with her for the promised payout." Jimmy said.

"Excellent Jimmy. This is a better answer. When you are finished with your group today, send me a comprehensive report outlining what we have discussed," Mr. Bouchard said.

"Of course. I will have my report completed and sent to you tonight sir." Jimmy replied.

"This is wonderful news Jimmy. I knew I could count on you to oversee this job. I will review your report this week and let you know my recommendations for moving ahead. Thank you, Jimmy. Speak to you soon." Mr. Bouchard assured and hung up the phone.

Miss Larsen rapped lightly on the glass doors and waited for Jimmy to give her the entry signal. She stealthily entered the room and made her way to one of the empty chairs close to Jimmy's chair and sat down. She was carrying a set of files with each candidate's name tagged across the top edge of each folder and she placed them onto the table top. She folded her hands on top of the pile and waited for Jimmy's undivided attention. Jimmy closed the file he was perusing and turned his focus to Scarlet.

"Was that Mr. Bouchard on the line? I thought I could hear his growling voice emanating from the boardroom." Scarlet asked.

"Yes. He seemed pleased with our progress to date. I told him that we would have a complete report about the group, on his desk tonight so after we have finished with the ladies today, I will need you for a few more hours. Hopefully, that works for you Miss Larsen." He smirked at Scarlet.

"You know the answer is yes. I know Mr. Bouchard does not like to be kept waiting, ever!" she responded.

"I also mentioned to him about June and Gary Spicer from Whistler, and our concerns with June's immediate health issues. I told him that we would like to do a trial run with the two of them to test the waters. He is aware that Gary Spicer is willing to die for his wife and family." He said.

"We do not know that for sure as of yet Jimmy. What if they wimp out and stay home? What then?" Scarlet said.

"Then we'll cross that bridge when we get to it. Even though I have never met him I am certain that he will do what is asked of him to please his wife. I've also looked over their financials and they are a family that could really use some extra money." Jimmy said.

"So, the immediate objective is to get them to carry out their undertaking before she is too weak or sick to complete something of this scale. It's easy to carry a bag around town, however; it is much scarier when you know your bag has an explosive device inside. Needless to say, the Spicer's are time sensitive." Scarlet added.

"Copy that." Jimmy glanced at the time and said, "The ground transportation should be arriving within the next half hour so let's get everything ready for today's session. We have eight women returning this morning for the final orientation and out of them I believe that four of the eight will do what is needed from them. How about you Scarlet?

How many do you think will be totally on board?" Jimmy said.

"For the bosses sake, I hope for eight out of eight. From what I have witnessed this week I agree with your assumption of four people. Louise Gagnon, Diane Fletcher, Cindy Denton, and Willow Smythe. They are my four picks for just the women alone, however; if the husbands come through and bite into this scheme, we may get Ivy Miller and Lexy Winehouse to take part as well. Peggy Woodford clearly is on her way to crazy town and June Spicer may not be healthy enough to implement our plans. This should make for an interesting day." Scarlet said.

"You got that right. Let's reconvene when the guests have arrived and settled in the boardroom. Till then, if you need me, I'll be in my office." Jim finished.

Soon after Jimmy's office phone rang to notify him that all of the guests were in the boardroom settled with a beverage and a tasty morsel of some kind. He left his office and walked slowly down the hall to the boardroom and swung open both doors at once for a dramatic effect. He entered the room like a celebrity heading onto the stage in a Las Vegas Hotel for a big show. Jimmy was a polished performer, and he knew he had a winning smile and the power of persuasion on his side. Now, to see if he could get the ladies to really commit to the plan by having each of them sign a Government Document confirming their participation in the program and where to send all of that money that was to be paid to their families. When people sign government paperwork it just makes everything feel important and as if there is no backing out after they've agreed to the terms and conditions.

"Good morning, everybody. It is so nice to see you all looking so rested and relaxed this fine day. I spoke with the big boss this morning and he wanted me to share with you his admiration for your commitment. He is elated that you have agreed to help rectify some serious problems we are currently facing in our country. It's not as though crime is on the rise in the country right now, but it is more about the types of crime that are gaining traction that needs to be remedied. That's where you all come in. A new kind of Canadian hero. The old and the weak become the powerful and the strong. What a contrast, don't you think?" Jimmy held his hands open and facing the group.

Out of nowhere Peggy Woodford stood up and began clapping. She beamed like she got an "A" on her report card and started to sing O Canada. The group was caught off guard, but they all dropped what they were holding and leapt to their feet, and they all joined in the singing of the National Anthem. When Peg had finished, she sat back down in her chair and beamed with pride.

"Oh, my goodness Mrs. Woodford. What a lovely rendition you performed for us. Such an honour." Jim commended as he faced Peggy and gave her a half bow out of courtesy. “Thank you to all of you ladies that have given us your valuable time and attention.”

Scarlet was sitting in her usual position in the room, but she did manage to get the waterworks pumping for effect. “This is what separates us from other countries around the world. Our culture is one that cares about this country and about each other. This has been an amazing experience to share with you ladies. I will always remember and cherish this time. Thank you.”

The next couple of minutes was spent mutually acknowledging how great all the participants were and why God was on their side. Then Jimmy got down to business and took back control of the meeting.

“After today’s meeting you will travel back to your respective homes and go back to your lives, however; you need to remember that you are NOT to put all of your affairs in order just yet because this could seem very suspicious to your family and friends. We have all heard the stories of people that are planning to commit suicide who begin giving away all of their valued possessions and this sets off red flags to anyone close that is really paying attention. The secret to all of your successes will be to continue living in a completely normal way, whatever your normal happens to be. No phone calls to someone you have not spoken to in forty years just to see how they are doing. Just live your life exactly as you have been living it. Change nothing. I am curious how many of you have told your families that you have late-stage cancer?" Jim said.

June Spicer raised her hand and said, "I have told my close family that I am sick, but I have not told anybody except my husband Gary that I have been given approximately six months to live."

"That's it? Just one of you told one person. You all know how to keep a secret. I must tell you all that I am really impressed." Jim said.

"It wasn't that hard Mr. Smits. I had my condition confirmed to me in the last six months so I haven't had time to get out there and look for as much sympathy as I could garner." Willow replied.

"I guess that would be true of a few of you, is that correct?" Jimmy said.

He looked around the table and watched as the women all nodded their heads in an affirmation when Jim made eye contact with them. Jimmy was relieved that the task group would not have to search out any persons exposed to the truth by the ladies. The Special Projects group had been monitoring the women and their correspondence since they were selected by the government task force to participate in the scheme. They had to be sure that the women did not expose the group to the general public at any time during the assignment. "Loose lips sink ships," Jim thought to himself.

“When it is time for you to support the Government with your assigned task, we will send a handler that will come to your city to coach you through all of the details. They are experts in many areas but be aware that they are not experts in compassion because of their military backgrounds. They have been trained to teach you what you need to fulfill your individual assignment and give you the tools to get in and get out of the selected target. If we need you to travel to another city, they will escort you at all times until the mission comes to fruition. They are not baby sitters and will not be able to help you perform your duties due to the risk of being recognized or complicit in it. Once you arrive to the site of the chosen quest, it is all on you. This of course brings me to the next item on the agenda which is, do any of you believe that your significant other would want to help you do this if they were given the opportunity?” Jim said.

The first to respond was June Spicer. “Gary would help me in a second. He still won’t let me open a car door so I can assure you that he is so chivalrous he would never want any harm to come to me, so yes, Gary would participate.” She said.

“I thought we aren’t supposed to discuss this information with anyone. If I spoke to Dennis, I know that he also would never allow me to do something crazy that could possibly harm me, so I believe he would come to my aid.” Willow said.

"Michael would not get involved in any way. He is a law-abiding citizen, and he despises people that try and take advantage of others and would see this as an act of terrorism and would most likely turn me into the authorities. I agreed to get involved simply because of the compensation that you have offered. I will be dead and gone from whatever kills me first but to know that my family will be financially set for life is a strong reason for me to move ahead with this plan." Ivy stated.

"Does anybody have anything else to offer up at this time?" Jim said.

All the ladies seemed to be nodding affirmations to Jim and each other regarding the abetting that would be taking place, and it was unanimous that all but Ivy would have the support if required. Peggy Woodford hopefully would still have some cognizant brain function left before she needed to perform her assignment. The Special Projects Director knew that Peggy would be the first person to be assigned a posting and he also knew that there was an exceedingly high rate of failure to be expected from a person who had such short-term memory loss. She would be moved into the number one position to be first to carry out the endeavour.

"You will be given a government issued phone that you are only to use when speaking with this department. NEVER use this phone for anything else, ever. If it rings and it doesn't say my name on your screen, you do not answer.

You tell me or Scarlet, or depending how far along you are in the process you talk to your handler, who will be available to you 24 hours a day. Now for the next couple of hours we will need to have you fill out some forms naming whom you wish your proceeds to go to after you have passed. Once we have all the paperwork in order, I would like to take you all to the hotel's private dining lounge and share a meal together. We have had the Executive Chef make a dinner for you based on what you all said were your favorite dishes. It will be a stupendous night of decadent dishes and wine pairings from around the globe. I am really excited about this meal. So, without further ado, let's get the forms filled in and move ahead with our day, shall we?" He looked over at Scarlet and saw that she was already passing out pens and papers to the ladies, ready to help with any questions they may have. Tim Dixon walked into the room and headed straight over to the ladies and also started helping with the paperwork. A few hours later they all had the forms filled in and the group was ready to return to the Royal York and get freshened up for their send-off dinner. Everyone headed down the elevator and out to the waiting limousines.

"Scarlet, Tim, please do me the favour of shredding all of these documents. The last thing we want is any evidence that we were ever in this building. Get the movers and cleaners in here tomorrow and let's get this place emptied. I want no trace that we were ever here. When you are both finished, please come to the hotel, and join us for our celebratory feast. The ladies are going to have the time of their lives." Jimmy said.

Jimmy's driver dropped him off at the hotel's front entrance and he made his way to the private dining room, reserved for special guests and celebrities, to make sure that everything was set up and to speak to the chef about the dinner plans. They had already done a food allergy check on the guests to be sure of a flawless dining experience. Jimmy stopped one of the servers that was scampering about getting the room set and ordered a double shot of bourbon. He sat down at the head of the table soaking up the ambience while waiting for his drink to arrive. The server brought the glass back to Jimmy on a shiny silver drink tray and proffered it up for Jimmy. He held it in the air as if he were toasting somebody, said cheers, and then downed the robust glass of liquor. The heat of the alcohol rushed through him, and he savoured the sensation for a moment, then he had to get his head back into the game. As he stood up Scarlet was just walking into the room with her briefcase of file folders. Each folder had a participant's name on the cover with details of their selected assignments inside; after the dinner Jim planned to meet with each person, do a quick analysis, and make sure they had a solid idea of the directives. They all would need to study the mission notes carefully and be prepared to review the data with their personal handler when the time came.

Soon after the guests began arriving to the dining room and found their name tags on the table for the seating placement. Within thirty minutes all of the ladies had found their seats and were ready to start their dining extravaganza. The servers expertly delivered the food course by course to the table and the Chef, Erin Moore, came into the room and described each plate in great detail. The ladies were all in awe of such a glorious meal, and many of them had never had a meal like this in their lives. Jimmy contemplated to himself at one point thinking that this was akin to the famous painting, The Last Supper, because all of these seniors were heading to death's door within the year. It was a sobering thought. Just over an hour and a half later the lights were dimmed as the servers entered the room together carrying a flaming Baked Alaska and placed in front of each guests. The ladies clapped and exchanged smiles and laughter. The dinner was going exactly as Jimmy had envisioned. The lights were brightened up and liqueurs and coffee were brought to the table. Jim looked over at Scarlet and gave a head nod which she read as "let's get the first one moving along." She slipped across the room and stopped at Peggy Woodford's seat and placed her hand on her shoulder and whispered in her ear, "Could Mr. Smits borrow you for ten minutes? He wants to review some critical information with you before you head back to your room tonight." Scarlet said.

Mrs. Woodford was having a lucid moment and agreed and stood to follow Jimmy into a private room to discuss her file folder. When she returned to the room Scarlet would immediately head to the next person on their list and escort them to the private room for their personal review. In no time Scarlet and Jimmy had completed the task and were ready to relax for a few minutes with the rest of the group. Jimmy was a tremendous showman who could tell fabulous stories and spin a yarn about any topic. His knowledge of the Canadian Government procedures was vast and impressive to the women, and they all sat back and allowed Jim to entertain them with his wit and sense of humor.

Soon after, most of the women were ready to retire for the evening. One by one Jim and Scarlet wished them well and exchanged pleasantries until they had all gone up to their rooms for the evening.

"Well, how do you feel that went?" Scarlet asked Jimmy.

"We are moving along nicely, however; it will be a true test to see if any of these ladies are capable of executing our plans without buggering up the works. The acid test will be Peggy Woodford, and she will be the first in the history of this nation. And, if it works, it could possibly become a whole new way to eliminate messy problems." Jimmy added.

Chapter Five

When Peggy returned home to The Glebe, a suburb of Ottawa, she was feeling exhausted and ready for a few days in her own bed and eating her own food. The limousine turned off Bank Street onto Third Avenue heading down the street to her house. She gazed out of the car window at the house and smiled that she remembered this was her house. She had trouble with her memory lately, but she could visualize the day she and Martin bought the house when they moved to Canada from England back in the early eighties. The car rolled to a stop, and the driver got out and came the around to open the door for Peggy and to gather her suitcase from the trunk and escort her to the bright red front door. She stood for a moment and looked at the door knob and it seemed like she was waiting for the door to magically open all by itself but that wasn't going to happen.

"Mrs. Woodford, would it be alright with you if I borrowed your keys to open the door?" The driver asked. He held out his glove covered hand and beamed a bright and happy smile at her, "Would that be, okay?"

"Yes. Of course. I need to find my front door key. It's a big red one with a picture of Betty-Boop on it." She replied. She faced the driver and opened her purse as wide open as it could go without splitting into two pieces and showed the purse interior to the driver and said, "Do you see her anywhere in there? Martin got me a big key so it would be easier to find inside my bag. Oh, there it is, down in the bottom." She acknowledged.

The driver gingerly slipped his hand into the gaping purse and fetched out the set of keys. No sooner was he was sliding the oversized key into the lock when the door swung open to reveal Martin who was home awaiting her arrival. She looked at his face and presented him with a warm smile and leapt into his arms and kissed his face. "Oh, my goodness Martin, I'm so glad to be home. I swear to the Lord above I don't want to take any more trips without you. No how, no way."

The driver rolled the bags into the entry foyer and moved them to one side out of their way.

"Is there anything else you require Mrs. Woodford?" He asked.

"No, thank you. You have been so kind." She expressed in a pleasant manner. She walked over to the entrance hall table and rummaged around in a small porcelain tray and found a loonie and walked back over to the driver and placed the coin in his hand and whispered to him, "This is for being such a wonderful young man. Your mother would be proud of you." He turned around, winked at Martin, and scurried out the front door.

"Oh, my darling how I have missed you. I am thrilled to have you back home where you belong. By the way I have invited the boys and their families over for a visit this evening. Not for dinner, just a drop-in to see you and give you a chance to see the grandchildren. I hope that will not be too much activity for your first night back?" Martin said.

"Oh, my goodness, that is a wonderful idea. I can't wait to meet them." Peggy said.

"Great. Now let's go sit on the couch so you can tell me all about your stay in Toronto. How was the Royal York Hotel? Was it all it was cracked up to be?" Martin queried.

"It was magnificent. The nicest hotel I have ever been to, Martin, in all of our travels over the years that place is really something to see. They gave each one of us proper suites with bedrooms and bathrooms and fresh cut flowers each day. It was a treat to be allowed to see how the rich live because I have never experienced anything like it in my life. We've had to struggle to get by our entire lives, and then you see rooms like the one I was staying in and realize how much higher up the ladder of life one has to be to achieve that level of success. It was staggering to say the least." Peggy explained.

The two made their way down the corridor to the family room attached to the kitchen and could smell the aroma of something tasty that Martin was cooking up.

"Oh, my goodness Martin, you baked something?" Peggy said.

"Yes. I made you something called monkey bread. I got the recipe from a lady at the bakery the other day. I won't lie, I didn't make the bread myself, it was frozen. Thought you might like a sweet treat for when you got home, and the grand kids are going to love it." Martin told her.

She got to her favorite resting spot in the house and curled up in ball in the corner of the sectional sofa and pulled a blanket over herself. Martin had gone to the refrigerator to get her a bottle of water but by the time he got to the sofa Peggy was asleep. He reached over her and rearranged the blanket and kissed her on the forehead to which she moaned and purred like a kitty cat. He was a tough and gruff old man, but he was making sure that Peggy knew that he was over-the-top happy to have her home. He sat down beside her resting body and put her petite feet onto his lap and began to rub them gently with his warm hands. He continued to massage her feet until his eyes closed.

Martin was drifting back into his past thinking about how he and Peggy had met so many years ago. Martin was raised by his parents in Portsmouth England, and Peggy and her parents were from a nearby city called Brighton. As it turned out, Martin's mom and Peggy's mom were both competitive Gingerbread House bakers and had been involved for years travelling the circuit of baking competitions throughout southern England. During that time Martin and Peggy were regularly dragged to the competitions, which they hated going to, but when they finally met and spoke to one another at a contest in London, they hit it off. From that day forward the two would ask their mothers if they could attend the events as a helper and before long, they both knew how to bake and design gingerbread projects of their own. Some years after that, Martin and Peggy made it into the top ten at a competition in Brighton, but that was as close as they got to the Gold Ring. What they did find out for certain was that their love for each other was real and their mothers actually got along rather well. When the two lovebirds had finally finished with their educations they planned to be married. They got hitched in Brighton and honeymooned in Portsmouth, at his parents' house. It took a while for the young couple to get jobs and steady incomes, but it did come to them over time, and they were able to save enough money to buy a place of their own. Martin's mom Harriet cried for days because she and Peggy had become so attached and so in-sync with each other. Even when Peggy was about to walk out the front door to her new home Harriet held her arm excitedly and looked her in the eye and whispered to her, "Oh my God. You're pregnant!"

"What are you talking about Mom? No, I'm not." Peggy responded.

"You might want to go see the doctor and have a test. You know I'm in tune with you and I'm telling you you're preggo kiddo." Harriet speculated.

Peggy and Martin drove the few blocks down the street to their new home. They were filled with pride to see what an amazing accomplishment they had managed. Home owners, what next, a family? The next morning Peggy made the appointment with the doctor to take a pregnancy test and see if Martin's mother was right. She was with child. She beamed a big smile because she would have Harriet right down the street to be there every step of the way. It brought her great comfort knowing that.

Years later Martin's mother got old and passed on. Peggy's mom moved into a home when her father passed, and she was on her own and so it was at that time when Peggy and Martin decided to move to Canada. Martin was offered a position in accounting in a government job in Ottawa, Ontario and they couldn't pass up the opportunity to live in a completely different country from where they grew up. So, they moved to Ottawa to the house on Third Ave and have been there ever since. Two sons and four grandchildren later they savoured a modest middle-class lifestyle and made the best out of what they had. They were humble and they were blessed with healthy children and grandchildren. Life was good and then Peggy got the news regarding the cancer. Just to make things even more difficult and painful she was also diagnosed with Alzheimer's. They would fight this together, like everything else in their lives.

He awoke to the sound of the front doorbell. He went to the door and opened it to the ruckus of both families arriving at the same time. Eric and Sandra and the two girls, and

Simon and Margaret with their son and daughter. Suddenly the house came alive with energy added into the space in as the four children romped around and begged for grandpa's monkey bread. Peggy came to with all of the commotion and was gleeful to see the family together. She was having amazing clarity that day, so this visit was perfect timing. She was able to be there physically and mentally.

Martin was a devoted family man, but he was a husband first. He spent his life being sure that he gave Peggy what many women hope for which is security. He was boring and exceptionally predictable, but he gave her a wonderful sense of protection and she felt blessed because of it.

As the night moved on and little screams of joy began turning into yawns, Simon and Eric knew it was time to head home. The group of bodies made their way to the front door and went through the ritualistic saying goodnight thing and suddenly Martin and Peggy were standing in the house alone. Peggy turned to Martin and said, "I've got a great idea, let's go to the boudoir and fool around."

"That is music to my ears." He answered.

***

Three days later Peggy received a phone call from Luc Bordeaux. He was assigned to be her handler for the upcoming activity that she was to perform and then secure the money for her once she had completed her mission. He spoke with a heavy French accent that sounded like he was a character from a TV cartoon show. He gave her a place and time to meet with him so they could begin their mission strategy. He instructed her to meet with him at the Chateau Laurier Hotel in downtown Ottawa which was less than ten minutes from her home in Glebe. She took a taxi and was delivered to the front doors of the hotel where she entered the building and headed to Room # 1021. When she got to the door Peggy was overwhelmed with nervous anticipation and found herself conjuring up the courage to knock on the door. Peg was pleased that her mind was working perfectly that day so she was convinced that she would remember everything that they were going to discuss. She was now ready. A shaking hand reached out and rapped on the door. The door swung open to reveal a small man standing at about five feet six inches tall and weighing not much over one hundred fifty pounds. She somehow thought they would all be giant sized men like Mr. Smits, however; such was not the case. "My name is Luc Bordeaux, and I am a member of the Ministry of Defenses' Special Projects Group, and I will be working with you to complete your assignment." He held out his hand, grasped hers and shook it hard. His accent was strong so she knew she would have to pay close attention to him to be sure and not miss anything important.

"Please, come in and sit down," he instructed. He pointed to the large sofa, and she made her way across the room and sat where she had been directed.

“My name is…” she was about to tell him, but he hushed her.

“This is not important. I was told you are Peg, yes?” He confirmed.

“Yes. Peggy Mar…” again he hushed her.

“I do not need this information. This will not help either of us with your assignment. Now, let’s get to work and review the information package provided to me and see if we can get through all of this efficiently. Once I finish, the opportunity for you to speak and ask any questions will be allowed. Until then, we are better to just learn and prepare for what is coming next, yes?” Luc said.

“Okay Luc.” She responded.

Luc opened the file pocket and pulled the contents from inside and spread them onto the coffee table between the two of them. For the next two hours Luc rattled through the info package at lightning speed, or so it felt to Peggy, and he finally said, “So, do you have any questions?” Luc said.

So, the scenario was - ultimately, a young man from McGill University in Montreal, Tom Shields, had developed a new fertilizer that could help farmers grow almost double the yield of hay they had been used to growing each year with no side effects to the livestock whatsoever. This was the biggest breakthrough in decades in agriculture but there was a major setback in this discovery that was the owner of this new formula was going to give it to Agriculture Canada for free. This was a wonderful thing for the people of Canada, but it was a terrible thing for Leveque Chemicals Ltd. who had been providing Canadian farmers with their hay fertilizer for the past two decades. If farmers had a product that was free and more effective, it would virtually run Leveque Chemicals into bankruptcy within a year. They would have no viable way to compete with a company giving the product to farmers every year moving forward. They had tried to convince Tom Shields to sell his new development to Leveque Chemicals for millions of dollars, but he refused and said he was not interested, and that the money meant nothing to him. He was far more concerned with helping fellow Canadians benefit from his discovery than being rich. This was not a working solution for Special Projects Group because in order to grow and pay for a country, you need donations from private supporters that can help stimulate the country's economy without having all of the red tape that surrounds the government and complicates getting things done in a timely manner. Hers was to be a remarkably simple task. She would wear a ring on her hand that appeared like ordinary jewelry, but it would have enough poison to attack the central nervous system and Tom would simply have a stroke hours later and most likely would never fully recover. Meanwhile, other members of the Special Project Group could go to his labs at the university and remove the formula for the fertilizer and pass it along to Leveque Chemicals and life would continue. Unfortunately, since Tom Shields was not being cooperative to their plan, something had to be done. Luc simply had to spin a yarn to Peggy that made Tom out to be the big-bad-wolf so she would suspect that Jean-Paul Leveque was a total creep and wanted to profit from these findings.

Luc explained in detail how this man Tom Shields was nothing short of a criminal terrorist that had to be stopped so that all Canadians could benefit from this amazing discovery and not just one man. Peggy Martin ate up his story and believed every word. She was determined to get this deed done quickly to stop Tom Shields from destroying the Canadian agricultural market place. She now knew that he was a menace and he had to be stopped. Luc went over the details of their planned trip to Montreal to visit the university where Peggy could blend into the crowds and walk down the corridors with the students, posing as a grandmother just visiting her grandson who was attending classes at the campus. She would go into the large lecture hall and sit in the back and wait until Tom's lecture was complete and then she would walk up behind him, take the protective cover off the poison ring, and accidently trip and fall into him at the front of the room in front of anybody still remaining in the lecture hall so that no one would see anything different happen to him. Hours later the serum would begin to take effect and he would fall into a stupor, be rushed to the hospital, and Leveque Chemicals would then acquire the formula and begin mass manufacturing of the new product. More crops for less cost, how can that be a bad thing? Luc gave Peggy detailed instructions, but he never wrote anything down or sent her any written communications. He kept telling her that he would be there with her, so she had nothing to worry about. They covered the dates and times once more based on what their intelligence had predicted Tom's schedule to be. Luc knew that this had to happen quickly because Tom and his fellow scientist were set to reveal the discovery at the end of the month at an Agricultural Convention in Montreal, Quebec. There were no guarantees on Tom's timetable so they had to go on some speculation, but Luc knew that they could get Peg close enough to touch Tom with the deadly device and be done with it, or so he hoped. No matter what Peggy did or didn't do Luc knew too well that he had to be successful, or he would pay with his own life.

"Do you have any more questions right now Peggy? Are you feeling brave?" Luc questioned her.

"Absolutely. I can do this for my country. I am ready." She replied.

"Excellent. I will contact you next week with flight details and then we will meet at a predetermined location in Montreal. If you have any questions or begin to feel nervous, please call me and we can talk our way through any obstacles. This is so easy to do Peggy. Just walk by him and tap him anywhere on his body. It is just that easy, okay?" Luc explained.

"I will look forward to your call Luc. By the way, how soon do you deposit the money into a foreign bank account in my family's name?" She inquired.

"The minute he drops dead from complications from his unexpected stroke." Luc said. "The money will transfer immediately."

She stood up, shook Luc's hand again and left the room. She climbed into the empty elevator and noticed what she thought could be a camera, so she dropped her head down, so her face was not exposed. She found herself trying to be clandestine for the first time since she was trying to hide candy from her children. This was a new way to think and act, and she was titillated by the thought of it. Peggy the Spy.

She walked out the front doors of the hotel and had the bellman call a taxi for her ride home. She slid into the seat and told the driver her address. Twenty minutes later she pulled up in front of her house and breathed a sigh of relief. She made it back to the house without having an incident. Now it was time to go in the house and make some dinner for her and Martin. "Maybe pork chops with apple sauce," she thought to herself. Peggy entered her house that night and was already having a challenging time remembering some of the details that Luc had told her that day. She fought her own mind as it tried to play tricks on her about where she was and who she was with that day. She had to keep these explanations clear and separate in her mind for the trip to…she couldn't remember. Where was she going next week. No big deal. That man…what was his name again…he would be there to help her. It would not come to her. She did recall that she was going to make pork chops. She went to the kitchen and made dinner for her and Martin. After that, who can remember these tiny details.

***

The following week Luc called Peggy on the Monday to check in with her and see how she was feeling. A woman answered the phone, "Hello." She said.

"Hello Peggy. It is Luc calling, how are you doing today?" He inquired.

"I'm sorry, who is this?" She said.

"It is Luc Bordeaux from the Special Projects Task Force." He replied with an agitated voice.

"Oh, my goodness," Peggy said in a soft and pleasant manner, "I think you have the wrong number. This is the home of Peggy and Martin Woodford. Sorry." And she hung up the phone.

Seconds later the phone rang again, and Peggy quickly answered, "Hello, this is Peggy." She replied.

“Hello Peggy. This is Luc Bordeaux from the Ministry. How are you doing today? Is everything alright with you?” He asked.

“Luc I am sorry to tell you that you have called the wrong number. This is the home of Peggy and Martin Wood…Ford, and I do not know any Luc anything, so I bid you good day sir.” She grumbled and disconnected. She was so surprised that anyone had called her on that phone because she didn’t remember ever having anybody call her on it. She was also surprised that the same man called her twice. “What are the odds of that happening?” She thought to herself.

Luc instantly made a phone call to Jimmy to pass along his assessment of the current situation. Luc felt heavy in his heart because he knew that Peggy was in some serious mental trouble which would mean that some action must be taken to control the needed outcome. Luc was simply going to confirm with Jimmy who the next person was to contact. He recalled that June Spicer was diagnosed with only six months to live so he felt that June would be an excellent candidate. She lives in Whistler BC so she could still get a flight and be in Montreal before the convention. It would be up to Jimmy to give the final approval. He called Jimmy and said, “Hello Jimmy. Got an update I must share with you asap. I just called that Peggy lady, and she doesn’t seem to be all there Jim. She literally couldn’t remember who the hell I was although we spent the entire afternoon together a few days ago. I don't pretend to be a Doctor, Jim, but I think she is loco. It could be that it comes and goes but from my vantage point I think we need to scrub her and move on to June Spicer, the lady with just a few months left. We should use her while she can still walk Jimmy. Please understand Jim that these are only my humble suggestions. I will wait for your final decision."

"What a shame. All that time and effort spent on her, and she comes up a lame duck. But we were aware this this was a possibility. Oh well, I like your idea of bringing June into the fold. I will connect her with you to make all of the travel and information sessions needed. In the meantime, I guess we are going to need to make some staff changes. Let me get back to you." Jimmy said.

He called Serge Bouchard and waited for him to answer, "Hello Jimmy. How are things developing? I only want good news." Serge said.

"Of course, Mr. Bouchard. I have two items to run past you. First, I would like to switch two of the women because Peggy Woodford's Alzheimer's is taking over her mind and she is subject to making a costly error sir. Secondly, what do you want me to do with Peggy Woodford?" Jim said.

"To the first question, yes, change your candidates. The second thing, contact Dr. Cook and have him pay them a visit, at once. We do not want her talking to anyone." Serge said.

"Another small detail sir, is that her husband, Martin Woodford, may hear some lucid thoughts that possibly could be problematic for us so, should we eliminate both parties in question?" Jimmy asked.

"Yes. Kill both of them, and, quickly." Serge said.

Jimmy wasted no time contacting Luc to confirm the go ahead with the change in personnel. Luc would contact him when things were arranged. His next call was to Dr. Thomas Cook to pass on the essential information that he may need. The Doctor made his notes and disconnected. He was headed to Ottawa.

***

Two days later he arrived at the home of the Woodford's humble abode and slowed his rental car to a stop just down the street, so he had a perfect view of the comings and goings of the house. He moved the car around a couple of times just to garner any further information he could. He wasn't completely surprised by the inactivity because usually old, retired people don't go out much. He watched Martin leave in the car, but he returned within the hour. They were home bodies. "I will pay them a visit tonight," he thought to himself.

Headline in Ottawa Today: A small residential home in the Glebe district stunned the neighborhood when a gas leak explosion completely demolished the house, killing an elderly couple who were asleep in their beds when it happened. Damage has been estimated in the millions because of the vast spread of destruction to the neighboring homes. No other injuries have been reported. The police are still investigating the scene to determine if any foul play was involved.

Jimmy read the headline on his computer screen and smiled. “That Doctor sure knows how to get things done.” He opened his email and got back to work.

Chapter Six

June was lying in her bed when the phone call came. She wasn't shocked that the Ministry contacted her, but for some reason she had expected there would be more time before she was called to duty. June was concerned that she would not be able to be useful to anybody at this point in her life. Her health was changing by the day and the only thing she could do now was to battle the disease with painkillers. Lots and lots of painkillers. Some days it was all she could do to muster the energy to get out of bed and head to the kitchen for a cup of coffee, even though on many occasions her body would expel the savory dark brew back down the drain. She wanted to wean herself off coffee, but she just couldn't handle the headaches that she got every time she tried to quit. She was already a medicine cabinet with feet, but June could not take quitting caffeine while she was trying to fight cancer. How many challenges could she handle at one time? The voice on the phone said, "Hello Mrs. Spicer. This is Luc Bordeaux calling from the Ministry, how are you doing today?" He asked in a caring tone.

"As good as I will ever be Luc. What are your instructions?" She asked directly.

"I will be your handler Mrs. Spicer. We need you in Montreal for an event at an agriculture convention for a few days. Typically, I would meet with you in your city, however; we need you to be on a flight in a couple of days, so please pack a bag and I will arrange for your plane tickets. I will email all of the information to you within twenty-four hours. The hotel info will be included in the email. You know to not speak with anyone except the general niceties one would anticipate hearing from a grandmother. I will meet you at your hotel once you have checked-in and got your room key. Do you understand everything that I have just said to you Mrs. Spicer?" He questioned.

"Yes Luc. I understand. I will wait to hear from you in my room in Montreal in the near future. Do I have it correct Luc?" She said.

"Yes. Perfect. I will see you soon. Remember, if you ever need anything you call this number and I will make whatever you require happen, do you understand? No matter what, please call. We are all here to help you." He said.

"Okay Luc. I appreciate your attention. Thank you and I will look forward to hearing from you in Montreal." She finished.

June continued to lie on the bed staring at the ceiling asking herself, "What the hell have I got myself into this time?" She started her mental check list, where is the travel bag? What should I wear? Do I need a coat? Don't forget my meds. She dozed for a spell as she tried to decide what she would tell the family as to why she was heading out of town again so soon after she had just got back from Toronto to meet with the Ministry of Defense. She knew that her husband Gary was going to be giving her the third degree, but she knew all of this nonsense would be worth it to get the payday she had been promised. He could be mad at her for a bit, but he loved her too much and he would always come around to her way of thinking. She also knew that Gary wanted to be with her every minute he could salvage out of her remaining time on earth. She had an expiration date on her, and he wasn't going to waste any of it buggering around with Government Agencies. Money meant nothing to Gary so it never would have been a motivating factor for him, however; he wasn't the one who had been asked. June sat up on the edge of the bed, drank down some water and tried to shake the cobwebs out of her head. She slid her feet into her slippers, arose from the bed and headed to the kitchen to find Gary. Her nose was still acute enough to catch the aromatic smell of a pizza cooking in the oven. "Mmm, a snack. Perfect timing," she thought to herself. She arrived in the kitchen to see Gary happily preparing the treat and drinking a cold beer. "Do we have any more of those?" she asked pointing at the beer bottle in his hand.

"Is the Pope Catholic?" He replied in a friendly banter. He walked over to the fridge and got June a cold beer and placed it on the kitchen island. He zipped around the edge of the counter and pulled out a chair for June as she sat down.

"You don't have to do that all the time. I'm not completely incapable yet!" She chaffed with him.

“I will not have this discussion again. You are my wife, and I am allowed to help you, right to the bitter end. We are in this together, like we have been our entire lives. Our time is short so please do not waste it on being mad at me for loving you too much. This doesn’t seem like a good use of our time. Are you hungry?” He piped up, leaned in and kissed her forehead. She looked him in the eyes, and smiled and gave him a wink.

“Yes. I would love some pizza.” She kindly replied.

The two ate their meal and drank beer and relaxed in front of the TV for the balance of the evening. June was filled with trepidation about her upcoming trip to Montreal. She feared that Gary was going to grill her about having to travel again. He always had been one of those people who ask more questions than a nosy mother-in-law. How was she to explain this; when she simply thought she would say that a clinic in Montreal has a radical new approach to her type of cancer. He should buy that story. The government was paying any related costs so how he could possibly be upset about that - she just didn’t know.

“Sweetheart.” She began.

“Yes dear.” He replied.

“You will not believe the amazing news I got today. I was contacted by the Ministries Special Projects Task Force, you know the people I met with in Toronto, and they want to send me to Montreal next week to be a part of a test group to experiment with a new radical cancer treatment program that they have developed. They said it is a new procedure so I would only be there for a couple of days and then fly back home. Can you imagine my good fortune. People would kill to be given an opportunity like this don't you think?" She curiously asked.

Gary was a highly suspicious man and trusted nobody, so he took the news with a grain of salt and a dubious mind and said, "This sounds fairly risky June. In your condition shouldn't you be trying to spend time with family and friends and not some fly-by-night government agency that I've never heard of in my life. You are a grown-up lady, and you make your own decisions, but I have an opinion and I do NOT like it at all." Gary said.

"But what if this new treatment sends my cancer into remission? What if it can help me live another year. Then it would be worth the effort, right?" She cajoled.

"If I get to have you around for an extra minute, I'll take it sweetheart. I will take whatever the good Lord is willing to give us." He said.

With that, the two sat on the couch and he rubbed her feet. Gary gazed over at his wife and could still see the young woman he married so many years before hiding under all the wrinkles that had migrated across her face throughout the decades. She was still the love of his life. He chuckled to himself and thought about when the two had met back in

Regina Saskatchewan in 1960 at a travelling carnival show. Gary was given the job of guessing people's weight, which by all rights he had become highly skilled at guessing correctly. June was attending the fair with her friends and stumbled upon a handsome boy with black wavy hair and a dangerous smile. She took one look at him and was interested. She strutted up to him at his booth and started to chat with him but like so many young men they have no idea what is really happening, so she had him guess her weight. He looked carefully and said, "one hundred twenty pounds." She burst into crocodile tears and said to him, "Oh, how could you. I've never been so embarrassed in my life."

He didn't know what to do. He had never had this type of reaction before. He reached out and put his hand and placed it on her shoulder and said, I'm so sorry Miss, I didn't mean to insult you, I swear I didn't." He said.

"Well, you could make it up to me." She replied.

"Of course. Anything." He answered.

"Okay then. How about a kiss to make me feel better?" She said coyly.

The carnival motto went through his head, "Keep the customer happy and you keep the boss happy." Pretty simple rule. He turned and said OKAY, but she leaned in and kissed him right on the mouth. Gary suddenly realized that he had never kissed anyone but his mother. It was fun. Immediately he had sensations that he had not experienced before this.

Many thoughts raced through his mind but the one that stuck with him was that he liked it. He liked her. And he wanted to kiss her again, and soon. As she sauntered off to the rides, she glanced back over her shoulder to be sure that he was still looking and that glance confirmed it, he was hooked. Later that evening as the sun went down, the crew began cleaning up the area and taking the attractions down to move to the next small town when June reappeared and walked directly over to Gary and said, "Do you want to go walking after you're finished your chores maybe?" She asked.

"I would love to go walking. I'll be about thirty minutes before I'm done. Is that okay?"

"I am waiting all night for you mister. I like you so far so don't mess it up." She said.

They walked close to the camp and talked. June then reached out and clasped his hand tightly as if she was going to fall, and then, she did fall, almost. Gary swept her up in his arms and stared into her face in a concerned way. "Are you okay June. Did I trip you accidentally. I swear I didn't mean to June." He implored.

"I know you big silly. I just wanted to be sure that the man I'm going to marry will always catch me if I fall, and you did. I'm yours." She finished.

"June, do want to run away with me and join the circus?" He proposed.

"Absolutely one hundred percent yes." She said.

From that day forward they were always in each other's lives. Before long Gary went to the University of Manitoba and earned a degree in Sciences before returning to Regina and marrying the woman of his dreams. Children quickly followed and they lived in Regina not far from June's mother and father, who had both become fond of Gary and his regimented lifestyle. His blessing was that he was as predictable as the sun. Before long they had four sons and Gary said he was done with having any more kids. However, June wanted a daughter so badly that she accidently forgot to take her birth control pills and voila, she got pregnant. They had never known the sex of any of the previous babies, but this time June did ask the doctor to tell her. She sat in the chair across the desk from the MD and awaited the news. "It's a girl." The doctor told her. June screamed out so loud that a couple of nurses on the floor in the ward rushed into the room to see if she was okay. She was better than okay because she was going to have a little princess. Her life was now complete. A little angel with four big brothers to look out for her. Her life was perfect.

The two lived in Regina until Gary was offered a job at a new Shell Oil Refinery in Vancouver BC. The job paid double what Gary was making and the company had full benefits, which Gary had never received in his entire life. They knew that they would miss the family, but it was too good to be true, so they moved. Gary stayed at the plant in

Burnaby for the next 30 years until retirement. He always made enough money so that June could stay home with the children. It was her whole life, and she could not have been prouder. June was not a person who felt like she had missed out on a career, she was a homemaker and would brag about her motherly prowess in the home. The four boys all had two children each and Penny, her daughter, had four kids. After Gary officially retired from the plant the two moved to Whistler to be closer to Penny who had moved there with her husband who was the General Manager of the Chateau Whistler. June and Penny were best friends and did everything together. They had a symbiotic relationship that just worked, and Gary was elated that June was having the mother-daughter experience that she so desperately wanted. Life was perfect until earlier last year when June was diagnosed with cancer. Now every event became more important because the family was now keeping close track of time and June's health. Both were fleeting.

The movie had ended but Gary stayed seated on the couch and held June's feet in his hands. He was going to miss her so much when she was gone. The family would try to keep him busy with chores, errands, and some babysitting but it was going to be a lousy substitute for having June with him every day. His eyes filled tears as he envisioned life without her, but it was impossible. "You cross each bridge when you get to it," he said to himself. June began stirring about and came to and said, “Gary darling, are you okay? It looks like you have been crying.”

His inflated ego and his macho nature refused for him to be vulnerable, so he answered back to her, “I think my allergies are acting up. Maybe I should take an antihistamine.”

“Or maybe you should cry like most people do on earth. It doesn’t make you weak, it just makes you human. By the way, I love you darling.” She smiled at him.

“I love you too June, forever, for always.” Gary said.

“I assure you that I will be okay to do the trip to Montreal. I am rather excited about finding a new cure. I will take anything if it gives me more time here with you and the kids.” June said.

June was having a horrible time having to lie about the false cancer treatment, but she knew her time was coming sooner rather than later however if she was able to complete a task for the Ministry and collect all of that money. However, it would be an amazing legacy to pass along to her brood. She had to keep her focus now and morph into spy mode.

Her phone signaled that she had received a new message. June looked at the lit-up screen and read the attached note with the dates and times of the flights. She smiled when she saw the hotel that she would be staying at in Montreal was the Ritz Carlton, which is one of the only Five Star Hotels in all of Canada. She had always wanted to stay in a swanky hotel of that luxury, and next week it was finally going to happen for her. She went to her bedroom and began to pack. She knew the agency had said to wear simple plain clothing. Nothing flashy or designer couture. Just good old matching track suit tops with matching bottoms. Clothes that no one would ever remember. She completed her packing, closed the suitcase, and put it by the door for the next night. She was catching the red eye from Vancouver to Montreal in the first-class cabin, which would be wonderful because she knew that she could stretch out on the plane and get some rest. Later that night, a limo arrived at her house to take her to the airport in Vancouver. It would take a couple of hours to get there, check in and board the plane. Gary hugged her goodbye and watched as the driver escorted her to the car and opened the back door for her to enter the car. Quickly the door closed and so did the trunk and then they were gone. Gary was still angry with this decision, but he didn't want to fight about it and add any extra pressure or strain to June's life. He had to control his feelings.

Two hours later June pulled up to the domestic terminal and exited the car. The driver promptly placed her bag on the sidewalk and drove away. She walked inside the terminal and headed to the Air Canada first-class ticket counter to check in and then went ahead to the departure gate to wait until the boarding call was made. An hour later the first-class passengers boarded the aircraft and June quickly made herself cozy and fell fast asleep. Next stop, Quebec. The plane landed at 7:00 am EST in Montreal. On cue the man was standing in the airport with a sign that read, June Spicer. She approached the man who was donning a face mask and hat, so it was impossible to know his identity. She acknowledged him and he simply took her bag and headed to the waiting car. Moments later they were arriving at the Ritz Carlton where they were met by a league of bellman at the door ready to help June in any way they could. Check-in was a breeze and soon after she was gazing out the large window in the suite that they had provided to her for her short stay. She felt like a celebrity with all of the special treatment she was receiving but she didn't know that this is how first-class guests are always treated. Like royalty. June knew she could get used to this and, it felt good that she would be able to help her entire family live richer lives because of the undertaking she was soon to achieve. In less than five minutes of being in the suite she got a message from Luc Bordeaux, "see you shortly." Now she would sit and wait for instructions. June had never been this nervous. The Ministry had told her that it would be easy, and nobody would even notice her but that didn't settle her quivering nerves. Heading to the mini bar for a shot of liquid courage, she twisted the cap of a vodka bottle and downed the entire container in one shot and suddenly realized that she had never downed a bottle of anything in her life, in one shot. The warmth and confidence of the booze started to take effect rapidly and she smiled to have bolstered her wanning bravado. Now she was prepared to meet with Luc.

In under an hour there was a knock at her door, and she got up and answered. Luc came in with a file pocket and walked over to the sofa and sat down, then patted the seat beside him to indicate for June to sit down beside him for the briefing. Luc wasted no time and instantly began running through all of the information regarding their person of interest. June was taken aback because he spoke to her as if she had performed this kind of action several times before, however; she had not. Luc laid out the details of the plan and showed her the ring with the poisonous pin on the inside. The small cap was to protect her from the poisonous pin poking into her by accident, which would be awfully bad. He ran through the information and then facing June he asked, "Do you have any questions for me?"

"Firstly, are you going to be there with me?" She asked.

"Yes. I will be there but not with you. I will be there incognito, and we won't speak to each other, ever, if possible. I will be there to aid and assist but not to take part in any way. Your cover must be maintained as a little old lady here to attend an agricultural convention and sit in on some round table discussions on dirt and soil. You will be working alone June, but you only have to get up beside Tom

Shields for a second so that you can tap him with the ring, and then you are done. The ring's poison will look after the rest and there is no chance that anyone would know that you had administered Tom a fatal dose of poison. Tom may not even feel the pin prick. He will most likely think that it is a rogue body being tugged out by an article of clothing. Happens to people all the time." Luc stated.

"How will I know when the right time is to strike?" June asked.

"As I told you I will try to be close by to give you a nod, but you will know when you see him. I am hoping that we can make contact with him while he is still in the corridor before he enters the room to deliver his speech. I want you to walk around looking as confused as possible and if someone asks you tell them you were hoping to get a picture of you and Tom together. Then, when he puts his arm around you, pop the cap on the ring and hug him by the waist. It just has to barely break the skin for the poison to work. It is a highly lethal product June. If you accidently touch it during this procedure, you will also die so, please be very careful. Understood?" He affirmed emphatically.

"What if anybody questions me as to why I want a picture with him. What do I say?" She asked.

"Tell them he reminds you of your son or grandson. It works every time with little old ladies." He replied. "Nobody ever questions what the elderly are doing. You will literally be invisible to any security people if they even have any on-site security. This is not some important public address. It is simply a bright young scientist presenting his research to an interested group." Luc mentioned.

"I am nervous. I don't want to mess this up." She worried.

"You won't June. Everything will be just fine. Slow and easy, no panic." Luc reassured her.

The following morning June got up at 7:00 am, ate breakfast in her room, and was at the front door of the hotel at 8:00 am to hail a taxi to the Montreal Convention Centre. When she arrived, she went through the front entrance, checked in and collected her convention pass to get into the different lectures that were being held throughout the space. The main floor had every type of farm equipment that was possibly imaginable. If it was farm related, it was on display in this room. June was astounded by the array of information about the farming industry and pondered to herself how many shows like this one happen all over the country year-round. Once June had checked in and donned her attendee badge, she was free to move about the facility. She walked up and down the aisles and read all of the literature that was available for guests to take away while she paid close attention to the time. She had to be in the hallway outside of Room 101 in the main salon for Tom Shield's keynote presentation regarding his recent findings. She headed upstairs to get an idea of where everything was located and where the exit staircases were to be found. She quickly analyzed that she could take the picture, accidentally bump into Tom, and slip out of the building down the exit stairs directly to the outside world. She walked over and opened the staircase door and checked for security cameras. They had cameras everywhere. As soon as she took the picture, she would raise her facemask up to hide her identity. Two flights of stairs to freedom, or at least the street and the outside crowds. She climbed back up the stairs and returned to the upper hallway and saw a group of benches and went to go sit down and rest to catch her breath. Currently the hallway was barren, but she knew that when one thousand people show up and make their way into the presentation area, the room and hall would be bustling with people. She watched carefully to see if she could spot any security guards in plain clothes or in uniforms. She only saw one woman walking around for a bit talking on her hand-held radio, but she received a call from someone and vanished at once. Another look at her watch proved that the lecture would be starting in under thirty minutes. She just had to stay calm for less than thirty minutes. Seems so easy, but it is so hard when you are waiting to kill someone. The hall began to fill up with more people and more voices which had begun to raise the noise decibels higher and higher. Her heart stopped for a second…she froze solid. She looked over and saw Luc walking down the hallway with Tom Shields and his entourage and they were smiling and laughing like they were old friends. She told herself, "June, don't be looking to play super sleuth. Just get over and do what you have to do."

She saw that Luc was leading the group towards her position and knew she was right along the pathway of the entrance door to the lecture room. She mustered the courage and got up and pretended to fall down to her knees in front of Tom and his associates. It could not have worked out any better because Tom was the one that reached out to help June back up to her feet and made sure that she had got her footing back under her. "Oh, my goodness, you look the spitting image of my grandson Johnny. I swear I'm staring at his doppelganger right here, right now. This is crazy, is there any way you would take a picture with me?" She pleaded politely.

"It would be my pleasure Mrs…?" Tom affirmed, holding out his hand to shake hers.

"Mrs. Bates darling. Betty Bates." She replied smiling.

Luc reached out and grabbed her camera and said, "Get ready, now smile, one, two, three and click." The picture was complete, and June had managed to get the protective cap off the ring and poked her target without him ever making a squeak. This plan was coming together. June thanked Tom one more time and she slipped into the crowd and made her way over to the fire exit doors, down the stairs and stepped quickly onto the street. Without looking back, she continued walking for two more blocks until it finally felt like it was safe to take a breath and look around. She had done it. She had slain the dragon, and her family would receive one last gift from her before she passed on. Her heart was beating rapidly, and she wasn't sure if it was a heart attack or just a run-of-mill panic attack. Nonetheless, she had completed her duty. She felt the pride growing in her chest. She was unstoppable now. June stopped on the side of the road and hailed a cab to take her back to the hotel. Tonight, she would celebrate with a fine meal for one at one of the many sumptuous restaurants at the Ritz Carton. When she climbed into the back seat of the cab, she was still on cloud nine. It now seemed all so easy. "What the heck was I all worried about," she thought to herself. The taxi pulled up to the front of the building and the bellman opened her door so she could get out. She walked across the lobby to the elevators and decided she needed a drink and nap. After that, she would have that special dinner tonight that she had been craving.

Just before June was to head downstairs for her meal, she had received a text from Luc. It read, "Congratulations June. All is well. Tom Shields fell into cardiac arrest just before giving his speech and has been taken to Montreal General Hospital. He slipped into a coma and is being monitored closely. His condition is currently unstable."

June the Hitman. She wouldn't have believed this possible in her lifetime, but surprisingly anything can happen given the right motivation.

The following morning June woke early and had breakfast and headed down to the lobby. When she stepped out the door of the lobby the limo was waiting to transport her back to the airport and then fly back to Vancouver. The driver made his way to the airport and pulled up at the domestic departures area. The driver opened her door and had placed her bag onto the sidewalk, so she was ready to head inside to the ticket counters. June was delighted at how quick and efficient everything went inside the terminal and within what seemed like minutes she was sitting in the waiting area outside of her designated gate. She found herself having flashbacks of Tom Shields face even though they met for only a few seconds. She knew why his face was coming back over and over but it wasn't his face that bothered her, it was the fact that she knowingly killed a man that day. That was something she had not done before and that might explain some of the feelings of angst that she was experiencing. It was over, she would be home in less than twenty-four hours. Back to the safety of her house and her family. She boarded the plane and was overcome with guilt. "Would the police stop her flight and drag her off for questioning?' She wondered to herself. She was going to panic until those doors were closed and the plane was in the air heading due west. Then she could relax. The passengers filed by her one by one until there were no empty seats left on the plane. She had made it. The door was about to be closed and locked when a person from inside the airport interrupted the flight attendant. “Hold that door please,” she yelled out. “Do you have a Mrs. Spicer on your list?” She inquired.

“Yes. Mrs. June Spicer, she is in first class.” The flight attendant replied.

The ticket lady walked onto the plane and went into the first-class area and called out, “Where is Mrs. June Spicer seated?”

She was afraid to raise her arm. This was it. She was busted.

“Girl, you done forgot your cell phone in the terminal. Is this yours?” She asked, holding up June’s phone.

“Yes, it’s mine. Thank you so much for bringing it to me. You are too kind.” June said.

“Just doing my job June. Have a safe flight home.” She remarked and exited the plane.

June was dumbfounded. She was petrified. She needed a drink and stat. She pressed the call button, and the flight attendant came and asked, “Mrs. Spicer, is there something I can get you?”

“May I have a glass of red wine please?” June asked.

A minute later the woman returned with her glass of wine and placed down the paper doily and put the glass on top of it and walked away. June again found herself holding her breath afraid of what might happen next. Soon after the engines whirled into action and the plane left the ground heading for Vancouver. She felt like she had made it and leaned back her seat and smiled. She had pulled it off.

About six hours later the plane began its descent into the Vancouver area. They touched down and disembarked and June again looked for the man holding a sign up with her name on it and then they were on their way back to Whistler. She was in the back seat and feeling safe and happy to be heading back to house to see Gary and the family. She couldn't wait to be home.

Laurent Pillared was a hard-working man with many unused talents, until today. It had been quite some time since he had driven a flat-deck diesel truck but once you know you never forget how. The previous day he had received a call from Jimmy Smits who asked him to take a little drive to the city of Squamish, which you had to drive through to get to Whistler. Laurent was instructed to acquire a flat deck vehicle for the day. Once he had borrowed the truck he was to wait until Jimmy called him with further instructions. He always did exactly what he was told to do to the letter. Failure was not in his vocabulary.

An hour up the road after leaving the YVR airport, the limo driver mentioned to June that he needed to take a quick bathroom break and apologized profusely but he just couldn't wait any longer. The driver found the perfect place to pull to the side of the road where they had washrooms and coffee. He turned to June in the back seat and asked, "Is there anything I can get you Mrs. Spicer. Do you need the restroom or a beverage of some kind?"

"No thank you. I am good, I will just wait in the limo." June responded.

"Okay then. I'll be right back." He declared.

June stared off into the distance enjoying the breathtaking views of the Sea-to-Sky Highway and smiled because she felt so blessed.

Laurent pressed down firmly on the brake pedal as the flat deck continued to gain speed. He was afraid to turn the wheel in fear that the entire machine would flip over on the road. He was fighting the beast when he decided to down shift through the gear box to try and slow the momentum of his out-of-control death box. He managed to slow the truck considerably, but it was still going quickly, and he knew there was a treacherous sharp corner coming up by the lookout viewing area. Laurent grabbed the wheel and pulled hard to make the turn, but the truck went a smidge wider in the turn than he expected and then it crashed into the parked limo in the lookout parking lot and launched it over the cliff into the depths below. Three, two, one, splash, the car splooshed front end first into the Howe Sound at the bottom of the cliff. A massive wave of water shot up into the air and then the water began to settle out until there was only a ripple left in the ocean where the car used to be. In a flash the car submerged under the dark cool water and the only thing left were the bubbles emerging from the bottom of the water. In an instant, June was gone.

Jimmy Smits' phone rang. He looked at the screen and answered. "Hello there, how is everything going?"

"The police are still here at the scene doing the clean-up and speaking with witnesses. They are going to try and raise the limousine and retrieve the body tomorrow, if the weather is permitting. Otherwise, there is no sign of the passenger. Should I stay in Vancouver, or do you need me elsewhere?" Laurent questioned.

"You better head to Toronto. We have a task for Lexy Winehouse, and I would like to have you there as a back-up. Call me when you land." Jimmy said and disconnected the phone. He rubbed his chin and murmured to himself, "That Sea-to Sky Highway really is a death trap."

Chapter Seven

Serge Bouchard was born in 1950 in a small Francophone community of Saint Vital within the Winnipeg city limits. It is an area of the city that still has a large population of French speaking citizens. Serge grew up in the area and by his early teens became very aware that most of the surrounding areas of the city spoke fluent English and he figured out that he and his friends and family were truly a minority in the province. By his mid-teens he was determined to move to where French would be the primary language spoken and English would be the minority. Serge found out quickly that the majority of the province of Quebec spoke French, which appealed to his way of thinking. He had never wanted to separate the country into parts, but he did want the opportunity for him and his kin folk to speak, in what they felt was their native tongue. As a teenager he made himself a promise to live in Quebec one day and speak and write all of his correspondence in French. It didn't seem that impossible because Quebec was only two provinces over to the east from Manitoba, so it always appeared to be within his grasp.

Serge was a man who matured long before his time, measured from his calendar birth. By the time he was a teenager he loved wearing a school uniform and making sure that the shirt and slacks were neatly pressed, tie done correctly, shoes buffed to a high gloss, and blazer tailored to fit him exquisitely. He always wore his hair slicked back with hair products and short enough to pass as a military personnel. By his mid-teens he was confident because he was so bright. If he read a factoid, he could recall it with exceptional accuracy, which also made him somewhat of a show-off. He was on the debate team and the chess club, as to be expected, but he refused to get involved with any of the school politics. He never ran for class president, although he would have won every time. He had a way of getting other people to rally behind him and by grade ten he already had about five of the school's biggest and toughest boys recruited to do his bidding. He never wanted to fight with his hands, but he was contentious, always. Whatever stand the school board would take on an issue he would most definitely take the opposing viewpoint. It was as if he wanted to gain experience in battling everybody for everything. He kept a paper-route and worked in a local deli so that he would have spending money, not for himself, but for his committed crew of friends who would defend him to the bitter end. He knew that young men craved food, girls, booze, and drugs, and so he made sure that he had money to supply his crew with the first two. However, he was too young to buy booze and drugs without drawing attention to himself in a negative way. He wanted to be known as a young man with abilities to get things done and the power to influence his peers to help him be successful. When he hit sixteen years old, it was his fervent goal to buy an automobile with the money he had saved but his father wouldn't hear of it. Competitively jealous of his own son, because he had not been able to afford a car of his own, he was far too proud to have his son driving around town in his own personal set of wheels. Serge knew his father was stubborn and wouldn't budge on this issue, so he got together with his two closest allies and made them an offer they couldn't refuse; he would buy a car and have the two of them use it, but whenever he needed a ride, they would have to prioritize his needs first and foremost. It was a simple arrangement and his two friends, seizing the opportunity for their benefit, agreed to the conditions. Serge bought the car and his days of being chauffeured began. One of those young men was Jimmy Smits: a giant-sized person with a nasty disposition who was ready to defend his buddies in an instant. The other person was Laurent Pillared who had already gotten his driver's license and whose parents didn't seem to give a hoot whether he was home or out, so that made it easy for the two young men to be at Serge's beck and call. Jimmy had his learners' license and would soon be taking his road test, so the three were set up. Two driving friends and a car that was at their disposal: this was a match made in heaven. School was a breeze for Serge; therefore, he spent little time on homework and more energy on scheming about how to make more money. Serge had enough money to pay for the car's gas and insurance, but he needed even more money to make sure that his two allies had some cash in their pocket books in order to keep them interested in driving him around whenever needed. He met up with a young native Canadian from the Mohawk tribe to see if they could make a deal buying cigarettes from them at their discounted price and selling the packs back to people in his neighbourhood for a small profit, but just enough that he could keep Jimmy and Laurent in good standing with him, which worked out well. Before Serge knew it, he was selling cigarettes to his dad at discounted prices and his father never asked how or why, he just wanted the cheaper price on the ciggies. That was the case with everybody. If they were cheaper than at the store, people were interested. By the start of his senior year at high school he was a king pin. He was known to everyone, and no one ever bothered him because they knew that he had Jimmy and Laurent on his payroll. All was good until one day an old Italian man they called Bobo asked Serge to come by his restaurant after school for a chat. Serge nervously entered the front door of Giuseppe's and was escorted to a small private dining room in the back of the restaurant where he was invited to sit and have a talk. Bobo encouraged Serge to talk about school, what he had planned to do once he graduated and his future goals. Serge was no fool and it was easy to see that Bobo was maneuvering the conversation to his own benefit. He was outnumbered and by himself even though Jimmy was waiting in his car outside. Bobo continued to talk in a pleasant way until he got to the real reason that Serge had been invited to the restaurant that day. He explained to Serge that nobody makes money in this town on booze, drugs, cigarettes, or prostitutes except for him and his crew. A basic cease and desist order was being handed down to Serge with no one getting hurt, yet. Serge knew that there was nothing he could do but to agree with everything that was said, or he would run the risk of not leaving the premises alive. Not his favorite option. What he didn't know is that Jimmy had gone over to pick up Laurent and Luc Bordeaux and had returned to Giuseppe's and was sitting in the car out front.

"He's taking way too long Jimmy. What the heck is going on in there?" Laurent questioned.

"I agree. Too long. We need to go in there and bring out our friend, right now." Luc responded.

"Do any of you have some heat?" Jim asked.

"I do," disclosed Laurent.

"Me too," replied Luc.

"Okay then. Let's go get our friend, no matter what it takes, right guys?" Jim asked.

"We're in, Jimmy. Whatever we gotta do, we're doing. I have no problem smoking a couple of old Italian farts. We're not leaving without Serge, right?" Laurent announced.

"You got that right." Jim agreed.

Simultaneously they opened the car doors and stealthily slunk to the front door. “Jimmy, you go around to the back door and make sure we don’t get ambushed in there, okay?” Luc instructed.

Luc pulled the front door opened, stepped inside and surveyed the area in one sweep of his gaze. Laurent was standing beside him with his hand on his gun, hidden under his school blazer. As they began making their way through the restaurant a man from behind the long bar area yelled at them, “What the hell are you stupid kids doing in here? Are you here for some food, cuz you’re too young for us to serve you alcohol. Grab a table and the waitress will be by in a minute.” He bellowed.

“No, we aren’t here for food. We’re here to pick up our friend Serge.” Luc announced.

“Sorry fellows, nobody here right now except for the people you see sitting at tables. Maybe your friend already came and left?” The bartender maintained.

“Yeah, that’s cool, but it’s a load of crap. Serge is here somewhere, and he’s leaving with us so could you please go get him or tell us where he is?” Luc insisted.

“Like I told you kids, your friend isn’t here, so you better bugger off.” The bartender threatened as he hefted up a double-barreled shotgun and pointed it at the two young men.

"Like I said old man, where the hell is Serge? Take us to him or face the consequences. It's that easy dude." Luc said.

Before the bartender had a chance to think about his next statement Laurent pulled his gun out his pocket and shot the man three times, one in the head and two into the body. As he spun down to the floor, he tried to get off a shot at the young men, but he was too late, and his shots blew a hole through the ceiling. Another figure in the back corner wearing a black suit leapt to his feet and was trying to draw his weapon when, bang, bang, Laurent shot him twice in the body. He winced in agony and crashed onto the floor face first, so Laurent walked over to the motionless body, and he shot a third bullet into the man's brain. He turned his attention back to the patrons of the restaurant, which seemed to be emptying out rather quickly. He gave a nod at Luc and the two continued towards the back until they arrived at the last office before the exit door. They could hear mumbling but couldn't make out any real words. Luc reached over and opened the back door to let Jimmy inside. He looked at the closed door and tried the handle, but as soon as he turned the knob, someone inside opened fire with a small caliber firearm and let six bullets fly, one of which hit Jimmy in his upper arm. He was livid. He stood back a foot and burst though the locked door and stood in the doorway as Bobo attempted to re-load his gun, but he was too slow. Jimmy stormed across the room like a wild buffalo stomping on a tourist and punched Bobo hard in the face. He went numb in that instant and lost his grip on Serge, who was being used as a human shield. Before Serge could land on the floor, Luc scooped him up and plowed out the back door with his friend. Jimmy was still enraged and was now a menace to everything in his path. He reached down with his large and powerful hands and said to Bobo, "Let me leave you with something you will not forget." He placed his thumbs over Bobo's eye and began to press in and continued to increase the pressure until both eyes gave into the pressure and exploded. Bobo screamed like a woman in a high squealy voice and collapsed on the floor. His hands lashed in the air, but didn't connect and then he made the mistake of saying, "We'll get you for this, I swear on my mother's…" He never finished. Bang, bang. Jimmy unloaded a couple of shots into his head to be sure that he wouldn't be coming after them, ever. He turned around and was heading for the back door when more shots rang out. Jimmy was shot again, in his left buttock and aimed his pistol and shot the new arrival three times in the chest. He scanned the back room and hallway to be sure it was clear and staggered into the back alley where the guys were waiting in the idling car. Jimmy casually limped over to the waiting car and got in. Luc threw the car into gear and the men drove away with the faint sounds of sirens approaching from the distance. As the men hurried off, Jimmy who had been shot twice, looked Serge in his eyes and asked, “Boss, are you okay? Did they hurt you at all?” The car kept its speed and direction as the four beat their hasty retreat, but it was the first time that anybody ever called Serge “Boss” and he liked it. He had never seen himself that way but as of now he knew he had the start of a dynamic team. Serge was still in shock from the ordeal, but he couldn’t stop smiling. Maybe it was being called Boss or maybe that he was enough of a rival that another businessman wanted him out of the picture, but he knew at that moment he was going to be a big part of the future in his little town.

“No Jimmy. I’m not hurt. Everything is alright. How about you guys? Any damages to report?” He asked.

“No, I think we are all fairly good, however; I have been shot twice so I should probably look into getting those holes plugged up soon. Do any of you know someone that can stitch me up, so I don’t have to go to the hospital?” Jimmy implored.

“My next-door neighbour is a seamstress so she could most likely sew up any holes you got. We’ll have to dig the bullets out ourselves, but she could do the rest. We have some moonshine in the basement you can use to help you with the pain Jimmy. I hope that’ll be okay Jimmy?” Serge suggested.

“No worries Boss. Let’s head there right now before my body craps out or I pass out. Give us an address and lets’ get moving.” Jim insisted.

Soon after they arrived at Serge’s neighbour’s house. He walked up to the front door and knocked. Michelle answered and Serge explained his dilemma and she agreed to bring him inside to the basement. Jimmy had bled quite a bit, but it wasn’t gushing out, so they seemed to be fairly relaxed about the whole ordeal. They grabbed Jimmy and hauled him into the basement and laid him down on her sewing table. She had to contain herself from puking, but she managed to keep it together long enough to get Jimmy stitched up. The minute she finished she begged the boys to get out of her house before her parents came home and began asking questions. As Jimmy made his way to the door he whispered to Michelle, “We were never here Michelle. We are going to trust you to keep our little secret, okay? We don’t want to ever come back here and discuss this with you, understood?”

“Yes Jimmy. I understand.” Michelle replied.

“Alright. Then we will bid you adieu.” Jim uttered and clumsily made his way back to their get-away car.

As the four young men drove down the road, Serge couldn’t help but feel like this was a scene from a movie where one group of bad guys battles it out with another group of bad guys. They were all stunned that Bobo was actually trying to stop them from conducting their business considering they had never heard a word from any locals about the goings on. Bobo wasn't selling cigarettes to anybody they knew which was odd to them because they knew a lot of people in the Winnipeg suburbs and hadn't once come across opposition regarding smokes. It couldn't be because of ciggies. It had to be bigger than that.

"Maybe those Italians are selling drugs right out the front door of Giuseppe's. Order a pizza and get an eight ball of coke at the same time. Besides, drugs are going to make a lot more money than cigarettes any day of the week. No matter what, I hope there are no eyewitnesses that can put us at the crime scene." Luc observed.

"Just to be sure Luc, can you drive this car to Saskatchewan tomorrow and trade it in for another model. I don't want any trace of it around us, especially at school. I'll give you enough money to swap it out. Maybe we should get a white panel van and put a plumbing sticker on it to fake people out." Serge offered.

"You got it Serge. Laurent and I can exchange it in the morning. No matter what it is we'll find a different vehicle. I like the van idea though. It could be handy for transporting boxes of smokes." Luc added.

"Well boys, maybe it's time that we move on from the cigarette business into something a bit more lucrative. If we're ever to make some real money, we need a more profitable product to sell. I don't want us to make the stuff, just sell it. We can talk about all of this later. For now, let's get Jimmy to a safe place and let him heal up a bit. Are your parents at home Jim? Is it safe to take you to your house or do you want to stay elsewhere for a while?" Serge asked.

"If my mother finds out I was involved in a shootout she'll ship me off to the Canadian Armed Forces faster than you can say Pina Colada. What about you two, he said looking at Luc and Laurent, is there any chance I could sleep in your basement for a couple of nights just until I can walk without wincing?" Jimmy inquired.

"No dice dude. My mom will ask way too many questions." Luc declared.

"Ditto Jim. You know my old man. If he thinks there is foul play taking place, I'll be grounded for a month. What about the Travel Lodge down the street. The place is an old dump, but I bet you they would take cash for the room. No trace, no worries. Stay there for a few days and then just tell your parents you met some chick and went to Thunder Bay with her. That could work." Laurent offered.

"Okay then, it's settled. Let's head there right now and I'll pay for the next three days and then we can see how you're feeling after that. If you're better, then head home. If not, let's talk about it then. Alright?" Serge said.

The boys headed over to the local Travel Lodge and checked in and Serge prepaid for the next three nights as planned. They helped Jim into the hotel room and placed him gently on the bed. Before they could finish talking Jimmy was out cold and they knew that he'd be out all night. They went to the vending machine and bought a handful of snacks for Jim in case he woke up in the night needing some food. They put a few water bottles beside the bed and slipped out of the room without waking Jim.

Serge was still captivated with the name - Boss. He felt like a big wig at a major company in downtown Toronto. He had never thought about being the boss of company, let alone his close friends, but it had a ring to it that he liked. It identified him as powerful, and he was stimulated with the notion.

Over the next two years, the boys all graduated from high school and continued to work together on the sly. They had moved up from smokes to marijuana and ecstasy, which both generated far more revenue than tobacco ever had, and still was not a huge risk to be in possession of. They all tried to find a path that would work for them, but nothing had synced up as of yet. Not long after Serge met a girl at the mall one day and he was smitten. He loved everything about her and wanted to date her but there was a catch, she was moving to Montreal with her parents in a few months and Serge didn't have the means to make the transition, so he laid low and continued to go on dates with her when she was available. One Friday night Serge was finally going to ask Louise Demers to be his steady girlfriend at the movies that night.

He was going to meet her outside of the Cinemas at 7:00 pm. He got there early so he could go over his carefully planned words to impress her enough to agree to be his girlfriend but when she showed up, things were not as he had planned. She was with Guy Tremblay, an old classmate of theirs from school. Serge had not seen or even thought about Guy in a long time however, he was determined to go through with it whether Guy was there or not. The odd threesome walked up to the ticket counter and the lady behind the glass asked, "Which show and how many?"

"I want two tickets for theatre number one please." He spoke.

"Oh, it's okay Serge. Guy has already purchased my ticket but thank you for your kind offer." Louise affirmed.

"Hey, it's the least your boyfriend can do for you, am I right Serge?" He replied and slapped the back of Serge in a brotherly gesture.

"What the hell are you talking about, boyfriend? Since when are you two a couple, a thing, an item? When did this happen?" Serge was incensed.

"About a week ago. He called me out the blue and asked me on a date and then one thing lead into another, and he asked me to go steady. Isn't that amazing!" Louise glowed.

"I don't get it. I have been asking you to go steady for weeks and then you suddenly go on one date and he's your guy. This is really cruel." Serge said.

"I'm sorry Serge, it wasn't my idea to hurt you in any way but when Guy asked me to wear his promise ring I just had to say yes. You understand don't you Serge? It kinda just happened. No malice was ever intended." Louise said.

"Alright then. I'll just be on my way then." Serge declared.

"Oh Serge, don't be like that. We've been friends for way too long to let something silly like this come between us, right?" Louise added.

"This isn't something silly Louise. This is my heart. I came here tonight to ask if you wanted to stay here in Winnipeg rather than moving to Montreal. I came to offer you an alternative, but you kicked me in the nuts. I will always remember this day, for the rest of my life, as the day you crushed my heart. And now I must bid you adieu. As for you, Guy," he said as he swung his attention to Guy and faced him straight on, "I will get you for this. I don't know how, and I don't know when, but I will have my revenge on you. Even if it takes one hundred lifetimes, I will make you rue this day. I am a man of my word; you will pay for this betrayal." Serge finished, turned, and stormed off.

"Holy crap, he sure got a bee in his bonnet, hey?" Guy said.

"He is a bit of a weirdo. It makes me want to sleep with one eye open for a while, or least until we move to Montreal.

Oh well, you ready to catch a film?" She offered jovially and off they marched arm in arm into the theatre.

From that day onward Serge became a different person. His interest in getting married and having children disappeared. His new life's purpose was power and money. He well knew the fastest way to power was with lots of money -that would now be his life's work; getting money to hire powerful people to work in his camp.

The following month Louise finally moved to Montreal with her parents so her dad could start his new job and his new life. Through the grapevine Serge had heard that not much after Louise had left town so did Guy and the two continued dating. He snickered to himself when he found out that Guy was trying to become a local politician of some kind, but Serge had not learned all the details. He knew he was an amazing liar so he should do very well in that area, however; he still wanted to break Guy's spirit, somehow, some day. All good things come to those who wait.

Serge woke up one morning and decided to begin a new group to counter act the government and all their nonsense and waste. He began a new and progressive movement to fulfill his own personal agenda. His creation, the Juste Droite Armee, or in English, the Righteous Right Army, (RRA), served to create havoc in the House of Commons. He would stand with whomever opposed the standing government, on any issue that came through Parliament. He would now be a tick on the rump of the Bloc Quebecois and oppose every idea that they had until his money ran out. However, over the years, his business had continued to grow because the Canadian people had spoken and it was clear that what they wanted more than anything, was drugs and alcohol. He was determined to provide this commodity to every Canadian he could reach out to for as long as it took to muddy the waters of any political party that would support his archrival, Guy. He realized that over the years he had become a terrible person, and he wanted to crush the hopes of many politicians, one campaign at a time. Serge had made up his mind to destroy Guy and whatever party that he was involved with and be a black fly in their Chardonnay for as many years as possible. Serge had never fallen in love again after Louise because he lost the ability to trust women anymore. They were all liars and will destroy you, given a chance. He focused on making money and didn't go on dates anymore. If he wanted the company of a woman, he did it the old-fashioned way and hired a prostitute who would go home at the end of the evening and not get the opportunity to cleverly insinuate their way into his life where they could ravage his heart. Those days were over. Now, he wanted money and power, and the opportunities that blossomed from those tools.

There was no longer any room left in his heart for love. It was a fools game.

Chapter Eight

Lexy Winehouse had full mental capacity even though she had Stage 3 cancer and was diminishing rapidly. Her weight was dropping, and she could only eat tiny amounts at each sitting. She was able to consume a banana or an apple along with a few sips of water. Although she tried to follow her doctor's advice and consume more food, she was afraid of all the nocuous effects it would have on her tummy. Lexy hated feeling sick in her stomach after each meal, but apparently this was her lot in life now. Hence the fact that she really tried to eat only when absolutely necessary. She had given up on alcoholic beverages a few years ago, but she still found herself craving a drink now and again. She decided that she would just give in to these impulses and suffer the consequences. The rough part of that reality is that she would have some horrible reactions to liquor and found that she could be ill for a couple of days afterwards however, she still found it impossible to fight off the powerful urges she would get, especially for a cool, crispy beer. Lexy had only had a few beers that she could remember in her entire life yet now her inner cravings for beer were at the top of the list and once all those hops and yeast got inside of her, she would feel like vomiting, sometimes for hours. On the days that it didn't have an adverse reaction in her stomach, she was on cloud nine. Her long-time sweet tooth had pretty much diminished to nothing. Sugary treats went the way of the dodo bird many years ago and she began suffering in her mind, just thinking about the loss of her freedom. To not be able to snack on a chocolate or a cookie just didn't seem fair to her but, it was her new reality. On her last visit to her physician, he was alarmed and concerned about Lexy's weight, but she was feeling defeated in her food battle. Her entire life went by, and she was constantly fighting with her BMI but now that she had cancer the pounds refused to stay on her petite frame. Lexy often pondered if she would simply get too skinny and might pass in the night from lack of sustenance. "Here lies Lexy Winehouse, passed away from skinniness," her headstone would read. The side effect of not eating well is a lack of energy to do anything at all. Most days she was content to watch TV shows and movies for the entire day. Her once vibrant lifestyle became a mere shadow of what she used to be before her diagnosis. Her memory was still strong with no problems on her recall of the past and how to do things, like driving a car, however; she was convinced it was just a matter of time before someone took that little avenue of pleasure away too. If Lexy couldn't drive herself to her bridge club and her senior activities, she would rather fall off the edge of a cliff. She still loved to cook but she didn't have anyone to serve her culinary treats to, outside of her husband Richard, since the kids had grown up and moved out. They had three children but one of their sons had passed away at seventeen years old in an accidental drowning at their back yard pool: Robert had snuck back into the pool after everybody had gone to bed for the evening. It was assumed by the police that he had gotten a cramp and was unable to make it to the edge of the pool for safety. The family found his lifeless body floating in the water the following morning and it was too late. He died that day and Lexy was forever devastated. They say that time heals all wounds but clearly who-ever coined that phrase didn't lose a child when he was just a kid in the beginning of his life. She mourned his life for years after and had to be medicated for several years to combat the depression and the urge to harm herself. She did finally come to grips with the death and understood that it was an accident and that she wasn't responsible for his passing. "If only I was there," she'd tell herself. It remained a jarring event in the family's history. Lexy's two other sons, Jeremy, and Colton, both joined the Armed Forces. Jeremy became a member of the Canadian Air Force and learned to fly all types of aircrafts but specialized in helicopters. Colton became an Infantry Captain in the Canadian Army. Both boys were younger than Robert at the time of the accidental drowning and were able to put the death behind them without having the same lasting devastation as their mother. The boys always hung Robert's Christmas stocking on the fireplace mantle each year to show that they still thought of him. Jeremy and Colton continued the tradition of baking him a birthday cake, his favourite being chocolate fudge cake, every year on his birthday. As to be expected once Robert drowned, Lexy was obsessively overprotective with Jeremy and Colton in the years to follow. Each time the young men came home for a visit they knew all too well to avoid talking about anything that had to do with swimming or water activities to be sure that they didn't set mother off and run the risk of having her fall back into the dark hole that she had fought so hard to crawl out of it. The boys always kept things light and never spoke of any near misses in their military lives that they were both experiencing. Both boys loved their careers in the service and wouldn't have chosen any other job. Jeremy got married to a wonderful girl named Barbara and they had one daughter. Colton finally came to grips with the fact that he was gay and explained to his mother that it had nothing to do with the type of breakfast cereal that Lexy had served them all for twenty years. "Come on Mom," Colton would say to her, "If it was the food then shouldn't Jeremy be gay as well?" He would ask her.

Like all moms who wanted peace and harmony in their household, they also wanted grandkids to dote over. Unfortunately, Jeremy got posted in Germany and moved away and Lexy only got to see her granddaughter, Charlotte, on occasion. That of course would all change one day, like it often does in the military lifestyle. Here today, gone tomorrow for who knows how long. Lexy always hoped and prayed that they would come back and live in the Niagara Region, but it never materialized. Jeremy had requested a transfer back to Canada once he found out his mother had cancer, but the stars were not aligning to make that dream a reality. Barbara was in the process of coming back to Canada with Charlotte to stay with Lexy and Richard at their family home so she could help out with things as the cancer progressed through her frail body, but that was still a month away. In the meantime, Colton would come home from his post at CFB Trenton Ontario and spent as much time as he could with his mom, but he could only visit when his commanding officer would allow him the time away. Their time together was usually filled with angst because the boys knew that her expiration date was rapidly approaching. So, when Lexy was not feeling herself and would be in bed for large periods of time, both boys took to sitting on the edge of her bed and would read Charles Dickens novels to her, as she truly adored his work. She would always say, "He is the greatest writer of all time, so if you are going to write a book just plagiarize his work and you will have a "Best Seller" on your hands. Her bad luck was that neither son was talented in that arena, so she didn't have to concern herself with not getting an opportunity to finish one their novels before she passed. Nevertheless, they had turned out to be good Canadian citizens and Lexy couldn't have been prouder of the both of them.

Lexy met Richard many years earlier at a vineyard in the Niagara peninsula not far from the falls in wine country. Lexy was with a few of her girlfriends, and they had traveled down from the Kitchener/Waterloo area to partake in a wine tasting. They paid their tasting fee and headed over to the bar to sample the different wines and Richard happened to be the on-staff sommelier, which he did every summer while attending the University of Waterloo for his degree in Optometry. He waxed poetic to the ladies and explained each wine in great detail as he poured glass after glass of the magical elixir, until finally the girls were as ripe for the picking as the grapes, they were sampling. Richard was smitten with one of Lexy's girlfriends at first until the million-dollar question was asked and she did not answer the way he agreed with. Which band do you like better, The Rolling Stones or The Beatles? His eyes lit up when Lexy said, "What a silly question. There is no comparison. It is the Beatles without a doubt." Lexy affirmed. He looked at her and knew she was the one. In that instance he fell hard for Lexy and immediately asked her on a date. Her friends were surprised by this invitation, but they all knew Lexy's type and he fit the bill perfectly. She was currently living in Mississauga, but he committed to come to her place and meet her parents and family so that she, as well as her mom and dad, would be comfortable. Richard still had three years remaining to complete his degree, but he was born with the gift of patience. He was willing to wait for as long as it took for him and Lexy to be together. Two weekends later Richard was standing in her parents living room asking permission to date their daughter, which her dad was highly in favour of, considering his mature attitude and his future earning potential. According to her father, he was a catch. One date led to another date, and so on and so forth. A few years later Richard graduated and started working for an Optometrist with a well-established practice with hundreds of patients and new ones continuously coming in. Soon after he was offered the chance to buy into the practice and he jumped at the opportunity. With his work future well in hand he asked Lexy's father for permission to marry his daughter, which he happily agreed to. Now he just had to convince Lexy to say yes, and happily, she did. Soon after the wedding they moved to Niagara-On-The Lake, and they bought their first house with a white picket fence, shutters on the windows, and a bright red door like she had always dreamed of having. Only a couple of years later his partner wanted to retire and he offered the balance of the practice to Richard for a lofty fee, but he was prepared to work hard for a while and pay off the debt knowing that this practice was going to generate substantial amounts of capital for their future. By the age of thirty Richard was able to pay off the purchase debt and then he got to paying off the mortgage. That's when Lexy announced to the family that she was with child and their families celebrated. Nine months later Robert, their first of three, was born. Lexy became a stay-at-home mother and never looked back. It was always her dream to be a good mother and an amazing wife. She took her duties seriously and was present for every little milestone that happened in her children's lives. She never missed an event no matter what was going on in her life. She adopted a super mom mentality and proved her efforts daily to her family. Their lives were storybook until Robert's unfortunate swimming pool accident. That was when Lexy and Richard realized that they were as vulnerable as the rest of the world and sometimes bad things happen to good people.

Lexy's phone lit up when the doctor's office called to set up an appointment and discuss further treatments for her condition. Lexy was becoming less interested in the care because she didn't feel like it was making any real difference to the way she felt every day. She felt guilty that she was taking the MDs away from really sick people who may still have a fighting chance, because she knew that it was curtains over for her, according to the specialist that she had seen this year. They had given her a zero percent chance of recovery. So, with that in mind, she simply asked for heavy duty pain relievers so when the end stage had arrived, she wouldn't sit around all day suffering. That scared the daylights out her. She probably had strong feelings about it after the loss of her son and the depression that had crept into her soul and beat the stuffing out of her for a couple of years. She only wanted meds that made you happy, even at the cost of not really knowing what was going on around her. She confirmed the appointment and hung up the phone only to have the screen light up again. She assumed it was the doctor's office calling her back to give her some kind of reminder, but it wasn't, it was Jimmy Smits. Lexy hesitated for second, she was scared for some reason to answer the phone, then she pressed the button and said, "Hello Mr. Smits. How are you today?" Within that moment she knew why she was afraid to answer, and it was because she realized that she feared her own demise and that's what Mr. Smits was to her now: her own personal Grim Reaper, a soothsayer of death.

"Hi there Lexy. Have I caught you at a suitable time?" He asked.

"It is the perfect time Mr. Smits. How can I be of assistance today?" She queried.

"I am going to need you in Toronto next week for an orientation meeting to discuss some future endeavours we have planned. Can you be there next Tuesday? It should be for one night only. I want to go over some ideas we have, and it would give you the chance to meet your assignment handler." Jimmy said. "Does this sound manageable to you Lexy?"

"Oh my, I just made a doctor's appointment a moment ago for the same day, but I will contact them and cancel it at once. So, yes, I am available for you on Tuesday." She answered.

"Excellent. That is what I love to hear, co-operation. Miss Larsen will send you the details of your transportation and lodging for your stay here. I think we can cover everything in one day but if not, please be available for a second night, if you don't mind." Jim said.

"No problem at all Mr. Smits. I will see you on Tuesday." She replied and disconnected the call. Instantly the butterflies in her stomach flapped around as she mentally prepared herself for the upcoming mission. She wondered if she was to be a suicide bomber and would never come home again, or if she would be given the simple order of placing a package in a locker somewhere, to be detonated later. None of it mattered now, she was committed to doing the job assigned to her and she would get it done! Although Richard had made lots of money over his tenure as an optometrist, Lexy was still enthralled with the idea that her two remaining sons could become millionaires and have a far easier life. The military was a wonderful opportunity, but it did not pay well enough for their sons to retire early. This job would solidify their futures without a doubt, and she needed to know that everybody was going to be okay once she had passed. This was her time to be courageous.

Lexy wandered into the kitchen and found Richard watching a CFL game while eating some mac and cheese at the table. She came up behind Richard and placed her hands on his shoulders and began softly massaging him. He breathed out a happy sigh and said, "Oh yeah, that's the ticket. Wonderful timing my darling, I was just saying to myself I would love a back rub, actually a rub of any kind would be nice." He placed his hands on hers and gave them a gentle squeeze to show his appreciation and affection. He stopped chewing on his food and leaned his head back against her chest and allowed her to continue the tenderness as she worked her way up his neck to his temples. She pressed in with a touch more pressure to stimulate him and he instantly thanked her for the kindness.

"Richard, I have a meeting with the Ministry in Toronto this Tuesday. They say it might be two days, but they are hoping it will just take one day. My contact has arranged the transportation and the hotel. I hope they put me up in the Royal York Hotel again. That place was absolutely stunning, and the rooms are magnificent. I wonder what it would be like to be able to afford to go to places like that for the rest of your life. You know, living in luxury." She spoke. She leaned over and kissed him on the forehead and whispered, "I Love you, Richard. You are a good man."

"I love you too Lexy. There is no denying that I am concerned that you are traveling again so soon after your last trip. You have barely had time to get your strength back. Are you sure this is a good idea?" Richard asked in a concerned voice.

She tried to do her Russian voice and intoned, "Me, I'm strong like bull. No troubles." Then giggled at her acting attempt.

"I just worry that you will become weak and burnt out and, in your condition, it is hard to bounce back from anything, you understand what I mean?" He worried.

"I promise to pace myself accordingly. No evening jogging around the U of T track. On the last visit we were either in the boardroom or in the hotel room and I can't imagine this trip will be any different. There are some final preparations that they need to review with me and then I will come back home. The last trip was terrific because they looked after me so attentively. I felt like royalty." Lexy explained.

"Well, you know best. I'm happy that they are taking care of the driving back and forth to the hotel. I sometimes dread driving on the QEW to Toronto. It's so fast and narrow." Richard added.

***

On Tuesday morning at 7:00 am the limousine was waiting in the driveway for Lexy to make an appearance. The driver approached the front door and knocked lightly. Lexy opened the door and set out with her single piece of luggage in her hand, which the driver took from her and escorted her down the stairs to the waiting car. She slipped into the back seat and found a soft blanket that she pulled up around her neck and promptly fell fast asleep until she heard the driver say, "Mrs. Winehouse, we will be arriving in just a minute. I thought you might like to allow yourself a chance to shake the cobwebs out, so-to-speak." He suggested.

"Thank you." She replied.

Lexy stared out the window at the city zipping by and pondered what her assignment was going to be. Was she going to be a hitman? She still had pent up nerves because she didn't know if she would have to go to another city, or even a different country. Lexy was not a world traveler and she got wound up sometimes just going to the grocery store, and now she may leave the country and exterminate some bad people. She felt a little sick to her stomach. Just what she didn't want on this trip, was a sick tummy. She arched her back and practiced her breathing exercises that the nurses had taught her to calm herself down, but to no avail. Maybe she would settle down once she got into the hotel room and laid on her bed for a bit. It had worked in the past, so it should work now. She started imagining that they would provide her with a firearm, although it was inconceivable. She had never shot a gun in her life. And what about the bullets? She didn't know how to load a gun. Lexy didn't know where to buy bullets. She inhaled deeply and exhaled for as long as she could. Again, easy calming breaths. Hopefully, they will give me a suitcase filled with dynamite or whatever type of exploding stuff they use nowadays to blow people up. I can put in down where instructed and make a run for it, oh that's right, you never run away, or you will attract suspicion. Drop off the suitcase and calmly walk away, not to garner any attention.

"Mrs. Winehouse, we are here." The driver quietly and calmly told her. He walked around the car and let her out. He passed the bag to the bellman, and he was on his way. Lexy felt a bit better because she had some familiarity to this hotel from her earlier visit and it helped ease her angst. Lexy checked in and headed up to the suites where she had stayed before. It was a different room number, but the inside of the room was similar to what she recalled. Finally, she could take off her shoes and lie on the bed for a minute and clear her head. As she stared up at the ceiling Lexy realized that she was no longer nervous, she was now terrified. "What the hell am I doing here. I should have opted out of this nonsense long before this, because now I'm trapped in downtown Toronto." Her heart was beating hard and fast, and she began thinking, "Am I going to have a heart attack right here in the hotel room?" Thump-thump…thump-thump…Panic was setting in. She wondered if she should call her husband. No, how about the front desk? Her breathing was getting harder to push air out and pull it back into her lungs. Oh, my goodness, I hope that I don't die here at the Royal York

Hotel. Lexy was fighting hard to take in little gasps of air…the room was getting darker…her heart was going to explode, and then…Lexy blacked out. She floated around the top edge of the room; she was terrified that she was going to melt right through the glass and be floating outside of the building. Twenty floors up and she was going to be soaring through space. She couldn't help herself anymore, she had to hold her breath and try to land back on the bed without crashing down to the floor. And then, darkness.

Five minutes later her cell phone illuminated and began to chime, she knew that she could hear the phone, but how, she was dead. The chiming stopped and she was still in total darkness until, there it was again. The phone chime, she mustered her strength and opened her eyes to find herself lying on the bed in the hotel room. Lexy let out a laugh because she was convinced, she had died, but apparently, she had not. This panic attack was a clear and telling sign that her body and mind now had a mind of their own. She picked the phone up in her hand and pressed the answer button, "Hello, this is Lexy."

"Hello Lexy, this is Laurent. I will be your handler for this task. Let's meet in your room tomorrow morning at 9:00 am, if that works for you?"

"Yes, of course Laurent. I will be ready. See in you the morning." She said.

She realized that night that she was at peace to meet her maker.

***

The following morning Laurent was knocking on Lexy's hotel room door promptly at nine o'clock as agreed. She opened the door and he headed to the sitting area in the suite. Sitting on the sofa he motioned for Lexy to take a seat beside him and opened up the file pocket he was carrying. He pulled out a photograph of a man she had never seen before and some architectural plans to a large-scale building with red lines indicating a proposed walking path through the building's interior. Laurent's strong French accent made it tricky to follow his instructions closely, but she continued to ask questions so that she completely understood her assignment. It was clear that she was going to enter a high-rise office tower in Montreal and go to the twenty second floor and take a package to the women's washroom and place it in the handicapped stall which backed onto the wall of the office of Jean Claude Moulin, who would be sitting on the other side of that same wall a mere ten feet away from the explosive device that would be detonated once Lexy had got herself to a safe distance away. Laurent spent hours going over the details in order to attract the least amount of attention to herself. If the police were to check all the CCTV cameras in the city core where the "accident" was going to take place, they certainly didn't want Lexy arriving in a limo.

She was instructed to wear ballet-slipper pink track pants with a non-matching Northern Reflections sweater. The two fumbled with a head scarf that she was to have on to keep her face hidden at all times on the street and in the designated building in order to remain anonymous. She was told to take a city bus to a nearby stop and walk to the building and enter through the parking garage underground ramp. She would go in through the doors to the elevator core and ride it up to the floor above the office of interest and then walk back down the nearest stairwell and enter the women's washroom from there. Laurent had a dummy bag, with nothing dangerous inside of it so Lexy could feel the weight of the bag and to be sure that she could easily carry it for the duration of the task. They worked with the bag, adjusting its shoulder strap to find a comfortable carrying position so Lexy could make the trek without running out steam before she could get the task completed. After several attempts they found a suitable strap length that would accommodate her comfort. Laurent had Lexy walk around the suite and sit in different chairs and stand up and sit down over and over to ad nauseum to make sure she had a sense of how it felt to move with the bag full. Once they were both happy with the bag, they began to discuss its contents and what was going to happen the day that she delivered the package to the office building. He explained to her about the active material she was to courier and how volatile it was and what she would need to be careful of to make sure the package (and her) arrived in one piece. Laurent had ample experience with different dangerous materials, so he tried to give Lexy the C-4 101 crash course so she understood what not to do until she made it to her target site. He told her not to allow the package to get too hot or sit in direct sunlight for a long of a period of time and covered off the other maintenance concerns to be sure she didn't have it explode before it was placed correctly. He showed her the remote control and how to activate the package so she could set the bomb off from a covert position using an electronic signal from the parking lot directly across the street. Nobody would pay any attention to an old lady digging through her shopping bag on the side of the street for a couple of seconds and that would be all the time she would need to press the button on the remote and ignite the package. Laurent had samples so Lexy could touch and feel the remote and get used to its' weight and feel and what each buttons' functions were. After an exhausting amount of time Laurent believed that Lexy understood the equipment and was ready to complete everything with some modicum of confidence. He looked at her as she practiced once more getting the bag over her shoulder in a comfortable position so she could make the trip effortlessly and suggested, "How about if we break for something to recharge our batteries and reconvene in two hours, would that be okay with you Lexy?"

“That would be wonderful. I am famished and everything on the menu here is amazing.” Lexy replied.

“Alright then, I’ll be back here in two hours. See you then” he stated and headed down the short hallway to the exit door and left.

Lexy had been told that Jean Claude Molin was a despicable person who was a king pin in a world-wide human trafficking organization that would steal children from countries all over the world and then sell them, ensuring that they were moved into other countries that spoke different languages, with dissimilar cultures so the kids would never be able to find a way out of the system until they had been used to a point where their value would diminish to zero. Then they were disposed of in a variety of ways, usually death. She was led to believe that eliminating Jean Claude Moulin would have a serious domino effect and could help eradicate this world-wide crime for good. If this man was killed there would be thousands of children set free and less children would disappear without a trace around the world. That is what Lexy was being told, however; it was a far cry from the truth. Jean Claude Moulin was Guy Tremblay’s right-hand man who was responsible for overseeing most of Guy’s operations world-wide. He had nothing to do with child abduction or the enslavement of people anywhere, but Lexy didn’t know that. Jean Claude oversaw Guy’s shipping and mining operations around the globe. He was highly educated and had been involved in the shipping of containers and bulk goods for years and was well versed on mining of precious metals and the transportation of them to other countries. He had never traded or sold a human soul in his life, and he wasn't about to start. His connection to Guy Tremblay was simple in that he was a key individual who happened to be working for Serge Bouchard's archrival. Serge knew all too well that one needed surround themselves with people who were smarter than them and Jean Claude was exactly that, however; he knew if he wanted to hurt Guy's businesses, he would need to start at the top echelon to create the most havoc. By taking out one of Guy's top executives, it would be an extremely difficult role to replace, so he was selected to begin the reign of terror that would herald the demise of his operations. There were others on Serge's death list, but Jean Claude was going to be an excellent starting point. Serge was determined to have his revenge on Guy Tremblay for stealing his girl and ruining his chance in life for love.

Two hours later Laurent rapped on Lexy's door, and the two resumed their planning. They discussed the transportation and where she would be staying while she was in Montreal. She was to arrive on a Tuesday, do the deed on the Wednesday, and head back to Toronto on the Thursday morning and would be transported back to Niagara on the Lake. They needed to make sure that her arrival time to the office was precisely coordinated so that Jean Claude would be in the building at the correct place for the highest level of success. This would be communicated to her via cell phone so there would be no mistakes. Go to building, drop off bag, head to parking lot, press button. Laurent was pleased with his tutelage because Lexy actually seemed to be reasonably capable. The two had a cocktail to celebrate her enormous triumph and wrap up any loose ends. Soon after Laurent left her room and called Jimmy from the hotel lobby. "Hello Jim. Just checking in to bring you up to date on the training session with Mrs. Winehouse. She is well prepared, and I strongly believe that she will be able to complete her obligation without incident" he said.

"This is wonderful news Laurent. How soon do think she could head to Montreal?" Jimmy asked.

"If I had my way, I would send her today, but I know things don't work like that. She is of sound mind and body so the sooner the better, next week if the dates work for you Jim." He explained.

"Excellent. I'll get back to you with dates and times. Splendid work Laurent. We'll speak soon." Jim said.

When Lexy arrived back to her house the next day, she was exhausted. She managed to walk in the door and make it to the couch before she dropped herself on the sofa and quickly began to slumber. Richard left her alone and covered her with a blanket and waited for her to wake up and fill him in on all the goings on. Little did he realize that Lexy was planning to murder somebody in Montreal the following week.

Her mind awoke and she was familiar with the surroundings but chose to lie still on the couch until she had thought of a great yarn to tell Richard, because she knew that he was going to ask a lot of questions. Especially when she told him that she was going to heading out of town again rather soon. She didn't know exactly when, but Lexy was hoping that all of this would end sooner rather than later. She pried her tired eyes open to find Richard sitting very attentively on the chair beside her, anxiously waiting to chat with her. The two exchanged dialogue for a couple of hours but Lexy was being guarded in what she could and couldn't say without revealing too much information. "Not to worry sweetheart, I'm just heading out of town for a couple of nights to kill a human trafficking monster," her inner voice was saying. She of course told Richard that she was heading to Montreal for a radical new cancer treatment that the Ministry was providing, and she would only be away for a few nights so he shouldn't worry at all. He was clearly at a point where he didn't want to rock the boat, seeing that he was continuously told that Lexy had only one year at the most to live. Wasted words and heated arguments had no place in his relationship anymore. He just wanted her to live her best life or, whatever was left of it.

The cell phone face lit up on a Sunday night and Lexy answered promptly. She was briefly given instructions and was told that the transportation arrangements were to follow. She was to fly out of Toronto next Tuesday returning home on Thursday evening. "Short and sweet," she thought to herself. She could feel a surge of anxiety wash over her while she stood in her bedroom contemplating the upcoming task. Did she have the mettle to do this? She was a little old lady. Why would anyone ask this of an old woman like me? Then her reality came rushing back into her head in the manner of cash dollars that was going to change her children's' lives, that's why. She packed her bag that night, so she wouldn't have to think about the trip until the morning when she was to be picked up at her home.

Lexy landed in Montreal on Tuesday afternoon and went directly to the Ritz Carlton and checked into her room. Soon after she had figured out how to turn on the TV, there was a knock at her door. When she swung the door open Laurent was standing there and said, "May I come in Mrs. Winehouse?"

"Of course, Laurent, please, yes, come in." She fumbled and stood aside.

"I will be onsite tomorrow to assist you, but I will not be visible. I will provide you with an ear device so you can communicate with me at all times. But don't forget yourself and start speaking to me accidently while you are by yourself, or people will think you are crazy. Okay?" Laurent instructed.

"Yes. I understand." She replied.

"Lets' go over the package one more time." He said and began to recap the usage instructions of the explosive and the remote control to make sure Lexy was armed with knowledge on their operational procedure.

Lexy then questioned, "What is this red button beside the red light?"

"Do not push that button or the package will explode. That is the direct switch, which are usually used by suicide bombers or their ilk. You press that and your day will be ruined." Laurent coached.

"What time should I be there tomorrow? I mean, in order to have the bomb in the right place?" She asked.

"Jean Claude takes his lunch every day at 12:00 noon. He only stays away for one hour before he goes back into his private office on the top floor and returns to his work. He does this each day like clockwork, so we are confident that our intelligence is strong. You need to have the device in the women's washroom by 12:40 pm and it needs to be put into the handicap stall so the device will be against the wall. He is directly on the other side of the wall so the device can do the greatest amount of damage. If someone is in the stall ahead of you, just wait. If she hasn't left the stall by 12:55 pm start pleading with her that you are going to poop yourself and you need the special needs stall, I'm sure they would understand. Right?" He confirmed.

"I can't imagine that will be a problem, but I will do as you ask." She replied.

"Excellent. Have you reviewed the bus schedule? 455 Rene Levesque Bld. West is fairly close by but give yourself ample time. If you arrive early just grab a coffee but cover your face as much as possible without being obvious. Any other questions Lexy?" Laurent asked.

"No more questions. I'm as prepared as I'll ever be. When will I see you again?" She queried.

"Never. This is our last hoorah. So, Mrs. Winehouse, I bid you adieu." He said and walked out the door of her room.

She walked over to the bar and poured two fingers of bourbon and emptied the glass. "Now to try and get some sleep," she thought to herself.

***

The next morning came five minutes after she had sunk her head onto the pillow, or so it felt like it. She was feeling weary this morning and decided to have a shower even though this wasn't a typical shower day for her. The warm water and the wonderfully fragrant soaps and lotions provided on the shelf were rejuvenating to her body and mind. She couldn't remember the last time a shower was that empowering but she was pleased that it was helping with her growing fear, which was building by the minute. No big deal, she was expecting this. She had to press on and get out the door. She donned her unassuming old lady ensemble and strapped the package over her shoulder. She checked for her room key, the device, her purse, with the bus fare inside the change purse. She was set. Headed down to the lobby and stepped onto the street. Swiftly her bus arrived at the stop and whisked her away to the destination on Rene Levesque Boulevard. It seemed like she had just sat down when the driver was warning her that her stop was next. She gingerly exited the bus and walked down the block to the correct address. The time was 11:45 am. Seemed too early to head upstairs and hang around in a bathroom. She saw a nearby bookstore and ducked in to browse. Before she knew it was 12:30 pm. Time to insert the communication earpiece into her ear. She stuffed it in the ear cavity, and it instantly came to life. "Hello Lexy. Do you copy, over?" Laurent said.

"Yes, I copy, over." She replied.

"You should be heading down to the underground parking right now. You need to haul ass Lexy." He ordered.

Lexy was taken aback. She hadn't been spoken to like that since she met Laurent and was having a hard time figuring out why he was being so abrupt. She scurried down the ramp and entered the elevator core as ordered. The door opened and she selected the top floor and waited. Soon after, the doors opened, and she stepped out and made her way to the bathrooms as planned. She stepped inside and was relieved to see that the handicap stall was unoccupied, and she swiftly stepped inside and locked the stall door. Her heart was beating faster and faster again as it did days before and it made her nervous. She sat on the toilet and began to take slow controlled breaths while she opened the top of her bag and checked her device. She reached her hand in and switched the power on, and the red light came to life. Perfect. Now all she had to was wait for Laurent to tell her when it was time for her to leave. Thump-thump, thump-thump. She could not believe her bad luck. She was having another panic attack, so she thought. As she sat there waiting for the signal she whispered, "Laurent, do you hear me, over?"

"Loud and clear Lexy. I am in front of the building and will let you know when he has entered the building. Once he is up there, we just need a few minutes to be sure he is back at his desk, okay, over."

"Understood, over." She responded.

She was feeling apprehensive but there was something weird going on. Her body wasn't feeling right. She looked at the device to double check the light, it was on. She reached in her pocket to retrieve the remote control…that's odd…she was sure that she put it in this pocket. Overwhelming panic gripped her. She began to ravage through all her pockets in search of the little remote control, but then it came to her, and she had a clear vision of where it was, on the table by the exit door of her room. Her heart sank deeper. What had she done? Thump-thump, thump-thump. These heart beats were stronger than any that she had ever felt in her life. As she sat on the toilet something was happening to the left side of her body. She was begging to slump down and could no longer lift her left arm. “Holy shit, I’m having a stroke,” she thought to herself. She was correct as she slowly lowered herself down off the throne and onto the cold tile floor. Her right arm still had some movement, so she grabbed the package and pulled to towards herself.

“Lexy, the target is on his way up. I’ll let you know when it is time for you to exit the building.” Laurent instructed.

Lexy tried to answer but she couldn’t speak. Something was wrong with her mouth; her tongue wasn’t working quite right. Lexy immediately knew she was in deep trouble. She reached out with her right arm and was stunned that its’ motion was seriously compromised. She managed to get her hand to the device’s control switch. The bathroom floor was getting colder as her body continued to sink further down. She felt like she had been turned into a puddle of jelly. She again tried to communicate but only gibberish came out of her mouth, she was having a major stroke and there was nothing she could do about it. A moment later the earpiece crackled, and Laurent said, “Okay Lexy, it is time for you to set the device and get the hell out of there, over.” He instructed.

He waited for an answer. Where was she? What's going on? She was fighting to stay conscious at this point and was struggling to keep her eyes opened. She glanced at the red button, moved her hand over, and pressed it.

Chapter Nine

Serge was pleased with the results when Jimmy called him with an update on the current project. Although he had money resources beyond measure, he was still a skinflint at heart and was always seeking out ways to avoid paying for anything. The recruitment of the women in their program had not cost him a dime until this point except for the cost of the hotel rooms and some airline travel, which was chicken feed to man like Serge. He was eager to move ahead with the project and was hoping that he could continue without having any further issues like what had happened with Lexy Winehouse. He was not interested in trying cover up any mishaps along the way, but he knew that completing the type of work that these women had committed to doing was going to have it's up and downs and he was acutely aware that there would be collateral damage. It is impossible to eliminate human beings from earth without stirring up some questions as to their whereabouts. Richard Winehouse was screaming from the rooftops about the disappearance of his wife after she went to Montreal for a quick medical procedure and never came home and had yet to be heard from or any idea as to her location. Richard had no means to track her down because the cell phone the Ministry had provided to her was also missing and its location tracker was not activated, so there was no way for him to find Lexy. He contacted the Ritz Carlton in Montreal, but they explained to him that she checked in but had never checked out of the hotel. Richard couldn't imagine that she was involved in the explosion that took place in a downtown Montreal office tower, however the authorities had found nothing that could link her to the crime scene. It was going to be a long while for investigators to discover Lexy's DNA in the woman's lavatory on the top floor of that building. It would take some time to review the CCTV tapes to see that she had entered the building but had never exited the premises. However, the truth was that eventually her blood was going to be found at the crime scene and that would add a whole new angle to the event. When the police discovered that she was at the building for no reasonable explanation whatsoever, she would become a person of interest. Then they would need to piece together why this little old lady was in the bathroom where the explosion took place, and this could be extremely difficult to piece together. The real concern was that the Canadian Authorities were good at their jobs, and it was only going to be a matter of time until the police would be knocking on Richard Winehouse's door asking him about his missing wife and why was she at the scene of the crime? This was going to set off a plethora of questions that Richard didn't have any answers for, but he had enough information to help the police with their investigation and send them in the direction of the Ministry of Special Projects, which potentially could create an entire new line of questions to be answered.

His phone lit up, and he answered, “Hello Sir, how can I be of service?” Jimmy asked.

“I have concerns regarding Richard Winehouse. When the authorities find their way to this man, he has some information that could possibly be problematic for me. Contact Dr. Cook and arrange for him to be neutralized. No traces.” Serge said.

“I understand. Consider it done. Anything else sir?” Jim obeyed.

“Yes. Jimmy you are doing an excellent job. You have taken this idea and made it a real winner so far. It’s working. Let’s amp up the duties on the next task and see how they work together. Try your next level assignment.” Serge stated.

“Thank you, Serge. That means a lot to me.” He recomposed himself because he was thrown off by Serge’s compliment. He was used to Serge being business 24/7 and wasn’t used to Serge noticing anything personal. “I will roll out the next project with two candidates immediately sir.” Jimmy said. He was pleased that he was being recognized for his hard work. He called the doctor and instructed him to go to Niagara on the Lake and have a sit down with Richard Winehouse.

***

Jimmy and Scarlet met at a local bistro in downtown Toronto and ordered coffee and scones. They got caught up with the personal niceties and Jim laid out the action plan to be set into motion. Their meeting was to exchange the details so they both could make the necessary arrangements to get started.

***

Dr. Thomas Cook was contacted and given instructions to head for Niagara on the Lake and drop in on Richard Winehouse. He caught the next available flight to Pearson airport in Toronto. When he landed, he rented a car and began his drive down the QEW South to the destination in a calm and orderly fashion. Dr. Cook was never one to panic before performing his most desired duty. He stayed as cool as a cucumber. He took his exit and headed down the road to the Niagara on the Lake area. After driving around in circles and slowly dissecting his way through the streets to check out his routes of escape and after an extensive search of the surrounding area he drove past the house and saw the front porch light was on and TV flashes were visible from the outside as he went past. Richard was home. He continued to sweep the area and found a place that he could abandon the car and not be noticed if he diverted through a small, treed area out the back of the house and snuck in that way. One hour later he saw the front porch light extinguish and waited one more hour for good measure. He then crept out of the rental car and, quietly as he could, closed the door. Down around to the wooded area he slid in between the trees until he was standing behind the house. All looked clear with no lights on in the interior of the home. He deftly made his way across the backyard and headed for the back door of the house. He walked up quietly and pulled his handy tap key out and quickly had the door open to the house. What the good doctor did not know is that Jeremy was staying at his dad's house in his old bedroom to keep him company while they waited to hear if any news became known about the disappearance of Lexy. The doctor slid his way through the house and looked in the bedrooms and happened to come across Richard's bedroom and stood in the doorway and made sure there was no movement. He instantly filled the syringe he had brought with him with a lethal dose of poison and began to step into the room and walk over to the bed when his head felt like it had exploded. He cast into long dark and narrow hallway with one small light at the end. What the hell was happening to him? The light grew a little bit, he was starting to get his bearing back when he felt the same pain as before, a sharp stinging pain to the head. He snapped out of his temporary funk for a split second to see Jeremy walking toward him with a roll of duct tape and a cast iron frying pan. Dr. Cook instantly knew what that sudden inability to function was, he had been hit in the head by a heavy object and he also knew he could not allow that tape to be wrapped around his hands or he would be dead. If not killed by his current target, for sure someone from the Ministry would see to it. He swung his legs forcefully forward as Jeremy came towards him again for a repeat strike at him with the frying pan and caught him off guard and collapsed onto his back on the floor and had the wind knocked out of him. This was allowing the doctor a few more seconds to regain his bearings and withstand the onslaught. He knew that any second Richard was going to be arriving, eager to see what the heck is going on in the hallway. Richard burst into the hall with a small caliber handgun and aimed it directly at the doctor and fired. The gun made a clicking noise but no projectiles emerged from the gun because Lexy had unloaded the gun months before so she wouldn't be tempted to shoot herself rather than go through any cancer treatment. He fired the gun six more times with the same result, click, click… The doctor quickly recovered the hypodermic needle and plunged it into Richard's unsuspecting arm and drained its contents. Richard instantly felt the surge of the lethal drug and slumped to the floor. Jeremy was just about to sit up, having regained his breath and was struck from behind in the head by his father's handgun that the doctor had recovered off the floor. Grabbing the roll of duct tape, he bound Jeremy's hands and feet together and taped over his eyes and mouth. He left him on the floor and went down the street and collected his rental car and brought it back to the house and parked in the rear of the home outside of the garage. He popped open the trunk and slung Jeremy into the cavity, leaning with his numb arms to close the lid. He wheeled the car out of the driveway and headed down the street to the closest park or field so he could stop and rest for a minute or two. He reached back his hand to the back of his head and gingerly touched the sensitive area and was met with a wave of pain that shot through his body. He drew back his hand and instinctively looked at his fingertips only to find them smothered in blood. The doctor knew he was injured but he was not sure how severely at this moment. He found an empty parking lot behind a closed auto dealer and stopped the car. Eyes were fighting to close, and he knew the fight was futile. Could not resist the temptation and his eyes shut, and he drifted off. It was thirty hours later when his eyes opened, and he found himself still completely alone in the parking lot behind the dealership. He heard a thumping sound coming the back of the car when remembered that Jeremy was still alive in the trunk. The doctor reached over his morning cup of coffee, which was ice cold, but he needed fluids of any kind, so he gulped it down. What was he going to do with Jeremy in the trunk? There was no doubt in his mind that he was in need of some medical attention, but he needed to dispose of the problem that was currently stored just feet away. Looking around for a length of garden hose he decided upon an easy solution. He grabbed the duct tape and put the garden hose into the tail pipe and taped it on securely, he then took the deadly end and placed it in the front of the car. He turned on the engine, placed the hose in the window and snugged it up and closed the car door to make the seal. The fumes immediately began to do their work and flood the car with deadly toxins and Jeremy will simply fall asleep and never wake up. This act will hopefully end the streak of bad luck that has been running through the Winehouse family as of late. He sauntered down Niagara Boulevard for a ways and stopped at the Sterling House Bed and Breakfast and took a room for the night. He had a shower and wrapped his head firmly with bandages and took a few pain killers and went to bed. If he woke up the next morning, he was going to consider this an exceptionally good day indeed. If he didn't, he had it coming.

***

The story was they have found the location of the group responsible for stealing millions of taxpayers' dollars away from the elderly nationwide on a yearly basis and, enough is enough. There was a big rally and picnic planned to have an opportunity to meet with the dignitaries and share some food and fun, but they knew it was all smoke and mirrors to get the trust of the elderly so they could gather their personal information and continue to steal all of their hard-earned money away from them. Jimmy and Scarlet knew that there would be several high-ranking officials and it would create a chance to have many of them in one place and at one time, so the setting was ideal. The participating women would be told to yell out negative comments when the party members began speaking and hiss and boo, and they knew that they would be hauled off by the security guards that would be stationed throughout the grounds during the event.

The part they would not know is the handy little portable chairs they were given were actually made out of explosive materials which are capable of extensive range of destruction from each unit. The security guards will never be expecting the seating material to be explosive, and it can passed through a metal detector. The plan is to have the two ladies move into strategic positions among the crowd at specific spots on the grounds and when the party members begin gathering and giving their speeches, the ladies will activate the devices and walk away quietly. "The only fear I have is that some good Samaritan will stop one of the ladies from getting away and bring their chair back to them because they think the old lady forgot it and then it would mess up our intended target area. No matter, the destructive range should be quite effective as long as the explosives are close to their designated target zone." Jim said.

"Our next two candidates are both of sound mind so I think they should be capable of staying with the portable chairs until they are given the signal to move away, and since they both are quite fit, we won't need to worry about them maneuvering through the crowds or falling down. I think this will go smoothly." Scarlet professed confidently.

"Let's hope so. I know we are having tremendous luck right now and I don't want to jinx it. Everyone on our active list has been successful or, successfully eliminated. It almost feels like we're good at this." Jimmy brazenly laughed out loud.

"Okay, I'll make the travel arrangements for Willow Smythe and Louise Gagnon to be in Montreal the day before they are required. We can lead them into thinking that they are helping all the seniors in Canada if we can crush these money mogul monsters and stop them from taking the money right out of their families hands. They have to be stopped, but how?" Scarlet giggled and shook her fist in the air.

The two collected their belongings and headed for the exit door. Once they were outside, they both walked away in different directions.

***

They had to arrange for two different handlers to implement the onsite work which would mean that Luc Bordeaux would head to Quebec to guide Louise Gagnon and Laurent Pillared would fly to Victoria BC and help Willow to get prepared for their task. The plan was to make sure that the women were made aware of the fact that there would be two people working simultaneously on the endeavour, for the first time. They would not need to hang out together and sit in the audience together, but just knowing that they would be helping the Ministry to accomplish this quest of squelching some of the truly evil people in the country, was going to hopefully inspire them as they went through the procedures. A team building exercise - of sorts. The handlers would visit the women and go through the procedures and ready them for the political picnic event to be held in Montreal in Le Champ-de-Mars off Saint Antoine East Street the following month which was a few weeks away leaving little time to get finalized. Scarlet made all the travel, hotel, and flight arrangements for the group and began to dispatch the required information to the necessary parties. The folding transportable chairs would be dropped off in the participants rooms once they had arrived in Montreal so the devices would not have to go through any screening beforehand. The chairs would be equipped with a micro-chip that would receive the signal from a transformer to set the devices off, which would essentially be handled by the back-up team on site to make sure on positioning to create the most amount of collateral damage when the devices exploded. There was a high potential for the team not to make it out of the park alive but that was on a need-to-know basis and the ladies just didn't need to know. They didn't want the women to be worried about their own humanity and survival as much as they wanted them to be focused on the task at hand. There were going to be thousands of people there that day, but their focus was on just one person in the crowd, Benoit Dupuis, who was Guy Tremblay's trusted assistant. For years now, the two had spoken every day of the week. The joke between the two men was they knew each other so well that they could take over each other's lives and nobody would know the difference; with the exception of their looks, so there would be a good chance that their wives would figure it out without needing a detective. The team knew all too well that if something happened to Benoit it would a big hit to the successful running of Guy's vast empire. His business wouldn't implode but it could affect Guy greatly and the day-to-day operations of his enterprises may suffer enormously. This is what Serge Bouchard was hoping for, Guy's organization to begin to fall into chaos, one step at a time.

Chapter Ten

Willow Smythe hadn't been on a plane in over twenty years, with one exception. Once she and Dennis moved to Pentrelew Place in downtown Victoria they had sworn they would only leave the island if they absolutely had to, which hadn't come up until Willow's trip to Toronto to meet with the Ministry of Special Projects just a brief time ago. Ever since her and Dennis had gone to spend some time in Thailand for a few months, years before when she got home to Canada, she kept having inner bowel troubles that just wouldn't go away. Even after having met with a battery of doctors all testing and probing her in many different ways and several tests to find the underlying cause of her ailment, they couldn't seem to find anything wrong, however; Willow had never been right again since her return from that trip. Her insides would seldom cooperate with her, and it became the bane of her existence. She was forever going to the bathroom where ever they went. Sometimes she couldn't finish off her grocery shopping without having to stop and find a facility to use in a hurry. Her simple life with her "A" Grade health was now compromised, and it changed how they were able to travel from total freedom to needing to be sure that they knew where all the public restrooms were at all times. Willow finally gave in because of countless accidents and began to don pull-ups, which is like a diaper for grownups, on a full-time basis. They did work wonderfully well; however, Willow was a woman filled with pride and felt like a slug when she would be traipsing around the world with a diaper fully soiled with God only knows what every day as they tried to visit monuments and tourist sites. She couldn't allow herself to get used to the horrible sensation of having excrement in her pants as she moved her way through the world. So, she and Dennis decided to give up on long trips and stay put in Victoria and the surrounding areas for their future trips. Day trips only. Now that the Ministry had asked her to work with them on some projects, she understood that she would have to travel but she also decided to take it on the chin and get used to doing what she had to in order to obtain the big payday that would be coming her way. Her and Dennis were humble people, and she wanted the opportunity to change her children's lives forever with the gift of money. According to the Ministry, big money. There was no way that she and Dennis would be able to come up with a million dollars per kid, it just wasn't obtainable without the Ministry's help. Willow had already done all of the soul searching as to whether or not this was a good idea because it wasn't a good idea. Murder is still a crime no matter how you try to paint it, and she knew that. What she also knew is that she would be dead within the next year from cancer that she was convinced that she had caught some kind of virus that the doctors in Canada just hadn't come across before. Nobody had ever linked her cancer to the intestinal woes, but she had women's intuition, and she knew she was right. Nonetheless, she was diagnosed with cancer, and she was going to pass sooner than she and Dennis would like. The money was the carrot and she found herself chasing that dream even though she had no way of confirming that the Ministry would ever pay them. "Blind faith," she thought to herself.

She was only a couple of months away from her eightieth birthday and Dennis was eighty-three. The two had been married for almost sixty years and had never had a fight or raised their voices at each other their entire lives. The two met when they were teenagers when Dennis was on a hockey team that was to billet into players homes in Campbell River that Willow's brother played for. The local team put up the Port Hardy team and the two met at her parents dinner table before the big game. Later that night after the visiting team beat her brother's team 11 to 1, they came back to the house and stayed up late with the parents and played board games and told stories. Dennis had never seen a family like theirs's before. Happy, friendly, all the siblings were getting along, and they loved to laugh out loud as much and as often as they could. This was very new to a boy that had two brothers that hadn't had a heart-to-heart conversation in his life. Dennis simply adored this family and what they stood for, unity. Later that evening, as everybody was heading to bed, Willow asked Dennis if he would like to stay up a bit later and watch a movie with her and her brother to which Dennis responded instantly with a big yes! They all piled onto the sofa and started watching Escape From Witch Mountain and shortly thereafter Willow's brother Sam was out cold, so Willow snuggled in a bit closer to Dennis and asked him, "Have you ever frenched kissed a girl before?"

"Of course, I have, I'm eighteen years old you know." He said but he had never kissed a girl unless you were to add his female dog Sophie which had licked his face countless times when he would arrive home from school every day. Willow was almost sixteen, but she wanted to try kissing a boy and she saw her opportunity with Dennis. He would be there for a night and the next day he would be on his way home never to be seen again. The perfect rendezvous. No commitments and NO embarrassment. She repositioned herself to give her suave lover full access to her lips and he took full advantage. For six to seven minutes his mouth was on Willow's with his tongue pressed into her mouth. This was insanity, he had never felt anything like this before. He conjured up the courage and placed his hand on her upper thigh, he was a Demi-God. Wait till he told his buddies about this, but they would never believe him. "You're full of shit Dennis," they would taunt him. He was in unfamiliar territory when she took his hand and pushed it up under her blouse and let him rest his hand on her flat chest. His lower down man parts were going kooky. This was incredible until,

"Willow honey, it's time to turn off the TV and hit the sack. It's getting late and we have church in the morning." Her father beckoned. Dennis's throbbing was brought back under control once he heard the deep tones of her dad's manly voice. His hand was quickly removed from the fun zone and placed back onto his own lap, but with a huge smile and one last little kiss as her brother was coming to from his slumber. This was literally the greatest evening of his life, and he would see her in the morning. His mind raced for hours as he lay there thinking about what had happened and he was infatuated with Willow.

The following morning the family arose to the sounds of symphony music, and they all met at the dining room table to eat breakfast before they left for church which Dennis had never stepped inside the front door of in his existence. The family was taking turns naming the composers and the song titles in a game of "Name That Tune" with no real rules but the happiness was abounding. They invited Dennis to attend church with them that morning which he agreed to instantly. They would go to the service and then they would drop Dennis off back at the ice rink at noon so he could head home with his team. He entered the church with the family and could see the outpouring of love and joy being shared amongst each other and he wanted to be part of these good vibes he was feeling. He sat in a row with the family and seconds later the Pastor appeared on the stage followed by a large group of musicians and a choir of people that began to sing spiritual songs loud and clear. The part that really blew Dennis's mind was that all of the audience sang along with the choir with strong and unabashed voices. No feeling shy or silly with this group of people, they were going to sing to the Lord at the top of their lungs and sing they did. Dennis was spinning with all these new sensations being thrust upon him and then it happened...did he feel Willow's finger tips dancing around his open hand. Yes, he did, she was looking right into his eyes smiling and singing along with the other parishioners while she tried to touch his hand. He suddenly pulled back his hand in fear that her mother or father would be angered by such an action, but they were not. She looked right at him and put his hand in hers and held them up to the heavens above and continued to sing. Dennis fully embraced the feeling of praise that day and decided that he wanted this feeling to be part of his life from that day forward, so he decided to become a pastor once he graduated from school. They walked out of the church and headed back to the ice rink but when they got there the whole family got out of the car to hug Dennis goodbye. He had never experienced this kind of love for his fellow man before, but he was keenly interested in having this feeling continue to be a big part of his life. Once he had hugged the entire family he came to Willow and she kissed him on the cheek and said, "Whoever knows the path of life and where it may take you, but it was nice to have met you on this part of your life. You're really cute Dennis" as she leaned in and hugged him one last time. They all watched Dennis climb onboard the bus and he sat in a seat beside the window, as they waved goodbye with vigor. His visit had been life altering. A couple years later he graduated from high school and was still involved with his local church in Port Hardy, but he had never changed his mind about his interest in worship and becoming a pastor. He found an opening at a church in Campbell River and applied for the position just to get his foot in the door. Soon after he moved to Campbell River, found a place to rent and began his internship with the Christian Life Fellowship and so began his new life of service to the Lord. He also knew that Willow was still in high school but did attend the church services every Sunday, so he was planning to run into her casually one morning at the service. A couple of weeks went by and finally she came through the door with her family on a Sunday morn and she was even more beautiful than he had remembered. He couldn't stop staring at her, but he looked away so as not to embarrass her with his childish crush. Her mother finally noticed Dennis lurking about, and she pointed him out to Willow and said, "Isn't that the boy that stayed at our house years ago? It sure looks like him. He has aged a bit and cut his hair, but I am sure that's him."

Willow's eyes darted around the room to spot the elusive visiting boy that French kissed her all that time before, and then she made eye contact with him. She had heard the term "Love at first sight," but had never believed it to be true however, her heart was overwhelmed, and she smiled brilliantly and began to weep. She didn't realize that she actually had feelings for this boy, and she really missed him. She walked over to him and hugged him with a bear hug to show her keen interest in him.

"What are you doing here?" She asked.

"I have decided to give my life to serve the Lord, and you if possible." He declared.

"I have never forgotten that night with you in my parent's basement. You stirred something in me that I haven't felt since that night. I am glad you are back." She leaned into him and kissed his cheek.

"Is there any chance to buy you a coffee or soda after service this morning?" He asked her.

"I'm available for all of them. Every morning Dennis. My heart is full right now because of your appearance. I need you in my life." She finished and went back to sit with her family. She tapped the empty seat beside her beckoning for him to join them. When he did, they all looked over and smiled and nodded approvingly. He was part of a new family now. He smiled and secretly hooked his little finger around hers and she leaned her body towards his and said, "Welcome back Mr. Smythe. Nice to have you back where you belong."

From that day to this, Willow and Dennis were always together. They spent their lives trying to be good citizens and good church members. They believed that the Lord would provide to them what they needed in life, and they had a chance to travel around the world supplying missionary help to less fortunate people around the globe. When the two returned home after a year in Congo with the church and teaching the word of Christ, they decided to get married. As to be expected the pair had children soon after and settled down in a small house in her parent's neighbourhood where they stayed for the next twenty-four years. Michael, Jacob, Mary, and Eve were all born at the local hospital in Campbell River and went to the same schools and had the same companionship that lured Dennis back to the town in the first place, and of course, Willow. Like so many families the children grew up fast and spread themselves all over Canada so by the time Dennis and Willow were sixty they were empty nesters. They continued to work with their community until Dennis was offered the opportunity to oversee the Parish at Christ Church Cathedral in Victoria. The two of them agreed to the position and made the move to the city which they loved and never looked back. They had found a blissful life that allowed them the happiness and friendships that they had always enjoyed throughout their lives. Unfortunately, cancer also found its' way into their lives and this time the Lord was powerless to stop it. Her faith was strong, but her body was human, and soon the disease began to ravage her internal organs, as the doctors had predicted, but she wore a smile for every Sunday service she attended. The only thing that Willow had to struggle with now was her ability to perform the action the Ministry had asked her to do, murder somebody. No matter what their crime, the church will find forgiveness. Not Willow, she knew that she would have a positive effect on the family once she was gone and they received the money promised to her by the Federal Government. She would do what she had to do in order to make her family's lives easier, no matter what was asked of her. This was going to be her parting gift to her husband and children. They deserved this money for all of the years that they sacrificed to try and enhance other peoples' lives.

Willow knew that she still had to explain to Dennis that she was needed in Montreal in the following weeks for a few days and she knew that she would be hit with resistance from him, big time. He did not want her to travel anymore without him or for any reason. He wanted to be her hero and be there for her through her last days on earth before she met her Lord. She conjured up an idea that the Ministry had a new radical cancer treatment that they were running trial tests with, and they desperately needed more test patients to try it out. This way she could tell Dennis that it could be of great benefit to her if the new drugs actually worked. She smiled to herself and felt it was a plausible story and, she waited for the opportunity to explain it all to him when she saw him later that night. A few hours after Willow received a message from Laurent to let her know that he would be coming to Victoria to discuss the upcoming piece of work and cover all the details. When he disconnected the line minutes later, she got an email with the travel details, dates, and times. It was her turn to help Canadian seniors fight back for what was theirs already, or, so she thought.

***

Louise Gagnon was relieved when she found out her task was to be staged in her hometown of Montreal. She was in the throes of feeling crummy a lot more often than she would like, but she could still walk and talk and cook for her family so Louise remained grateful for her current status. The slow deterioration of her body and mind in the last two years had beaten her down tremendously. She was a singer and actress from the time she hit the stage in her first high school production of Annie. She was the understudy for the lead role in Grade Eight but from that point forward, she practiced every aspect of her new found craft and put her heart & soul into it from then on. She only had the lead parts in all other productions she was cast for, and took countless hours of singing, dancing, and acting lessons to hone her skills so when she was graduated from high school, she attended Juilliard in New York and then attended the

Academy of Dramatic Arts West. Upon completion she was a well-rounded performer with stunning looks and charisma that could light up a room. She was special. Soon after her graduation from the Academy she was a working actress, doing TV commercials, daytime soap operas, movie of the week parts, and performing on stage in Los Angeles at least once a year for a fortnight, she caught the attention of an up-and-coming local real estate broker, and he waited by the stage door to applaud her brilliant performance in Pygmalion and see if there was a possibility of some flirting. She exited the theatre like a heroine of the movies to a large group of fans seeking autographs and well wishes when she noticed him. He was six foot three and had a wide shoulder frame, styled black hair, clean shaven square jaw line, and a deep voice when he approached her and observed, "I was spellbound by your performance and, enchanted by your poise. I look forward to seeing your next show, Miss Lambert." Then he disappeared into the crowd of waiting fans.

In that split second, he had made an impression on her, he was alarmingly handsome with a sexy voice. It was a nice start. When she was done with her adoring fans, she headed for her car. As she walked down the street the handsome stranger was still lurking in her mind and she wondered, "How can I find this fellow?" As she looked up the billboard across the street from her on the rooftop said, "If you want to maximize your ROI on real estate call Gregory "Skip" Winslow". Louise saw this as a sign, they were destined to meet.

One day after an audition she walked down the street on a beautiful west coast day and popped into the Realtor's Place Ltd. She walked up to the receptionist and asked to see Mr. Gregory Winslow. "Oh, my goodness," the receptionist said, "No one ever calls him Gregory except his mom."

"Alright, can I please see Skip?" Louise calmly whispered.

"Please have a seat and I will let him know you're here Miss…" she waited for the response.

"Miss Lambert, Louise Lambert." She added.

"Oh yeah, the actress," the receptionist said and pressed a call button on her panel.

She was totally fine and feeling noticeably confident when he walked into the waiting area and looked directly into her eyes, "Miss Lambert, what an honour to have an esteemed actress visit my humble working environment. To what do I owe the honour?" Skip said.

He was wearing a medium grey pin striped suit with a bright yellow shirt and a masculine patterned tie and matching pouf. He was handsome and stylish, a lethal combination. She was well rehearsed until she looked at him and she lost the ability to speak momentarily. "I came in to buy some real estate Mr. Winslow. I saw your billboard and I thought you might be able to help me." She responded coyly.

"Miss Lambert, there is nothing on my agenda for the next year that could stop me from dropping everything I am currently working on and dedicating all of my time to help you find that perfect piece of real estate that can enhance your life. That's what I do. So…how soon can we get started?" He said in a friendly and jovial manner.

"I was hoping today. So, how do we get started?" Louise asked.

"Well, the first thing we gotta do is for me to understand your specific needs, however; you need a clear head and a satiated tummy. Have you had lunch?" He cheerfully asked.

"No. That sounds like a great idea. Do you have a place in mind?" She queried.

"Of course, I do." He swung open the office door and held it open for her. She floated by him, and they headed up the street to a Four Season's Hotel and went into their restaurant and got seated. There was an incredible chemistry between the two of them. Louise asked herself if this was infatuation because of his looks and her own ego or was she truly falling for this handsome stranger. They continued to talk, and they kept matching up on all fronts until she nudged him about religion, the game changer/deal breaker.

"I was raised Roman Catholic, why, is that a problem!" He said.

She was in hyperspace now. A handsome man that would look lovely on her arm at the Academy Awards one night in the future and she could take him home to meet her mother without worry because he's Catholic. Her mind drifted off with thoughts of having his children and going on holidays in Europe and staying at picturesque villas and vineyards. She could just see the two of them driving up the coast to Carmel for weekends, her mind wandered, and she was tickled with the ism.

"No, not at all. My family is Catholic, from Montreal. Have you ever been?" She enquired.

"Not yet, but I feel there is a good chance that I'll be going there soon. Do you have any brothers or sisters?" He asked.

"No. I'm an only child which is rare for a Roman Catholic family from le belle province. Usually, mothers from Quebec have a few litters of kids before they're thirty. We were the "French-Canadian weirdos." How about you? Do you have any siblings?" She asked.

"Only child also. Always wondered what it would be like to have a brother or sister, but I got to do everything I ever wanted because there was no competition. I always had my parents' ear. They never missed an event for ninety percent of my life. Lots of attention. I loved it. How about you? Parents make it out to lots of life events for you?" He asked.

"Absolutely. My mom skirted me around town all my life to dancing, singing, and acting events and auditions. They had the funds to put me through two fine arts schools and paid all of my bills and tuitions. Yeah, call me selfish but I loved my childhood as a single child. Only thing that is tough now is having my parents so far away in Montreal, so I don't see them often. That is what it takes to climb the ranks to stardom, be prepared and be seen." She stated and made a mock salute.

"Well then, I guess the only thing left for the two of us is to find out what kind of home you want. Do you mind if I ask you some questions to give a more focused search for your new home?"

"I will answer all of your questions Mr. Winslow and yes, I am free for dinner on Saturday night." She said and winked at him.

Skip knew he was falling hard for this woman he just met but, he could not resist the temptation. Over the next year the two were inseparable and soon found themselves talking about moving in to a house together. Louise said she could not because her father would disown her if she lived in sin. If they were to live together, they had to be married. Skip agreed and they caught a plane to Montreal so he could ask her father for her hand in Holy Matrimony. He approved and they were married in their local church that week and returned to LA to continue their new life. Less than a year later she got pregnant which was shocking because the two were the most self-centered people on earth, but they were. She had Domino nine months later, and a new chapter of their lives began.

Louise got the good news that she had been cast in a new movie that was to be filmed in New York City for six months. The two had ample money so they had opted to have a live-in babysitter to stay in the house while she was away making the film, to help Skip with little Domino. Unfortunately, California is a volatile place with unpredictable weather and events. A fire started in downtown Los Angeles in a neighborhood several miles from Louise and Skip's home however, the winds were high, and sparks began to fly into the night sky and ignited fires all over the city. A brush fire started down the street from their house, and it seemed harmless, but it quickly became a big and out of control fire and began to ravage the streets of the community until Skip could smell smoke in his house. He rushed onto the street to find the entire neighborhood was ablaze with no visible means of escape. He darted back into the house but what could he do? The house was beginning to burn, and he rushed to Domino's room and lifted her out of bed but where was he to go? He looked out the windows and all he could see was flames. Where was he to go? Glass began to crack and explode into shards flying through the air. The nanny was now standing beside him and screamed, "What do we do now Mr. Winslow?" She grabbed him and wrapped her arms around him and Domino and held her breath.

He looked back at her and answered, "Now we meet our God." An eruption of flames consumed the three of them as they stood there and then they were gone. They and hundreds of other souls were lost in the blaze, and Louise became a widow that night.

Louise never returned to LA after that day. She flew back to Montreal and lived with her mom and dad for the next few years. For work she would perform in Cabarets and Clubs and do the odd play, but she kept to herself for many years until she met Rene Gagnon. He had come to have a beer with his buddies after work one night. He owned a small car dealership in Laval and had been successful at it for twenty plus years. He was plain and was losing his hair, but he spoke with a silver tongue that was capable of charming the pants right off a lady, many times in his life. Rene was well traveled and could speak five languages fluently, so he was charismatic and loved to dance, which most men are allergic to at the best of times. He was bold and bland, a very unlethal combination. She ended up falling in love with him because he was steady and predictable. That is all she could handle in her life right now. She had hung up her ego when she decided to hang up her own Hollywood star, which made Rene ideal. They courted and a year later they were married. Louise had fallen on tough times in the past, but her future was looking grand. One month after the wedding she announced she was pregnant with their son Claude. Her new life was cast and now all she had to do, was live it. She lived a happy and fruitful life, and their son Claude grew up and got married to handsome young man named Jean. The two lived together in Montreal for many years but eventually moved to New York City so Claude could be closer to the big city art scene since he had become an art dealer of many types, but his passion was watercolours and acrylic on canvas. When the two men learned of Claude's mother's ailment, they began making arrangements to move back to Montreal to be with his parents, but Louise insisted on the two continuing their work and their love of involvement in the art trade in a cosmopolitan city where there was an abundance of interested clients to buy and sell painting and sculptures to. Louise felt they had worked too hard to give up their success and sit a hospital room waiting for the end to arrive. Louise assumed that when she was admitted to a hospice that the boys could come and pay their last respects rather than having the two of them sit bedside and watch her dwindle away to nothing. This wasn't going to happen on her watch. She was far too proud to have her family see her fade to black on a hospital bed.

Louise knew that she still needed to have a discussion with Rene about her involvement with the upcoming task she was to perform for the Ministry of Special Projects. The fortunate news was that she did not have to leave town and have Rene worry about her being away from home for an extended period of time. She would be able to leave her house one morning and simply head to Le Champs-de-Mars, do her part in the completion of the duty and head back home that same evening. It couldn't get any easier. The toughest thing to do now was to create a viable story that Rene would believe so that she could go to the rally in the park without being accompanied by her husband, because, of course, he insisted on being with Louise whenever she left the house. He was retired and had time on his hands, so he became a doting husband and a chauffeur for her and was a reliable means of transportation, as well as a set of hands to carry whatever she happened to buy on her outings. He was her rock, so what she needed now was an indisputable reason for her to go downtown by herself. She decided that she would simply tell Rene she was going to meet with a man from the Ministry to discuss a potential cancer treatment that the government was developing. She had assumed that she was not going to stay downtown overnight so Rene would certainly understand but she would still have to explain to him that she was going to the appointment alone. The last thing Louise wanted was to have her husband in tow as she was trying to plant a device in the park and then walk quickly away. He would just slow her down and distract her from the goal at hand. She also didn't want to explain what she was really doing for the Ministry because she couldn't risk compromising her potential payout to her surviving family members.

Two days later Louise got a call from Luc Bordeaux who planned to meet her at one of the Ritz Carlton guest suites to review the procedure for this mission. In the meantime, Laurent Pillared contacted Willow in Victoria and made plans to meet in the Empress Hotel, downtown Victoria, to discuss her participation in the upcoming task in Montreal. Willow was to catch a plane to Montreal the following week and would stay two nights, previous to the political rally that was happening in the park near old Montreal. This detail was to be very straight forward because they just needed to have their portable stools with them and then place them in the assigned strategic positions to inflict the most carnage possible but making sure to vaporize Benoit Dupuis and several other key political figures that had been robbing the senior citizens of Canada from right under their noses. Louise and Willow wanted to make a difference to other Canadian seniors and stop this group of thieves from stealing their pension money, the security for their futures. It was a chance to fight back against these people repressing and stealing from the elderly. Their fight was righteous, and they wanted to help others in any way they could. Neither woman wanted anyone to die but they had a lifetime of paying too many taxes and watching their paycheques dwindle away each month, leaving less and less to take home to their families. It was time for a little payback and this group of liars was a really effective way to start. Knowing that these horrible people were skimming money from the seniors' pension fund every month was just too much for them to not get involved. It was just shameless that these thieves were robbing hard working retirees.

Arrangements had now been made for both women to meet their individual handlers that week in preparation for the assignment the following week. Once they were both advised on how to carry out their tasks, they were to meet in Montreal at the Ritz Carlton the next week to make final preparations. Louise and Willow had a common goal and they wanted to get it over and done with so they could both get back to their normal lives and shed the cloak and dagger scenarios.

Chapter Eleven

A common trait amongst many magnates is their inability to trust anyone, ever. Hence, Serge's Juste Droite Armee, (RRA), was made up of a dozen dedicated souls who had pledged their service to this man in exchange for ample funding and an opportunity to do what they all loved to do, kill people. Some people belong to golf or tennis clubs, card groups, a choir, or a book club, but no ordinary club was going to quench their thirst for blood. They had purpose because it was their job, nothing personal, but lethally effective. They enjoyed a mutually beneficial arrangement with Serge, and certainly had no intentions of this changing. They all liked the roles they currently played within the organization and had tremendous respect for Jimmy Smits, who was their direct supervisor. The team's goal was to get it done, which usually meant having to do away with someone or more than just a someone, without asking why. Just do the job, get the paycheque, live the sweet life with all the spoils. One thing that they all had to sacrifice however was having a conscious. It wasn't kill or be killed, it was kill or don't get paid. Serge had no exceptions to the rule. He had somewhat of a kind heart because he did frown upon the sanctioning of young children, which was to be avoided at all costs unless they just had to kill the little tykes. It wasn't a glamorous business, but the team loved their current dynamic and were prepared to be successful at all costs.

This, of course, pleased Serge because he could still run his businesses to generate legal profits and keep his personal feud with his sworn enemy, Guy Tremblay. His goal was a simple one, screw up Guy's life as much and as often as he possibly could. No matter how busy he was in his personal or business affairs, he would always find the time to try and create havoc for his rival. For many years he tried to be a fly in the ointment of Guy's life, but he had never really had the resources to cause the level of mayhem he was wishing to inflict until he and Jimmy invented a team that could dedicate themselves to the goal of making Guy's life miserable. Step by step the RRA were beginning to have an impact on Guy's companies and his personal life as Serge continued to eliminate his closest allies and disrupt his chain of command. It was a slow process, but it was starting to have a noticeable impact with Guy, and Serge knew that removing Benoit Dupuis from his stable of talent was going to have a devastating effect on Guy's operations. Benoit was his second in command and was exceptionally integral to his organization. With Benoit being snuffed out it would take some serious time to find a replacement that had his credentials and capabilities. Benoit was well educated and exceptionally skilled in every aspect of Guy's global vision for his companies, and for the future of politics in the province of Quebec. Guy had decided to run for political office so that he could get a foot in the door and have a more effective opportunity to run his vast groups of corrupt companies. Once he became a member of Parliament, he would be granted access to information that could bolster certain aspects of his businesses. He was still considered an honest hard-working Canadian, but this position would grant him opportunities that, in the past, would have been hidden behind the veil of democracy. This would solidify his position as a trusted member of the Canadian Government which would provide him all the spoils that go with that title. First you get the money, then you get the power, no matter what you might have to do to achieve it, then fill your pockets with as much moolah as you can without getting caught. Serge was well aware of the adverse impact Benoit's death would have on Guy, but he knew, like in his own company dynamics, he would be replaced by another ruthless person, whose number one priority was personal gain, no matter the cost to others. These leaders knew to surround themselves with as-like thinkers just for that reason of making sure that if someone is relieved of their duties that there is already somebody else in the wings prepared to take on that position, thereby maintaining a smooth and seamless transition without effecting the company's operations. It was a slow process, but Serge was finally gaining some traction by interfering with Guy's inner circle, however; he also knew that Guy was very capable of retaliation, and he knew that it wouldn't be long before some hired hitman was going to be coming after him and his inner circle. Serge made sure to fortify his intel as often as he could but all it would take was one young person that wanted a big payday or promotion to walk up behind one of his team and snuff them out in a split second. Then Serge would be trying to find the perfect replacement from within his inner sanctum. He contacted Jimmy Smits to discuss the situation and to see if Jim felt like they should be on high alert based on a vengeance factor. Serge made the call to Jimmy to review the current status and to seek out problem areas and nip them in the bud. Jim agreed with Serge about heightening their security and to be vigilant with the Special Projects Team to watch their backs. The two men both concurred that once Benoit was eradicated there was going to be some push-back, or possibly some pay-back to follow. Guy was not going to take this sanction well and he was not going to take it laying down. He would be ready to fight but his next problem would be trying to find out who he was fighting against. With all the hits being done by little old ladies, with no connection to Serge in any way, it was going to be difficult for Guy's team to track down the responsible parties. Even if they were to find one of the participants, the women had no idea who they were really working for because they still honestly believed that they were employed by the Federal Government. This simply meant that it was still going to take a lot of time and investigation to find out who was truly responsible for the hits on Guy's team. Another common thread among really rich people is their ability to outsource to get things done. Serge realized that once Benoit had been disposed of, there were going to be repercussions because Guy was going to want answers, and to know who was behind these accidental misfortunes happening to his elite team. What Serge did not know is that with Guy's unlimited resources he had already been informed by his team that something odd was going on and was recommended to increase his security. The whole group was on high alert to pay close attention to their surroundings for a spell just to be sure that these deaths were not attempted hits on his staff. He knew that Benoit was on the road going from city to city and making public appearances which made it more difficult to keep a watchful eye over his precious assets. He had assigned a security detail to travel with Benoit, for the time being, just to keep a higher level of safety, however, Guy knew too well that if somebody out there wanted you dead it was exceptionally difficult to protect your valued assets. Benoit was not a big fan of having a security team march through the streets with him everywhere he went but he also knew that he was vulnerable out in public and needed to accept the additional strongmen to keep him safe. Guy still had aspirations of taking over the province of Quebec in the House of Commons by adding in his own hand-picked team to help him rise to the top and remove the Block Party from power for the last time. Guy had his own ideas on how things should be run in Quebec, and he was preparing to gradually take over the House of Commons one seat at a time. He knew it would be a gradual process which meant that it would happen slowly, and he was a patient man. Currently, time was on his side, or so he thought.

***

The following week Willow arrived in Montreal as planned, two days before their task, so she could have a full day to go to the Le Champ-de-mars and become familiar with her surroundings. She checked into the Ritz Carlton Hotel and headed directly to her suite. When she opened the door, she could tell that someone else was already in the room with the TV on showing local news in French. Willow cautiously tread down the main hallway and rounded the corner into the main living/dining room area to see another elderly woman sitting on the sofa sipping on a drink.

"Hello there, do I have the correct room?" She inquired.

"Bonjour, hello." She replied back with a mild French accent. "I am Louise Gagnon, and you must be Willow Smythe from BC. We met before in Toronto at the Ministries offices'. I didn't mean to take you by surprise." She reassured.

When they had met with their handlers the previous week, they had both been told that this particular job was going to need two people to execute the plan. Both of them would work together to place the devices in strategic locations in order to ensure that the packages would deliver the maximum carnage. They had received instructions on how to activate the device once they had arrived at the park at the predetermined time and place. They knew their placement did not have to be exact, but they had been given a ten-meter range where the armed device should be placed. Once the packages were activated, they would have mere minutes to evacuate the area and be a safe distance from the blast. At least that was the plan, how this would turn out the day of the event was yet to be determined.

"Oh, it's quite alright. My handler made it clear to me that we are working collectively at the site, but I didn't realize that we would be sharing a room." Willow noted.

"I was only just told that we were sharing a room this morning. The Ministry thought it would look less obvious if we stayed in the same room and hung out together by day to make it appear that we are old friends just getting away for a couple of days. I know that we need to head down to old Montreal for lunch and then walk around the neighboring area for a bit to get they lay-of-the-land for this week's agenda." Louise said.

"I would love to get out for a wandering time. Do you mind if I quickly freshen up?" She asked politely.

"I was just about to say the exact same thing to you. I will meet you back here," as Louise pointed to the floor, "In ten minutes."

They caught the elevator down to the main level. As they made their way across the hotel's immaculate lobby Willow reached out and grabbed Louise by the hand and said, "Hey, Louise, do you want to do a little test with me? The Ministry has told us over and over how we are completely invisible to everybody, so let's put it to the test." She finished.

"Okay, how do you suppose we do that?" Louise asked.

"Do you see that door over there that says "Staff Only" on it? Well, how about you go into that area, and I will go through the restaurant and head into the kitchen and let's see how long it takes before we are removed from those areas. When you are discovered, say that you are lost and are looking for your friend who is also in search of the toilets. Let us reconvene here. If no one speaks to you or gives you directions, give up and head back here in ten minutes anyway. I am curious if anybody even says a single word to us. Are you good with this ploy?" Willow asked.

"I'm good. See you soon." Louise said.

Louise stood patiently by the active staff door and waited for a staff member to walk through and then she skirted along behind into the depths of the hotel. It was a long hallway with a white tile floor and white walls with a rubber bumper running along both sides as far as she could see. It was a service corridor for sure with many insets with doors that some were open and most of them closed. She had decided to herself to walk down the hallway in an assertive manner, so she didn't appear feeble or lost. She marched down to the end of the hall and took a right at the end of the "t" and walked until that corridor also ended. There were three doors in different directions but one of them swung open and a young man carrying an enormous sized serving tray swept by and said, "Bonjour madame." And continued on his way. She smiled back and replied, "Bonjour."

She went down the short hallway and could see a large well-lit open space and continued forward and entered what turned out to be an industrial sized kitchen with people focused on all types of food preparation, as they were spread out all over the massive space. She could see a group of men standing in front of the burners and ovens preparing food, and another man was banging and bumping pots and pans around in the dish pit. She stood there for a solid thirty seconds before a handsome young man approached her and questioned, "Excuse madam, are you looking for something or someone?"

"Oh, thank goodness, I've been looking for the women's toilets, can you show me where they are please?" Louise said.

"Of course," he replied, "Follow me," as he led her back down the vast hallway she had already visited. He stopped in front of a door marked, “Women’s Staff Only,” and he walked away.

“Merci!” She shouted back as he instantly disappeared.

As luck would have it, she needed to take a minute for herself and use the facilities. While she was in the bathroom washing her hands two young employees came into the bathroom wearing their uniforms and continued to speak to each other throughout the entire duration without looking at her or even saying a single word to her. The Ministry was right, they were invisible. This just gave Louise even more resolve to get these money mongers who were stealing from Canadian seniors. She had to fight for other seniors. She exited the bathroom and made her way down a hallway that she was sure she had been down before but, alas, she really was lost. “Excuse me, can someone show me back to the lobby, I’m quite lost right now.” She said to a group in a meeting room.

“Please madame, follow me,” offered a man seated at the table. He escorted her down the hall to the large double doors leading back into the lobby. Swung the door open, stood to one side, and “Voila.”

“Thank you, young man. You are too kind.” Louise murmured as she re-entered the lobby. Her eyes darted around the splendor of the interior design and architecture looking for her colleague. She meandered over to a small settee sitting alone by the elevators and she plopped herself down and kept searching for Willows' whereabouts. The hotel was busy with many people coming and going. Hardly a moment went by without someone walking to and fro. Interestingly enough, not a single person ever stopped to ask her a question. She knew it was only a few minutes, but this was the Ritz Carlton, so shouldn't one expect the best service possible. She wondered when Willow would return. She leaned back in seat, relaxed and took in the experience. As she inhaled deeply, she became intoxicated by the aroma of a fresh bouquet of flowers filled with lilies, which were one of favourites.

Willow had walked through the restaurant and tagged along behind a waiter who was carry a tray of empty dishes back to the dish pit and she stayed up tight in tow and simply kept walking once they went inside the room. She headed straight through the kitchen staging area and walked down a hallway to an exit door which read: Alarm Will Sound If Opened. She pressed the door handle lock and pushed the metal exit door open and to her surprise the alarm did not sound off, rather, absolutely nothing happened. She didn't know if it was broken or, just not activated or, even possibly the door just didn't make any sound at all, and the warning was false. She shut the door with a loud slam and one of the men with a chef's hat poked his head from around the corner, looked directly at her, and disappeared back into the kitchen area and continued to work. She continued past the kitchen pass again and had to move aside for two waiters bringing trays out to one of the dining rooms as she stepped to one side but still no questions were asked of her. She headed back through the large double doors leading out of the kitchen and was approached by a handsome young man wearing a suit and tie with a name badge and he said to Willow, "Excuse me Madame, but you should not be back here for it is far too dangerous. You might be hit by a flying croissant or something scary like that. Let me help you find whatever it is you are looking for." The stranger said.

"I am simply trying to find my friend who is waiting for me in the lobby. Could you take me there kind sir?" Willow said.

"Of course. Please, allow me," and he swung his arm in a follow me this way please, kind of motion.

She followed him around the corner and into the lobby and saw Louise sitting on a sofa across the room. "Oh, there she is. Thank you for helping me, sir." She walked to Louise and the two made their way to the front door of the hotel and they left the building. The second they were on the street they discussed their findings of the ability to walk around the hotel into restricted areas and not one person gave them a challenging time. Every person they met treated them with compassion and offered assistance. The Ministry was right. They really were invisible to the world around them. Nobody bothered them and when they were spoken to, they were met with kindness and respect. This proved to the both of them that day they could literally go anywhere they wished and, they just had to keep to themselves. The two women oriented themselves directionally once they were outside on the street and decided to walk the two and a half kilometers to the park in the lovely weather. The two strolled casually along the streets peeking into shops and chatting about their lives and families. The taboo topic of cancer rose to the top and made an appearance but they both downplayed the seriousness of their ailments and tried to keep a positive outlook on the day. When they finally breached the topic of the Ministry of Special Projects, at first both women seemed reticent to open up with each other, but Willow reminded Louise that their time was coming sooner rather than later so if they felt like it, they could discuss in detail anything they wanted. What would the Ministry do about it anyway…kill them? They began to ask each other questions about what had been said to them by the Ministry since their indoctrination and it seemed that both parties knew very little. They both liked Jimmy because he was big and handsome and very manly and Scarlet because she was so polite and kind to all of them. They talked about the Block Party and their plans to steal millions of dollars in pension money from Canada's seniors, and they agreed that it was a grave issue that had to be dealt with and they wanted to help in anyway they could. If it meant dropping off a package in the park that could potentially cause harm to others, they were not happy about it but they both wanted to stop these individuals from causing more harm to the second most vulnerable group next to children. They were determined to help make a difference. Before long they were arriving at the edge of the park where the political rally was to be held two days hence and many people were actively setting things up and erecting a stage for the speakers to address the audience. The two of them stood and gazed around for a moment but noticed how big this park was and potentially how many attendees were scheduled to take part, and they both had a sinking feeling run through them…how many people would be injured by this explosive device going off in a park filled with innocent people. The two realized that this park could have several thousand people standing and watching when suddenly, KABOOM. It was all easy when there were no faces or souls connected to this horrific crime, they were about to commit but now as they stood on a rise overlooking the park, they wondered how many citizens would be evaporated by their hands? Now was not the time to be growing a conscience but now was the first opportunity to see how many innocents this would affect.

"Oh, my sweet Lord Louise, I don't know if I can do it. There could be so many lives lost because of us. I'm not sure that I can live with that. I know that I have less than a year before I expire but, to go to heaven with this dastardly act on my soul, I will not be forgiven by God. I want my family to get enough money to live out their lives with confidence financially, but this is an act of terrorism, plain and simple. I wonder how many mother's will be here in two days with their children in tow. How many kids could get hurt or worse than that, killed. What a horrible dilemma. Help Canadian seniors nationwide or potentially kill a bunch of women and children? This is quite a conundrum." Willow said.

"I am going to be completely selfish and do whatever I have to do and be sure that my family can profit from my passing rather than mourning me for years with empty pockets. People are killed all around the world every day for senseless reasons, so in this situation I may be the hand that strikes these people down, but I am willing to take the chance that God will understand why I did what I did. I think he will understand why both of us will do it Willow. We are mothers and we have lived our lives putting our families' needs before our own, so why the hell would we stop now?" Louise said.

"You are right Louise. Why grow a conscience at this late date. The Ministry wants this deed done in two days, so let's take a quick stroll around the park and survey the best escape route." Willow replied.

The two sauntered along the sidewalks and enjoyed the day like they had no idea the carnage they would be bringing to this venue in the next forty-eight hours. They found a path, where once they had placed their folding chairs in the correct positions, it could be an excellent way to quickly get away from the open park and have some protection from the neighbouring buildings. A hundred meters down the alleyway and right back onto a main street that they could make their way back to the hotel without drawing any attention to themselves. After the devices exploded all the people would be running from the site seeking out safety and the two women would just be two faces in a crowd. They knew from their training they would have to walk away slowly and not run before the devices were activated so they would not be noticed later by police investigators on the CCTV security cameras that were strategically placed around the downtown city core. Feeling like they had a good understanding of the park's layout and having confirmed an escape plan, the pair walked to St. Laurent Boulevard and caught a taxi cab back to the hotel. Within minutes they arrived back to the hotel, went ahead to the lobby bar and ordered two glasses of white wine.

"What are your plans for dinner tonight, Louise?" Willow asked.

"I do not have any plans as of yet. Do you want me to join you?" She smiled and winked at Willow.

"It would be an honor mademoiselle." She replied.

***

Luc Bordeaux and Laurent Pillared sat across from one another and listened intently to the two women. They had planted listening devices in their purses and pockets to hear what they were up to while they were together that day. The men were impressed by the fact that the ladies took the initiative to go down to the park and scope out the site and find a withdrawal plan. This type of preparation is what makes the projects go smoothly and that is what they were after. The other thing that they respected was the women testing out their invisibility at the hotel by walking into restricted areas and faced no opposition or resistance. They seemed to be free to move about the hotel as they wished without any consequences. The men admired their confidence to take chances and experiment with their new found stealth mode. The two colleagues listened intently to the conversations about the Lord and how the two ladies were still willing to carry out the immoral obligation even though they knew that there would be carnage in the park the day of the rally, and both of them had come to grips with their intentions. It was clear that Willow and Louise had made up their minds to move ahead and take the money and improve their families futures, over a group of strangers. Luc picked up his phone and contacted Jimmy Smits and said, "It's a go. We will review with the ladies tomorrow in the hotel room and I will contact you when we are done."

Chapter Twelve

Luc and Laurent knocked on the ladies room door at ten o'clock in the morning and began reviewing the upcoming plans for the political rally the following day. The women had been to the park the previous day and had a clear idea of the space and the surrounding areas including a potential plan to leave from the downtown park location. Luc went through a step-by-step detailed overview with Willow and Louise sitting around the dining table in their suite countless times to be sure that the information had really sunk into their minds. The two men were going to be on the ground at the park to help in any way they could, but they were not going to be seen with the ladies. They of course would be wired so the group could communicate with one another, but Luc and Laurent would not be taking part in the set-up of the devices, only the detonation when the time was right. The devices were a simple little portable round stool with a folding base that pops open to create a solid sitting stool for the user to comfortably sit on however, the top seat portion of the stool was comprised of a C-4 type material that was highly explosive and yet impossible for police or even police K-9 units to detect the deadly material. The ladies would carry the portable chairs into the park that day and Laurent had given both of the women a small remote like a mini-TV remote that once they opened the chair, they would tactfully attach the remote to an ignition trigger on the underside of the seat pan that could receive a short-wave communication to detonate the device. When the seat was opened and the remote was in place the bomb was set to go. Luc was to be sure of the position on the devices in the park for placement to ensure maximum damage radius of the device and also make certain that Benoit Dupuis was going to be in the expected blast span. Laurent and Luc would both carry an electronic detonator in case of any problems with the remote. Two would be better than one in this case, and they couldn't afford to have one remote not responding. The small portable chairs were going to allow the ladies to get inside the area and set up remarkably close to the stage when the speeches were about to take place that day. The ladies knew that they had to be in position before the presentations were to begin so their stools were strategically located. Willow and Louise were to enter Le Champ-de-mars while all the attendees were making their way to the stage area and take up two positions near to each other on either side of a weeping willow tree that was going to be the perfect place for the team to carry out their dastardly deed in plain sight. They had to be sure to not allow the willow tree to be in front of their stool placement so that the tree didn't act as a blockade. They needed to get to the park early enough in case too many people arrived early and took all of the vacant spots near the trees. Once they had the stools in position and the explosive devices armed, they would just casually stand up and slowly walk away towards the portable public washrooms to quietly slip away through the crowd before the units were detonated. Nobody would even pay attention to the two old ladies sauntering around the park that afternoon with thousands of people listening intently to the political jargon going on, so their escape plan was set. They completed a sound check on the communication devices and tested them in the room and found them to be functioning perfectly. The men made the ladies open the chairs, attach the remote and arm the devices twenty times to make sure they had a clear understanding on how the units worked. The two women sat on the stools in the room just to be comfortable and at ease with the units so they would be prepared for the day without too much squirming. The stools only weighed about five pounds each, so it wasn't going to be a problem for the ladies to lug the stools around with them the day of the event. The men did one last battery check on the remotes and the communication units and were satisfied that all was up-to-speed. They were ready. Luc and Laurent said goodbye and headed out of the room into the hallway where they vacated the building and prepared themselves for tomorrow's big event.

The two women sat in the living room of the suite and chatted about trivial things trying to keep the scariest day of their lives as far away as possible even though it was less than twelve hours until they had to plant their bombs. It was a bold move on their part but they both found themselves agreeing about the money and how much of a difference it would make to their families' futures.

"What are you going to wear tomorrow? I watched the weather channel, and it predicted that the temperature was to be about 20 Celsius with clear skies and a light breeze out of the east. I know that they want us to wear little old lady clothing, but those track suits can get so bloody warm and uncomfortable, and I don't want to be sweating all day." Louise remarked.

"I would love to wear a skirt and blouse but Luc told me to don my bright sunshine yellow stretchy track suit so I could become invisible in the crowd. I know that I hate wearing it, but it is only for one more day and then we are done with our cloak and dagger routine." Willow responded.

"Luc suggested that I wear the matching top and bottom baby blue track suit. He believes it will make my eyes pop." She giggled. "I agree with you however, it is just one more day and we can get back to trying to live with cancer."

"Are you hungry?" Willow asked her.

"Absolutely I could eat. I would prefer to just sit here in the room and eat and then go to bed early. I am still jittery about our day tomorrow. All of these things we are doing make my anxiety bubble over like a fountain. I keep hoping that I won't have a heart attack before we even get this task finished." Louise said.

"Have you looked at the room service menu? It looks more comprehensive than most of the restaurants I've eaten at in the past few years. I'm going to have chicken coco-vin with the mashed potatoes. I haven't had that in years, and I know it's going to be good if it comes from their kitchen. How about you? Any "Last Supper" type meals you have on your mind." Willow laughed.

"I am French Canadian, so I have to try the Tourtiere pie and see if it's better than the one I prepare for my family at home. It is a simple dish, but some chefs just know how to make it sing." Louise alleged.

"Sounds good. I'll call up room service and you can make us a highball. I'd love to have whiskey sour. Do you know how to make one?" Willow asked.

"Absolutely I do. One whiskey sour coming right up." Louise responded and began making the drinks.

Thirty minutes after making the call to room service, the food arrived on a trolly with all the fixings and the two sat down at the table. They ate in disbelief as each tender morsel was more delicious than the one before. They had a bite of each other's meals and fell in love with them for their exquisite flavours. The Ritz Carlton had delivered borderline perfection once again. Both women admitted to each other that they could not make these meals as good as the hotel had made them. Leaning back in their chairs, they reveled in the sensation. At that exact moment, life was good.

The following morning the pair awoke to a lovely clear and sunny day, just as the weatherman predicted. They both had coffee and oatmeal in the room and dressed in their recommended outfits and made sure to fix their hair but only wear mascara without any other facial adornments in order to appear old and humble. A simple appearance so as not to draw any attention to themselves. The two ate the breakfast and made their final preparations before they strapped on their fanny packs, grabbed the portable stools, and headed over to the park. Once outside, they decided to buy a water bottle to drink while they waited for the participants to gather and for the speakers to arrive. The two meandered down the city streets until they turned the corner and walked between two buildings and looming large was the open expanse where the event was being held. Suddenly their ear pieces went live, and Luc's voice said, "Just wanted you two ladies to know that Laurent and I are both here in the park with you today. If you look directly across the open area, you can see me sitting beside a statue wearing a bright green jumper." Luc waved his arm quickly for a second, so the ladies spotted his location. "Laurent is over between the two willow trees that we talked about with you yesterday. We cannot get behind the trees because they're too big and will have a negative impact on the explosive devices. They need to be out in front of the trees. Do you see Laurent," he asked and waiting for a positive nod of confirmation. The women looked around and spied Laurent and coyly affirmed that they had seen him in the crowd. Both women gained confidence knowing that someone other than themselves were here at the park with the same goal in mind. They didn't feel as alone and vulnerable with other team members present. The two started walking towards the stage area but they slowly began to separate from each other as they made their way to the willow trees. Many early risers had come to the park but both women were able to secure spots in the shade of the trees where they were within twenty meters of the temporary staircase that had been erected at the edge of the stage. There were still countless bodies running to and fro getting everything set up and ready. The roadies began doing sound checks on the PA system that had been set up for the planned speeches. "Test one two, test one two," the roadies voice echoed over the grounds making sure their sound equipment was ready to go. As the women moved about near the staircase, Luc was giving them the actual locations that he wanted them to be standing in before they took their seats and armed their portable stools for destruction. Finally, Luc said, "Okay Willow. Stop right there. Do not move an inch until the speakers walk past you and head up the stairs to the stage. Louise, I want you to walk to your left about five meters. Stop…right…there. That will be ideal for our two positions for the devices. Now please stay as close to those spots as possible until I let you know when I want you open your stool and add the remote control and be sure they are armed, which means a tiny little red light on the remote turns on.

The ladies could no longer see each other through the throngs of people that continued to assemble throughout the park. They could hear clearly through their ear communication devices but could no longer tell if the other assailant was anywhere close to their position. They had to believe that they had been placed into the crowd correctly to pull off the assignment with the desired effect. Willow and Louise were delighted that the real draw for the day had not attracted children to the event although the presentation had not begun as of yet so there was a chance that some kids would be in attendance, however, they had to let those guilty feelings go and remember what their objective was. The hot sun moved its way across the sky that day when Louise noticed that the politicians were to be arriving at any time to get the speeches started. Luc had moved his way into a position that he could see both women under the willow trees looking around like all the other attendees waiting for things to get going when Luc told her, "Willow, I need you to back up a bit and make sure you have a clear visual of the staircase so that there is nothing impeding our line of fire."

"Copy that. Moving a meter to the left. Tell me when I am in the right position Luc." Willow answered.

“Okay Willow, right there is good. I will let you both know when the entourage is heading your way and then you will both have about a minute to set up your stool and then get the hell out of there as quickly as possible. Both of you need to open your stools and just sit down right away so it appears that you are both tired of standing. Please do not engage in any conversations with anyone. If someone speaks to you just act confused and pretend that you cannot hear them properly.” Luc said.

The two women were in the assigned positions, and they stayed in their spots to keep the blast radius intact. They wondered if they were going to actually make it out of harm's way or if they were going to be too close when the blast occurred and would cause them collateral damage, as in their own deaths. It wasn’t a terrible thing because their families would be paid out and they would have done what they came to Montreal for and that was to eliminate some really bad Canadians. Wouldn’t be the funeral that the families maybe planned for, but it would still be the desired result, a huge payday. The crowd continued to grow minute by minute now and the available standing space was shoulder to shoulder. Even as the ladies sat on their stools, they couldn’t see much left or right, but they did have a clear view of the stage from where they were situated because it was elevated above the masses. A minute later music started blaring out of the audio equipment on the stage which was a clear indicator that things were about to begin. A short man with wavy hair trotted past and scooted up the stairs onto the large platform and headed for the lectern with the attached microphone and spoke to the crowd which gave him a thunderous applause as he introduced the keynote speaker for that day. Mr. Benoit Dupuis who, was to be taking the stage within minutes. He went on about the party and the support of the Quebec people and made some general comments with literally no content whatsoever, but the crowd was getting pumped up and they were ready to embrace the candidate that was soon to be speaking to them. Luc's voice came over the ear buds, "Okay, it is time to add your remotes to the seat pans and arm the devices. The entourage is going to be heading your way shortly."

"Copy that," Willow responded.

"Copy Luc, I am arming my device now." Louise said.

The women carefully used their fingertips to align the remote pins up with the receptacles on the underside of the stool and pushed them into place. Both of them checked the stool and they had the red light showing they were successfully armed and ready.

"Luc I am ready." Willow announced.

"Also ready." Louise confirmed.

"Okay ladies. Please stand up from your stools and slowly start walking to the portable toilet area you passed on the upper hill as you entered the park. You need to move quickly to get away from the inevitable doom that is coming." Luc stated.

Louise stood up and pretended to stretch her bottom and looked around like she was trying to find something like the bathrooms. She lowered her head and started heading in the direction of the toilets. Willow made sure she was moving slowly and steadily and began her journey towards to the outdoor toilets also. She slid back around the large willow tree and could see the tops of the porta-potties all lined up across the field and kept trudging along towards the bathrooms.

"Oh Miss, hello there, you forgot you're your stool." A friendly bystander yelled out to her. He was running up the small rise and quickly caught up to her and placed the stool into her hands.

"Oh, my goodness. Thank you so much but I was leaving it there because I am coming right back to hear the speeches and I didn't want to lose my spot in the shade. Thank you for bringing it to me." She said.

"Oh, I'm sorry, I can gladly take it back to the spot." He replied.

Luc's voice came over the earpiece instantly, "Do not let him take it back to your spot. We can't be assured he will place it in the correct spot. Hold your ground, Willow. I am on my way to you right now. I will be there in a second." Luc said.

“I’m okay with taking it back to my spot,” she smiled and took the stool back from the helpful stranger.

The man turned away and the music was playing again, and the keynote speaker was getting ready to make their grand entrance and one of the devices was currently twenty-five meters from where it needed to be. From out of the crowd Luc appeared and grabbed the stool from Willow and headed for the predetermined position that the stool was needed to be located. Willow looked off to the large parking lot and could see the grouping of black cars and SUVs all beginning to gather together to escort the dignitaries down to the main stage’s side staircase entrance. Luc was slipping his way through the crowd as quickly as he could, but the volumes of people had made it difficult to get to the strategic spot in a hurried time. Luc was just arriving at the tree when he could see that Benoit was surrounded by his followers closely and he was making a direct line to the main stage entrance. Luc was too late. He said on his communication device to Laurent, “I have the device in position, you need to complete the chore, no matter what.”

“If I detonate the device Luc you will be killed for certain. We can try again at a different location. We will just have to delay this sanction.” Laurent claimed.

“No. You must do it now. Jimmy is relying on us to complete this. It must happen now. I can see the entourage coming towards me right now. You have about twenty seconds to press that button." Luc responded in a panic.

Luc looked over his shoulder and saw two giant oak trees side by side with a weeping willow just in front them and the idea hit him. "I am going hide behind these trees and avoid the blast...I hope. You have to start the device in four, three, two, one, initiate the device." He yelled into the earpiece as he dove onto the ground behind the tree. A large ball of fire appeared right at the bottom of the staircase leading to the stage and then a moment later, it was gone. The carnage was immense! The two devices had performed their job remarkably well. Luc was lying on the ground behind the two oak trees when he began to regain some conscience thought. He was alive. He stayed still and did a mind check over to feel if he was injured. His could feel a burning sensation on the back of his legs and head but otherwise he was okay. He looked backwards at his legs and could see that the fire ball had burnt off most of his pants and had torched the hair completely off the back of his head. It was very tender, but he knew he could move, and he knew that he had to get moving from this scene right now. Luc made his way to his feet and started taking in his surroundings and saw the devastating effect the two bombs had on the stage and surrounding area. The devices had worked perfectly. There was no sign of Benoit Dupuis or his entourage. They had been vaporized. Luc needed medical help. He knew his body was in rough shape after the blast. He knew he had to get out of the area. His goal was to get to the street before emergency crews arrived and began helping people and whisking them off to nearby hospitals. “Louise, Willow, do you copy?” Luc said.

“Luc, Willow here, I copy.” Willow responded.

“Where are you? I need help walking. I’ve been badly burned, but I think I can make it to the street.” He groaned.

“Louise and I are in the small alley that goes to the main street over by the portable bathrooms. Can you see the portable toilets from where you are?” Willow said.

“Yes, I can see them. It is too far for me. I might have to lie down and wait to be rescued.” Luc said.

“We are on our way. We are coming around the corner and will be there in a couple of minutes.” Willow assured him.

When the two women rounded the corner from the back alley and could see the devastation caused by the explosive devices they were in shock. They had never seen anything like this type of carnage in their lives. There were hundreds of people injured laying around the open area and too many dead people to count. It was a scene from a war movie. The women were instantly in a state of disbelief, however, their minds kept pushing them onward. They had to find Luc and get him back to the hotel. Louise spotted Luc quickly thereafter and they trudged down the slope to meet up with him and they shored up his body under his shoulders and began almost dragging him towards the back alley they previously came down. They tried to keep the pace up as countless rescue personnel began arriving at the scene to aid and assist others. Luc was in rough shape, and he was literally being supported by the two women as they hoofed his body down the streets of Montreal trying to create some space between them and the rest of horrific scene from which they were escaping. They stopped for a second and Willow took off her sweatshirt and pulled it on over Luc's head so people going by couldn't see that Luc was seriously injured. They got a few blocks away and were about to hail a taxi cab when in their earpiece, Laurent's frantic voice, "Do you copy? Louise, Willow, do you copy?"

"We copy you Laurent. We are a couple of streets away from the scene at Rue Belmont and Union Ave. Where are you?" Willow responded.

"I am coming down the street in an unmarked white van. I will be there in a couple of minutes. Just keep moving forward towards the Ritz and I will find you." Laurent said.

It seemed like a split second before the white van pulled up beside the three and Laurent leaped out of the cab and helped the ladies get Luc into the back of the van. He shut all of the doors and casually drove away and headed for the Ritz Carlton. Laurent pulled up on the side street and told the ladies to get out of the vehicle. He explained to both of them to go back to the room and stay in the hotel that night. Tomorrow Willow was to return to her home in Victoria and Louise would go back to her house in Montreal.

"The Ministry will contact you this week on these burner phones. We will need to sort this out, but I will tell you that the outcome of the mission was a success. We were able to stop these thieves finally. Although Luc is badly hurt, the mission accomplished what we set out to do and that was stop the constant stealing of Canadian Seniors money. This is a momentous day for tax paying seniors. Thank you, ladies, for your loyalty. Safe travels."

The women climbed out of the van and watched Laurent speed away down the street and around the corner out of sight. The two looked at each other and Louise said, "I need a shower and a drink. How about you Willow?"

"Music to my ears. I'm going to need a couple drinks to get over that one. Let's head inside, shall we?" Willow suggested as she linked elbows with Louise, and they headed in the side door entrance.

Their memory was going, but it would take the rest of their lives to forget what they had seen that day. Maybe money wasn't the only thing.

***

Luc Bordeaux was a tough man; however, fire is also tough. The fire cloud that encompassed many people including Luc that afternoon in the park had burnt most of his skin off his legs, back, and back of his head. When the fire ball erupted, he dove behind the bases of two oak trees and covered his face but that was not enough to divert the powerful explosion and the relentless heat of the blast. The hair on the back of his head was gone, most likely forever. His legs suffer tremendous skin damage, and his back was charred but not devastated because he was wearing a light leather jacket that seem to have saved the skin on his back nicely. The jacket however was done and wouldn't recover from the bomb. Laurent managed to get Luc to a friend of Dr. Thomas Cook who resided in Westmount in Montreal and he was able to administer first aid to Luc soon after the blast had happened. Dr. Michele Lentin brought Luc into his home and took care of the burned skin as much as he was able. He portioned out a dose of a heavy pain killer and they put Luc into a bed to allow him time to recover from his wounds. It was clear to see that Luc was going to need a few weeks to get back to moving about but until then he was under the watchful eye of a highly regarded medical doctor. Laurent sat bedside with Luc and continued to speak to him as if he were awake and alert, but he was not. He had suffered some serious trauma, and it would take time for healing. Luc came to briefly, looked directly at Laurent and mumbled, "Was it successful?" He asked.

"Yes Luc, it had the desired effect." Laurent replied.

“Did Willow and Louise get out of harm's way when the blast took place?” He asked.

“Yes Luc. They are safe back at the hotel.” Laurent answered.

“Do they know that I am still alive. They must have assumed that I perished in the fire?” Luc speculated.

“They are my first call. I will tell them that you are okay and, on the mend, as we speak. My next call will be to Jimmy to bring him up-to-speed on the day's events. I will let him know of your heroism and dedication to completing the task at hand. I still can’t believe you ran back there and almost got yourself killed you crazy Frenchman. I am really glad you are okay. I know the team will rejoice in your team’s accomplishment. Next time, just run away and we can find another time to finish the job.” Laurent said as he held Luc’s hand tightly and wrapped both hands around Luc’s hand.

Laurent walked down the stairs, through the kitchen, and out the French doors onto the large cobblestone patio in the backyard of the home. He meandered over to a grouping of expensive all metal frame outdoor patio furniture with wonderfully comfortable seats and back cushions and selected one to sit on. He removed his cell phone from his pocket and called Louise Gagnon to discuss with her the results of the day and the aftermath. She answered on the second ring, “Hello, this is Louise, how are you doing Laurent?” She asked with serious concern in her voice.

"Things are okay, not exactly as planned but things are good. Firstly, the intended target was successfully sanctioned. The radio news has yet to give a full list of people fatally injured or just injured but there is still a lot of police, fire, and paramedics at the scene trying to sort things out. You ladies should be immensely proud of your work because the Ministry was able to accomplish our task to the desired effect. Secondly, Luc has been severely burned over fifty percent of his body, but he is with a doctor who has assured us that Luc will make a full recovery and will be walking about within a month. He covered his face when he laid on the ground behind the oak trees and he got partly protected from the blast, however, the back of his legs, back, and his head are all severely damaged and it will take a while for full recovery. Luc wanted you both to know that he was alive and recuperating and said he is looking forward to seeing both of you soon. Louise, you, and Willow did some nice work today. You are both valued and courageous women and your country thanks you for your assistance. You are both model Canadian citizens." Laurent asserted.

"I am happy that Luc is alright, and I know that Willow will also be delighted to hear that he made it out of there alive today. It is difficult to see such a vast amount of innocent people being vaporized as we saw this afternoon. It all happened so quickly that one's brain is still processing but I know that my subconscious saw all of it and it will come back into my mind. Of course, my main fear is that it doesn't haunt the remaining days of my life. It was like watching a scene from a movie except we all knew it was real. I can shake it off, but I am not so sure about Willow. She is a church going, law abiding citizen, and this will be difficult for her to find peace with herself because she knows that we are the reason that this horrible scenario took place. We don't have a lot of time left here on earth but what we do have shouldn't be riddled with self-loathing. Nonetheless, I am happy that we completed the undertaking for the Ministry and, how soon do I get my money?" Louise stated.

"My next call is to Jimmy Smits, and I will find out from him about the transfer of funds and the procedures to make it happen Louise. I will let you know at once. Just to be clear, you and Willow are physically okay, correct?" He asked.

"Never been better. Both of us have a ringing in our ears from the blast but we are both doing well." Louise confirmed.

"Thank you again Louise. I will get back to you soon." Laurent said and disconnected the call.

***

"Jimmy Smits here. What's happening in Montreal today. The news reported that there was an explosion at Le Champ-de-mars today killing at least twenty people and injuring over one hundred people. It must have been a horrific scene Laurent. Please tell me that you and Luc survived this horrible event unharmed." He said as if someone was listening to his call.

Instantly Laurent suspected that there could be a bug on Jimmy's phone because of the manner that he was speaking. It just wasn't the usual Jimmy way, so he played along.

"Jimmy, you wouldn't believe it. I was sitting on a bench and a few of the candidates came up onto the stage in the middle of the park and before anybody started speaking there was a huge blast and monstrous ball of fire that lashed out at the audience, took many lives, and left countless innocents dead or gravely injured. I had a friend in the audience, Luc, and he was ravaged by the flames of the fire ball. It was a macabre scene and within a minute police, firefighters, and paramedics began arriving at the scene to triage the injuries. It was a horrible thing that happened today sir. I am unharmed but Luc did receive burns over fifty percent of his body and it will take him a month before he will be able to rejoin us for any active duties. I took him to Dr. Lentin's office in Westmount for observation and I will leave him there for a few days until the city has had a chance to calm down a bit. The streets are mayhem right now and the local authorities are asking people to stay home, or at least stay away from the city, specifically Le Champ-de-mars park. What do you need me to do Jimmy?" Laurent asked.

"I am so glad that you were not injured. It is a shame about Luc, but he is young, and he will quickly recover.

Please be sure to drive Louise back to her home in Montreal and then drive Willow to the Ottawa International airport and have her fly back to Victoria from there just to stay away from all of the commotion going on there in Montreal. Once she is safely away contact me and we will discuss the upcoming agenda. Until then, be well my friend and keep an eye out for everything. Speak to you in a day Laurent." Jim said.

"Sounds good to me. I will pick the ladies up in the morning and get them both out of town. I have one question sir. Are we going to reward people for a job well done? I'm simply curious sir." He asked.

"Of course, we are. A promise is a promise…right." Jimmy sarcastically answered.

***

Back in the hotel room Louise was sitting in the living room watching the story unfold on the local news channel as the first responders continued their struggle to help victims of the blast. Every few minutes the reports were coming in from the scene with more information about who's alive and how many killed or injured. The overhead view that was shown by the news helicopter showed the circumference of the blast range and from the air you could see all of the bright red outlines of where human beings once stood. Most of the stage was destroyed and all of the attendees that were on the stage when the blast took place were eliminated, completely.

As the reports from the park continued to flow in Louise notice a familiar outfit that she had seen that day at the park. It was listed as a person of interest and then the TV showed an elderly woman in a baby blue track suit heading away from the blast thirty seconds before the blast occurred so there was reason to suspect that the woman had some prior knowledge of what was to come. The CCTV video of the woman was not clear, and it was difficult to make out her face, but the police had a suspect within a couple of hours of the explosion taking place. "Willow," Louise yelled out to the bedroom, "Did you dispose of your baby blue track suit since you have been back here today?" She asked.

"No. We just got here a couple hours ago. Why do you ask?" Willow queried.

"Well according to the local news, you are on camera leaving the scene just before the blast and, you are now a person of interest. We need to get our track suits out of this room right now and destroy them before we are affiliated to the crime. I know when we arrived back to the hotel, we came in through the side door so few people would have even seen us enter this hotel. However, if they did, they would have seen our ridiculous outfits and now we have to hope that nobody remembers seeing us in the hotel this morning when we left or, when we came back this afternoon. No matter what, we should stay in our room for dinner tonight and I will call Laurent to arrange transportation tomorrow." Louise said.

"It took me my entire life to get on TV and now I'm a fugitive. Just can't catch a break sometimes." She uttered in exhaustion.

Within a few minutes of their conversation Laurent called Louise. "Hello Louise, just making sure that you both know that I will come to your room tomorrow morning and pick you both up and take you both to your next destinations. Please stay in your room tonight and order room service. Do not answer the door unless somebody breaks it down, otherwise, stay put. I will take Louise back to her home and you and I will head for Ottawa so you can catch a flight to Victoria from there. Also make sure that you do not don any clothing that you have worn since you have both been here in Montreal. I will drive my car into the underground parking, and we will exit the building from there. Everything will be fine as long as we stay calm and get you both out of the city in the morning. Any other questions for me Louise?" Laurent asked.

"I understand. We will be ready in the am. See you then." Louise said.

She disconnected the line and was still watching the TV news and they had already found another CCTV camera view of Willow walking away before the blast. Their police force was fast and surprisingly accurate. Louise continued to watch the TV to see how soon her own picture was going to be turning up on screen. This was definitely an angle they had not considered. Getting caught by the Montreal Police Department. No matter to Louise she thought to herself. Once anyone found out that they are actually working the Ministry of Special Projects they would understand what was going on and how they had been helping the government catch criminals from stealing from the pension fund of seniors. Once people knew the truth, they would be exonerated of any wrong doing, or so she believed.

Chapter Thirteen

Brent MacIntosh was born in Grand Prairie, Alberta in 1960 to a mother and father that had lived their entire lives as farmers. They had grown a variety of crops over the years but the mainstay crop for the family was alfalfa. They grew up out in the rural areas and kept to themselves most of the time and would make weekly trips into town to collect supplies and groceries but much of the food they ate was grown on the farm. They had been blessed with four healthy children, so they didn't spend much time taking their kids to doctors' appointments, so they had no excessive costs for medicines for the children over the years as the kids grew up. Brent had three older sisters and he was the youngest of the siblings with two years between each child. The three girls loved horses and chose a life involved with all things equestrian and rode for their work on the farm on a daily basis and the eldest daughter, Tara, had participated with the Canadian Equestrian Team in the 1976 Olympic Games in Montreal, Quebec which was an honour that the family was ready to brag about any time somebody would mention the story. Brent however, had no interest at all in anything horse related and only rode a horse one time at a youthful age and was bucked off the back of a nasty equine and swore never to ride again for as long as he lived. Certainly, a far different type of boy than his three cowgirl sisters. With his pride severely damaged from the fall, he would spend most of his time studying frogs in the muddy edges of the fields after a rain and spending all of his time learning about algae and how fast it could grow and that it could dry out completely and then get wet and come back to life. Brent soon realized that the murky edges of ponds and the little creatures that lived in them began to fascinate him to the point where it was his only passion in life to learn as much as he could about the growth of algae and bacteria and how they could help the world if harvested correctly. All the way through high school Brent never did anything else except study until he stumbled onto a new interest that changed his life forever, natural foods that could potentially help human beings with body pain. He soon realized that the creatures that had been eating algae all of their lives seemed to live hardy and healthy lives that there had to be something of immense value to the frogs and other creatures that lived off of this food. From that he began to study to find organic food sources that could hopefully find natural products that could help people with chronic body pain that couldn't find relief from big pharma prescription drugs. When he was one year from graduation his parents did something that took him completely by surprise: his father announced that they were selling the family farm and moving to Tofino, BC to start a new job as a deckhand on a fishing boat. The family was in shock at first, but his reasoning was sound, it was time to try something completely different. The family had lived in northern Alberta their entire lives, but it seemed like an interesting thing to try out, so they sold the farm and headed west to the Pacific coastline. Two of his three sisters decided to stay in their hometown, but his third oldest sister Alice and Brent were close, and she was eager to try living a new type of life, so she made the transition to Vancouver Island with the rest of the family. Brent knew that he could finish grade twelve in Tofino and then attend the University of Victoria to complete a microbiology degree before attempting to do his own personal research on finding ways to create safer and non-addictive medicines to help the world's population with creating natural remedies to assist people with long term pain and suffering. He watched his best friend Jack's mother suffer through tremendous pain after she had gone through numerous surgeries to help her with chronic back injuries. The doctors had operated on her attempting to fix these long-term ailments but after she was over the healing process, she was addicted to oxycontin and could not shake the dependency for the rest of her life. Brent was convinced that God put all of the correct ingredients on earth and all he had to do was find the right combination so he could gift the remedy to the world. He never wanted a big payout for the research, he just wanted to help people like Jack's mother recover fully and go back to living a normal and healthy life. He sat with Jack's mom on a few occasions and watched her suffer until the drugs would hit her system and she could find some peace from the pain until she passed out. He held her in his arms and could feel and understand the level of pain and anguish she was going through, and it motivated him to find a cure. This was his destiny. His father worked at trying not to be seasick all of the time and he worked at trying to find the perfect formula to ease the suffering of post operative patients. After he graduated from UVIC he continued on with his research until one day he met an acquaintance from Tofino; a local beach bum surfer who ran a side business growing and selling marijuana to the locals. It gave him enough money to pay rent and allowed him to hang out and surf several months of the year. He mentioned to Brent how he had started using pot to get relief for his suffering joints and bones, aching from all the punishment that was inflicted by the Pacific swells. Brent began to question Ray as to the effects on his body and wanted to discuss the matter in more detail to which Ray gladly agreed to help because he was always interested in trying to mass manufacture pot as a human healing aid. This was right up Ray's alley. Use pot to cure people, what next, he thought to himself? The two men became close over the next couple of years as Brent and Ray delved into the study of medical marijuana and continued to grow different strains of the product to increase the THC levels beyond what the average pot smoker was used to dealing with. They were creating super pot so the product could consume the users pain until they were healed and then ebb off the natural substance without the fear of long-term addiction during recovery. The two men worked tirelessly on their research and at their little trailer in the woods they grew their greenhouse to a massive farm that supported over fifty full time employees until one day, it happened. The team after twenty plus years of trial and error had found a product that they were ready to put in front of the Canadian Food Inspection Agency, CFIA, and try to gain approval for sale in Canada and, potentially world-wide distribution. Once the CFIA had approved the product it would be ready for FDA approval and then, onward, and upwards. The original plan was to give the formula to the Canadian people for free and to not profit from the pain of others, however; Brent MacIntosh had been approached by a large pharmaceutical company out of Montreal by the name of Vortex Pharmaceuticals which started as a not-for-profit company, but since had been purchased by a larger parent company that was owned by Guy Tremblay. Brent had never heard of the company and had no idea of its' ownership with the exception of seeing Guy's name written on the bottom of the purchase agreement that was sent over to him to sign his company over. Brent was a simple farmers' son and so when he saw the offer from Vortex, he just about had a heart attack. He could have never imagined that someone would come along and offer him ten million dollars for a company that was purely research for the past twenty years but now that he had gotten his new non-addictive pain reliever medicine ready for CFIA and FDA approval he was pleased to know that all the years of arduous work were about to pay off. Brent was adamant that the new pain killer was to be available to all Canadians for pennies per tablet but what he did not know was that once he signed his company over to Guy and his team, they were going to mothball the entire project and all of the research because Vortex Pharmaceuticals was also about to release their new pain medicine that was a tried-and-true formula that kept all of the users of the drug in desperate need of the product. It had been proven on clinical tests over and over to be highly addictive however, its results were undeniable. Patients could cope with all types of pain including post operations for cosmetic surgeries. The last thing that Guy ever wanted was the new product Gongina hitting the market for half to a third less than his own company's product. The purchase of Brent's company was for one reason, and he had no idea that all of his time and effort would be for naught, and Guy had added in the non-competition clause so that Brent couldn't head back into the market place and simply remake and rebrand the drug under a new name. The lawyers had tied up all of the loose ends and were incredibly capable of making sure that Brent's company would fade into oblivion in short order. His life long work would be evaporated but his family would now have the money to purchase one of the big houses on Chesterman's Beach facing due west overlooking the wind, waves, and water. The only obstacle was that Brent had not signed over ownership as of yet and Serge Bouchard had no intentions of allowing that document to be signed…ever.

***

Jimmy contacted Serge to inform him of their success in Montreal in eradicating Benoit Dupuis from any potential political future. Benoit's demise was a major blow to Guy Lambert and his organization because he had staked so much of his company's future on him winning his election to the House of Commons, however; this was no longer the case. In the Le Champ de Mars Park blast they were also able to eliminate two of Benoit's personal aids that would spend every day of their lives with him for a variety of reasons, but they also knew everything that Benoit knew so there was a huge missing link in Guy's team. Serge had set him back years with Guy no longer having an ideal candidate to even attempt to be voted into the Quebec political arena. He would have to go back to the beginning to nurture a new candidate to replace Benoit and all of his experience and his time and energy already spent getting into the public eye and winning them over was going to be difficult to replace. Guy pondered to himself if he could somehow buy a new political figure to step in immediately because there would be tremendous sympathy from the Quebec people behind whichever new candidate they got to step into the role and try and maintain some level of consistency. It was a strong possibility but they would need to find that new person within the next couple of weeks so they could continue to participate in any speeches or political debates that were needed from that position. This was going to be a sensitive situation that Guy, and his team were going to have wade their way through. For now, Serge Bouchard had hit Guy in a challenging way that could potentially take Guy years to recover from. This is what Serge lived for now, crushing his enemies.

***

Over the next few days, the Montreal television stations continued to show all of the different angles captured by the CCTV cameras throughout the city showing two elderly women helping a man walk down the street from the scene of the explosion and then the three jumped into a white panel van and whisked away from the scene. The cameras clearly showed the ladies helping the man get away, but the cameras were unable to give any footage that showed the faces of the suspects clear enough to begin a nation-wide search to bring them to justice. Currently the Montreal Police Force had nothing but the blurry images to go off and try to build a case. They were going to depend on the public to assist the police in bringing these criminals to justice.

Meanwhile Jimmy Smits was communicating with Laurent to keep up to speed with Luc's recovery and, at the same time Jim knew that they needed a person on the West Coast to go see a man about a newly created pain formula that was currently going through the final stages of CFIA approvals. Serge was determined to squelch any transactions between Brent MacIntosh and Vortex Pharmaceuticals because he wanted the drug to be sold on the open market so it could compete directly with Vortex and their dominance in the prescription business. If this new drug made it to world-wide market, it would hit Vortex hard and would cost Guy Lambert millions of dollars and would seriously alter his company's market share. Unfortunately for Brent MacIntosh he was now just a hurdle to get over to make sure that he did not sign the company deed over to Vortex to be sure that it was dead ended. The easiest way to do that was to sanction Brent and with his passing it would be left to his surviving partner Ray who was virtually an idiot surfer dude with zero business acumen. The only trick was to be sure that Ray understood the smart move was to sell the company to someone who planned on mass manufacturing the drug and flooding the market with it rather than moth ball the idea and shelf it to stop the loyal fans of the addictive oxycontin from buying the better and cheaper alternative. Serge didn't want to be in the pharmaceutical business, but he would do what needed to be done to make sure that Guy couldn't add this product into his portfolio, even if it was to tank the entire company to eliminate any serious competition. He decided to make his move and have Jimmy send some of the team to Tofino to negotiate with Brent and see if they could get him to change his mind. If not, they would go to plan B, kill him. Jimmy decided to send Willow Smythe to complete the task because he knew that she lived only a few hours by car away from Tofino and she had proven to be quite resourceful when she was in Montreal looking after Benoit Dupuis. This was a simple show up at Brent's house, ring the doorbell, wait for him to answer the door, and put a bullet in his head. No negotiating or trying to convince him of anything. The only thing she had to worry about was not being seen coming or going from the scene. Seemed rather straight forward. Jimmy called Laurent and made the arrangements to get Laurent out to Victoria and have him meet up with Willow and drive to the west coast of the island. Jim had told Laurent to be clandestine for the entire trip so when he flew to Vancouver, BC he would steal a car so he couldn't be traced through any car rental agency. He could pick Willow up at a predetermined location and they could head across the island. The next call was to Willow who was still in shock from the scene they created in Montreal the week before, however; they needed to continue to complete assignments for the Ministry as long as the women were able, and alive.

Willow was sitting in her cozy space reading a book when she saw the face of the phone sparkle to life and display the familiar name of Laurent Pillared. She wanted to ignore the electrical device and pretend like they had never called but she could not. Willow was the most taken aback because she had already performed her duty for the Ministry, so what could they possibly want from her now she thought to herself. "Hello Laurent, how are doing?" She answered politely.

"I am well Madame Willow. How have you been since your return from Montreal?" Laurent queried.

"Honestly, I am having a tough time getting the images of the aftermath out of my head from that day. It wasn't the people running away in fear, it was the copious amounts of blood sprayed onto the ground and the walls of all the buildings and trees. It was as though someone came with a blood filled waterbomber and released their payload directly overhead as they flew by and saturated everything in its' path. I can't even remember if anyone screamed, or people were crying. After the explosion, my ears turned off for a few hours until I was back in the Ritz Carlton watching TV. It was a surreal experience that I wouldn't recommend to anybody." She explained.

"I'm not surprised Willow. The only people that ever really witness what you saw in Montreal are soldiers on a battle field. It is not often in any person's life that they see something like you have now seen. It will haunt you for some time now, this I can assure you." He said.

"Well thank goodness I don't have a long time left so hopefully I can shake it off. So…what's the purpose of your call?" She abruptly stated.

"The Ministry desperately needs your help. It will take just one night away from your home, and I promise you will never see any of us again. We would never ask this of anyone ever, but you handled yourself so well in Montreal that we knew you are the only person we know that could manage this responsibility. We need a man, who represents a big-pharma company selling addictive pain killers to women and children all over Canada and they are about to release a new deadly strain of medication into the open market, erased. He is about to sell his new formula to a mega conglomerate called Vortex Pharmaceuticals from Quebec and the product will go to world-wide distribution within the next month. Our goal is to stop the sale so the company will produce the drug themselves and keep it affordable to all Canadians. This product is getting FDA Approval for sale in the USA in under thirty days, so we have to act quickly. We must halt the sale of the new drug Gongina to Vortex, it's that simple. I need to pick you up tomorrow and then we need to head west to Tofino and meet up with the Brent MacIntosh, one of the two company owners and see if we can influence him into not selling the company. If not, we will need to take more drastic actions." Laurent explained.

"So why is this chemist going to listen to me?" She asked.

"Simple. Because you will be pointing a gun at his head." Laurent replied.

Willow finished the call and went to find Dennis and give him her new alibi. Her story was going to be that she was going to a women's spa with a friend to relax and get pampered. Dennis was at a point in his life that he never would argue with Willow about anything because he wanted her life filled with pleasant thoughts and easy dialogue. He knew he had her for a limited time now and he wasn't about to waste any of it bickering. As soon as she presented him with her spa idea he asked if she wanted him to drive her to the place which she quickly declined. They would only be one night and return the following evening, so Dennis didn't see this as anything but an opportunity to spend time with an old friend. She headed to her bedroom to pack a few things and she found herself packing a black jacket and black slacks and she grabbed a pair of matching gloves. She had never put this type of outfit together in her life. Who was she becoming? After she, knowing the CCTV cameras in Montreal doing playback on the TV, distinctly felt she needed to fade into the background. The baby blue and bright yellow tracksuits may be too easy for people to remember after all. Laurent had made it clear that this was to be a clandestine visit to the City of Tofino and her task was a house call. The black camouflage outfit was the perfect ensemble to don for this visit. She walked over to the walk-in closet and looked through an old bin of hats and scarves until the ideal item tumbled out and onto the floor. A balaclava. Perfect for ski trips or bumping people off. Some outfits are multi-functional.

The following morning, she had Dennis drive her to the Bay Centre Mall in downtown Victoria where she was to meet up with Laurent. Within minutes of her sitting down to a coffee he arrived and sat down and waited quietly until Willow had sipped some her coffee and eaten half of her scone before he gave the head nod that meant, we need to get moving along. She stood up and dumped her tray into the garbage bin and then the two strolled across the mall to the parking lot where his car was waiting. It was a big white Range Rover with shiny new rims and chrome bits all over the place. Willow was a humble woman who had never sat in such an opulent vehicle in her life. Her fingers fondled the leather seats, and she found the multitude of buttons to adjust the seat to create the highest level of user comfort. She was impressed. The big machine purred quietly as a kitten with a feeling of power and stability and Willow was already looking forward to the car ride to Tofino in this SUV. "This is a lovely car Laurent, is it yours?" She asked.

“No Mrs. Smythe. I am just borrowing from a friend of mine at the Vancouver airport. Do you like it?” He asked.

“Oh yes. It’s so luxurious. It should be a smooth ride up to Tofino.” She exclaimed.

“Well, we should be there in about five to six hours so please lean back and relax and play whatever music you wish. The car has satellite radio so you can pick any genre you like.” He said.

Later that night the two arrived at the Wickaninnish Inn for the night. Scarlet had made arrangements for a suite for the two of them for that evening. Laurent wanted the two of them to stay in the room to remain invisible. After they had eaten some room service Laurent explained that they needed to do some reconnaissance and look at the plant and drive past his house and check out the property and survey the grounds. He wanted them to be familiar with their surroundings which made perfect sense to Willow. They drove to a nearby warehouse area of town and found the factory which had a six-foot-high chain link fence surrounding the entire circumference of the property with a pair of swinging gates pad locked shut. The plant was far smaller than Willow thought it would be, but she didn’t realize that the building housed the research and development team and didn’t mass manufacture the product as of yet. Only a couple of lights in the yard and none illuminated inside the plant. The placard on the front of the fence read: Beware of Dog. Enter at your own RISK. Didn't appear to be a guard dog but animals could be sleeping somewhere else on the property, so it wasn't worth the risk to scale the fence and look around the grounds. They headed back towards the city and came into a humble little residential area while seeking the correct house for 450 Gibson Street. The two of them stared blankly at each other and looked again at the house and both could clearly see that this man was just a regular guy that obviously formulated a drug that was the next big thing, but he had evidently not been paid out as of yet. He was still struggling through life like the rest of Canada. They slowed slightly and did a drive by but there were lights on in many windows of the house which potentially meant someone was home. There was limited intel, and they did not know how many people lived in the house. Laurent eased the SUV off to the edge of the street down around corner and shut off the motor. "I want you to wait here for a minute while I go down the street and take a look around. I will simply go and see if I can establish access and how many possible bodies are in the house. If for any reason I'm not back in ten minutes you need to get the hell out here. There is a loaded nine-millimeter pistol in the glove box, and you know how to take off the safety and then once it's cocked you just point and shoot eleven times. Hopefully, it won't come to that." He said as he shut the door and quietly moved his way down the street.

She was filled with fear when she watched Laurent disappear into the back yard of the house. She had no more visual reference. Willow had to sit and wait for him return to the vehicle. She checked her cell phone to see the time and keep a watch on his duration. What seemed like ten hours was actually ten minutes, but he had not returned. She sat in the car and kept thinking to herself, "You're not a government agent. You shouldn't be doing this. It is not good for my heart or my weary soul. What the hell am I doing here?" Now it had been fifteen minutes. He went in the back yard and never came out. He has to be in the house. Where else could he be? Willow retrieved the weapon from the glove box and exited the vehicle. She quietly shut the door, crept down the side of the road, darted across the street, and slipped down the side of the house where the empty carport was situated. By this point she was having heart palpitations because she was a grandmother not a spy. Her brain just continued to gnaw at her, "Go home. Get out of here. You shouldn't be here." She suddenly heard loud male voices shouting back and forth. It was Laurent's voice without question telling the other person to go pound sand. This turned back into a rally of yelling and clearly somebody was getting punched or hit with something, but it was tough to tell from just sounds alone. She continued walking back into the yard until she was against the perimeter fence, and she could see that Laurent was sitting in a chair and the other man was standing over him and hitting him with a baseball bat. Her heart dropped, "What do I do?" She thought to herself.

Willow went to the front of the house and secured her gun in her hand in the jacket pocket. She was ready to do battle. She reached out and pressed the doorbell. The loud thumping of a human rang through the house as he swung open the door in an aggressive manner, "What can I do for you miss? Shouldn't you be in senior's home down the street? It's way past your bedtime granny." Brent said.

"I'm so sorry mister. I was trying to find my way back to the Bed & Breakfast, but I have become totally lost. Can you please help a stupid old lady find her way home…please." Her mind was so surprised to see this skinny unassuming young man looking so frail, yet he had just been beating her friend with a baseball bat and she wasn't going to allow that to happen anymore. The man unlocked the screen door and opened it a smidge and started to use his hands in the air to show her the direction when she pressed the cold steel against his bare hip and said, "I think I'm good now. Why don't we go inside, and you can introduce me to your friend in the kitchen." She said coldly.

"How did you know…" She shoved the gun deeper into his ribs and again commanded, "Let's go inside, now." She lifted the gun and smashed it down onto the back of Brent's head, so he was clear that she meant business. His hand rose and held the spot where he had just been hammered. He checked his finger tips and saw that the old lady had drawn blood from her head trauma smash.

"I said - move it sunny boy." This time he was cooperative and headed up the short flight of stairs to the second floor living room and kitchen area. They two came into the kitchen and Laurent was stunned to see Willow Smythe leading Brent into the room. He looked at her and she winked at him and then she raised the gun up again and crashed it into Brent's head sending him sprawling onto the floor in a heap. She spun around and said to Laurent, "Are you hurt? Can you walk? How are you tied right now? I need to get your bindings off before this guy gets back up."

"They are zip ties." He said.

She looked over on the kitchen counter and saw the knife block and she reached out and grabbed a serrated edge and pulled it from the block and began to cut away at his hand bindings. Instantly they were off, and the plastic restraints fell to the floor. Now Laurent could exact his revenge on the man that had tied him up and beat him with a bat in his own kitchen. He pressed his knees into Brent's back and grabbed more of the zip ties and secured Brent's hands behind his back and zip tied his ankles. He then hoisted him by his shoulders into the kitchen chair that he had just occupied. Now the tables had turned. He propped him up and glared at Brent with anger on his face. Willow had never seen Laurent display this look of seething hate for another person and it was scary, however, she had never seen a person beat him with a baseball bat. The two of them stood in the kitchen facing towards Brent trying to decide his fate when a voice from behind the two said, "Don't make a move or I'll blast yah."

Willow's hand was still holding her gun, so she simply turned around swiftly and aimed in the general direction that the voice came from and fired off a half a dozen rounds. A moment later a nine-year old boy collapsed onto the floor with three lethal bullet wounds to his body. They had no idea that Brent had a kid or someone else's kid at his house that night. He was the unfortunate recipient of numerous rounds of ammunition, and now he was dead. Laurent grabbed Willow by the shoulders and looked directly into her eyes and said, "We gotta go right now."

He pulled her down to the bottom of the stairs and told her to wait right there. He ran back up and pulled a syringe from him pocket that he had on the sleeve of his jacket and pumped the full dose into Brent's body. He was still trying to yell but Laurent had stuffed a gag in his mouth to keep him quiet. He leapt down the staircase and pulled Willow down to the basement and exited through the carport. When they could see no other people, they made their way back to the Range Rover that was still parked at the side of the street. Willow tossed the keys to Laurent as he hastily got into the

SUV and took off in a hurry. They drove through the quiet neighbourhood and headed out onto the highway and began to head back to Victoria. Laurent was sure to follow all of the posted speed limits and wondered how long it would be before somebody found Brent and the boy's bodies, dead on the floor. Hard to guess who was going to be the friend or acquaintance that was going to stumble into that macabre scene. The two drove for over an hour without uttering a word to each other. Laurent was simply delighted to still be alive. If it wasn't for Willow coming into the house, he was for sure going to be fish bait. She actually saved his life tonight and now he owed her a huge favour. "You doing okay there Willow?" He asked her.

"It really is a strange job to go out and kill people. I continue to wonder how you ever get over the finality of it all. My husband and I spent our lives respecting the preservation of life, not the destruction of it. Since I have been involved with the Ministry, I have seen certain death. Tonight, however the good Lord above is not going to forgive me. I shot an unarmed child six times, and I was responsible for twenty deaths at the park in Montreal. This is not the life for me. What is left of my life, I do not deserve to live. I am now the ultimate sinner. A murderer. I will rue the day." She ended.

The drive went slowly through all of the tight and twisty roads when finally, they came to a gas station, so they pulled in to get a drink of something and have a bathroom break. Laurent turned off the vehicle and Willow reached over and grabbed one of his hands tightly and asked, "I have a question for you Laurent. I want the truth. You owe me…I saved your life today. So, the question is, is the Ministry really run by Prime Minister Trudeau and, is the Ministry going to pay us all one million dollars per child in the family?"

"I do owe you my life, so for that I will give you the truth as I know it, because I am merely a pawn in this mighty machine. So, the answer to the first question is no, he is not. The answer to the next question is no, no you will not receive any money. I am not the boss, but I have never heard of that happening in the past. I'm sorry I had to lie to you Willow, but I am simply doing my job. I hope you can understand that." Laurent said.

"Of course, I understand. I am very aware how loyalty works." She said and headed into the bathroom.

Turning over in his mind about the frailty of his own life, Laurent heard a loud pop come from inside the gas station restroom. He reached over and opened the glove box, to see the gun was missing and knew that Willow already rued the day. He threw the car into drive and left the parking lot.

Chapter Fourteen

With the Montreal Police trying to find the parties responsible for the park bombing they had found a few different angles from the CCTV cameras showing Louise and Willow, but nobody could make out their faces. There was no evidence to connect them other than the clear proof that two elderly ladies helped an injured man out of the park after the explosion that day; and so, they were people of interest being sought out by the authorities. This meant that, moving forward, the two women were no longer usable in the Ministries plan. With the passing of Willow Smythe this only left one person remaining with knowledge of that lethal day and that was Louise Gagnon. Serge knew that it was time to retire Louise and hide her back in the suburbs of Montreal to quietly live out her life. Serge did something so uncharacteristic that nobody would have ever seen it coming. He made a money transfer of one million dollars into a bank account set up for Louise in the Grand Cayman Islands for her efforts. Louise received the notification and smiled quietly to herself and never mentioned the money transfer to anyone, including her husband, Rene. She instantly planned for the money to be transferred into an account for her son and simply told him that it was his inheritance money coming early and he was not to discuss this money with any living soul for the rest of his life. The next thing to be addressed was that Luc Bordeaux was severely injured and would need a few months to heal before he would be ready for active duty. Laurent was beaten up a bit from his confrontation with Brent MacIntosh but more importantly he needed to lay low for a while because of his ever-increasing exposure in public during cross country flights, rental cars, hotel rooms and besides, he was running out of fake IDs. He knew that there were CCTV cameras at the gas station that he and Willow stopped at on the way back to Nanaimo when she took her own life in the gas station restroom, but he wasn't overly concerned because the stolen car couldn't be traced back to him. His handy Covid-19 face mask concealed his identity but, he was actually at the park in Montreal, as well on the day of the bombing, and he was concerned that suddenly a wanted poster would appear with his face on it taped up to gas stations and corner stores asking, "Have you seen this person? If so, please contact the local police." It was time for Laurent and Luc to disappear for a spell and have other members of the task force step up and do their part. That is where Scarlet Larsen came into the fold. She was a loyal member of the RRA, and she had no qualms doing what was needed from her, no matter how grave it may have been. Scarlet had been training for this work her entire life and wouldn't hesitate to extinguish a life if that was what was expected of her. She was no shrinking violet when it came to following orders. She had been trained in hand-to-hand combat, all types of firearms, explosives, highly skilled in the use of knives whether for throwing or cutting and was a wiz on computers and social media which, all-in-all, made her into a well-rounded assassin. Her father had hoped that she would follow in his footsteps and potentially take over the family empire one day, but she had other plans for herself, Scarlet was highly driven to be the best at everything she did which left no time for a steady relationship in her life. She was tough to please and demanded the best out of everybody. A difficult combination in the dating world but she was always too busy to have a partner and dedicate the time needed for a happy marriage with children at her feet. Scarlet Larsen was ready for field work and was capable of doing important things with the right motivation and at the age she was at, money was a strong first. Secondly, the fact the team did enjoy doing their jobs which usually meant eradicating problems for good. Scarlet was now a product of her environment, which meant killing people. She was curious to meet the infamous Serge Bouchard one day just to see what kind of person he was and to thank him for the opportunity to do what she loved. The only problem that Scarlet had was she was alarmingly attractive, and this made her impossible for bystanders to completely miss and forget about her if she made an appearance somewhere in the public eye. Her skills were honed but her looks were eye-catching. The other person they were going to activate was Tim Dixon - he oversaw most of the team's computer work, but Tim was the type of guy you couldn't remember his hair colour as he was walking away from you. Boasting a total milk toast appearance, he was the perfect type of character for this business.

With the passing of Willow Smythe, the Ministry was prepared to activate two replacement field agents and Tim and Scarlet would dovetail into this role perfectly. Both of them knew what was demanded of them and they both knew how to get things done. They could also call upon Dr. Thomas Cook because he was ready to get back into field work after his skirmish with the Millers in Niagara Falls. The RRA had other agents situated from coast to coast that could be called upon, but Jimmy liked to keep the tactical teams small in order to draw less attention to themselves when they had to move around the country. Jimmy also liked to have complete control over each project, because smaller teams functioned more efficiently, to his way of thinking. Jimmy was also aware that he needed to inaugurate more seniors from his group for the upcoming tasks. He contacted Scarlet to have her connect with Diane Fletcher from Toronto and Cindy Denton from Vancouver and put them on alert so they could begin to mentally prepare themselves for action, whatever that may entail. The Ministry of Special Projects had many assignments that still needed to be checked off their list.

***

From the time Gary Blin was a teenager he was fascinated by electric power, how it functioned and all of the good things it was capable of doing. Sometimes he would spend a full day dreaming of what the world would be like without the use of AC current surging through his house and all of the other places where human beings spend their days contemplating life. He realized that he couldn't have lived in a world pre-1890s when big cities had just began to run 110 electric power and brought light into homes, factories, street lights, and gathering places like churches and restaurants. A world without light in the evenings was just a thing he couldn't wrap his head around. Gary was born in 1970 and lived in Mission BC where his dad worked the small power dam at Stave Lake, making a small amount of energy to be used in the small town of Mission, in case the city's main power supply was ever compromised. Since he was nine years old, his passion was for electric power and how it could change the world for people in so many positive ways. It started as a child with batteries; buying toys that used electric batteries; and then the frustration that would always follow, because the batteries died too quickly. He spent hours researching how to make cell batteries rechargeable so they could be used over and over again. That was the dream. It wasn't long before battery companies had figured out how to make batteries re-chargeable, but it was also the length of time a battery could keep it's charge that was a significant factor. Gary wanted to learn more about how to keep the charge for longer periods of time while maintaining strength while the battery was in use. Some batteries would re-charge, but they had no power to even operate the toy or piece of equipment on which he was experimenting. Within a couple of years, he had cut open hundreds of batteries trying to learn all the diverse types and all the components that go into a battery. He learned about wind mills, solar panels, water hydro power, nuclear power - to find out which power source would be the best match for long lasting battery power with the ability to recharge. Gary and his stepfather Clyde would spend hours going over the processes and trying to find out if they were missing some simple answer is? They had worked extensively with wind and solar products because they were easy to obtain and therefore could be brought to the house for testing. The hydro was tougher because not everybody had a steady water supply pouring through one's yard that they could up and re-route any time they felt like it. The two focused on batteries mostly because at the time the world was talking about the development of more electric cars on the road. They knew there would be mountains of work needed to create an infrastructure of a world that truly relied on electric vehicles to move people and products around. The two wanted to be the first to find a way to make better, longer lasting batteries and cars. Gary graduated from Ecole Mission Senior Secondary School in 1989 and attended Simon Fraser University (SFU) for the next four years while he completed his education in electric power. His curiosity continued to grow and between him and his father Clyde, they were determined to solve this age-old problem and keeping the batteries energized for the longest time possible. They were obsessed with the notion. Gary had worked extremely hard on his own interests in the field and had scored in the top percentile for grades and achievements which allowed Gary to be offered a job right after graduation with a Vancouver based company named Ballard Power. Ballard Power Systems Inc. are a developer and manufacturer of proton exchange membrane fuel cell products for markets such as heavy-duty motors, portable power, material handling as well as engineering services. Ballard had designed and shipped over 400 MW of fuel cell products to date. This was a fantastic opportunity for Gary to learn from a highly respected innovative power company. Like his father was always telling him, "Learn as much as you can from the smart ones. They're really not ever ready to give up their secrets, so when they do, listen carefully." This was going to be a wonderful chance for Gary to expand his education and understanding of the battery and recharging world that awaited him. Gary, like many young eager minded people, thought he was going to discover how to run a car on pure hydrogen and never pay any mind to emissions into the environment. All super clean energy. He climbed the ranks of the organization and after nine years he was promoted to Plant Manager. The only people over him were Geoffrey Ballard and the current President Randall MacEwen, which was the achievement of a lifetime, however; this is not what he was interested in doing. He was still in search of the "Holy Grail" of batteries that to-date had yet to be invented. He and his team had worked extensively for years on the concept of a hydro-electric car, but it had not been successful enough to change the world forever. He wanted more and Ballard Power was not going to help him get to his crowning achievement. He spent the weekend hanging out with his dad and doing a little fishing on Stave Lake beside the powerhouse and they both concluded that they were going to focus all of their energies into the one goal of creating their dream battery. They just needed time and money, and Clyde knew just the person to ask for a few million in seed money, Walter Hofmann. So that fateful Monday morning Gary headed into work in Burnaby and went into the president's foyer pre-function area and asked Miss Fleming, the president's secretary, to speak with Mr. MacEwen.

"Good morning my boy, how are you on this fine day?" all smiles and polish like the president of a major company should be, "Didn't realize I had a meeting with you this morning, but I am always delighted to see you. How can I be of service to you this morning?" Mr. MacEwen said.

"Sir, I need to tell you that I am resigning as of now. I didn't want to take you by surprise with this news, but I know there is no straightforward way to do this sort of thing. You and Geoffrey Ballard have been two of the best mentors I could have ever hoped to have but unfortunately my interest is solely in solving the dilemma of long-life rechargeable batteries. I know that this company focuses on hydro-like solutions for the future, but I want to continue my work and development on strictly battery power until I can solve the mystery. So, that is why I will be heading home. I walked in with empty pockets, and I will leave with empty pockets. I have read through my contract, and I am not permitted to work for any company in a related field for the next two years, however; it does give me the right to research and develop innovative ideas for some possible new products to the market. You have been an awesome boss and mentor, but I need to work on my own projects now. I don't have the time to waste trying to accomplish someone else's goals. I have always respected you and Mr. Ballard, and you have my word that I will not show up at any other competitor's for at least two years as per our contract. So…I guess I will get moving along." He stated and turned to walk out of the office.

"Just a second young man. You don't think it's going to be that easy, do you?" He said as he slid onto a small leather sofa and pulled out a cigarette case, pulled one out, lit it and began to blow smoke about the room. "You have been our number one son around here for at least five years now and you just waltz into my office and tell me you're out. I'm sorry my boy, but we have so much invested in you now we just can't have you disappearing to another company, can we?" Randall said.

"What is this…some kind of movie? I'm not allowed to quit. You can't force me to work here Mr. MacEwen. What are you going do? Lock me up in the basement?" Gary snapped back at Randall.

"Don't be silly Gary. We're all civilized here. I have spent millions and millions of shareholder's dollars creating, for you and your research team, possibly the best hydro power lab in the world. We have also paid you handsomely in salary, bonuses and lifestyle so that is why when I say things of this nature, it is because I want you to understand what we have gone through to help you solve some of the world's greatest mysteries and now you tell me that you want to go home for a while. You know full well why I am not letting you walk out of this facility, today, or any other day. Gary my lad, we have been watching you ever since we bought you that lovely apartment in Burnaby within walking distance to the office. How convenient don't you think? We have owned you since you started working for us five years ago when you graduated from SFU. Your professor, Mr. Kimball, works for us in sales, he was just one of the many plants we had at your alma-matter keeping an eye on you. Extraordinary talent cannot be wasted, and we knew you were just the type of young man we were looking for. You always had the fire in your belly; wanting to find the answers to riddles on your own terms. Gary, we created a place just so that you would find answers to some of the world's greatest questions and electric power has got to be solved. Gary, you have already spent ample time in finding long lasting batteries and maybe if you spent more time on finding hydro-electric solutions the world would be a different place. You have to realize that there are almost one hundred people who make their income off being part of the super-genius Gary Blin developer extraordinaire, so these are all reasons why I can't just let you walk out of that door and if you think that you will start doing something else, then you are mistaken," Geoffrey said as two menacingly large men entered the room dressed in somber garb and took their places at both exits. "So, you just tell me what's bothering you and I will get it looked after. It can't possibly be more money because the last time I checked your accounts you had over two million in your savings. No credit card debt. So, what the hell is making you feel so dissatisfied that you would want to walk away from your best friends. It must be something horrible. Please, you must tell me." He proffered.

"I want to spend all of my efforts on developing the long-life batteries. If we can just figure out the right ingredients inside the battery so it can hold its charge longer, it would be one of the great contributions to the world. Everyone would be able to resource clean energy quickly and easily. I need to delve into this for a while. It could be a week, but it could be more than that, I don't know until I know. You told me to spend all of my time doing the hydro-car prototype. Now I want to work on the battery idea for a while." Gary said.

"I think we can allow you time to work on another project Gary. It sounds like a wonderful idea indeed. Is your father going to be able to join us at the factory while you are in development?" Randall asked in a kind and engaging voice.

"I could ask him Mr. MacEwen. I think he would like that. We work well together." Gary replied. "I've gotta get back to work. We can chat more later."

"Perfect. You simply let me know if you need to talk more about this matter. Let's get to work on batteries." He shook his hands up in the air like a cheerleader.

"Okay then sir," and Gary went about his daily business.

Randall hoped that, as usual, his at-work genius kid would forget about the batteries within the next couple of days, however; sometimes these ideas lead to instances of great clarity. There was always the possibility that someone finds the secret formula to something in life and, presto, you want to get it out to the world. He always preferred when there was some profit that he could glean, and after all, Ballard Power was still a business. He had to think of his shareholders primarily, and possibly some for himself. The worst that was going to happen was the boy genius was going to put some thought into a plausible device that would be useful worldwide. He couldn't lose.

In less than a year Gary and his team had begun using different combinations of elements rather than just using the standard aluminum, cobalt, nickel, graphite, magnesium metal, and lithium with one exception, they also began adding precious metals like gold into the separator and the electrolyte: they began running tests to see if that could be the missing link. Once they had got all of the batteries built and assembled, they began running tests to see if the new combination between the cathode and anode made the difference they were looking for regarding length of use, and length of time recharging. These were the results that Gary and his team were most interested in.

The following day they got back the answer for which they were hoping. The test had proved that the new prototype battery actually lasted twice a battery types. These were life altering results and they spelled big bucks to the Ballard Power Company and its shareholders were all about to receive a financial infusion that was long awaited. This was splendid news for all. Even Gary thought it was cool but then he ate a sandwich and went back to his office. Now his mind could be free of the outside disruptions of thinking about batteries. Now Gary could concentrate on hydro-electric cars again.

What this all meant to ownership was that Ballard Power could be in possession of a major breakthrough in rechargeable batteries. This of course would mean millions upon millions of dollars coming in every month from world-wide sales of the product. The profit was staggering, and the work force needed to produce it would be massive around the world wherever the raw materials would be the easiest to mine and transport. All of the electric car manufacturers would want to talk about making a deal of some kind, considering some major USA cities were striving to become fossil-fuel free in the next ten years. Phone calls from billionaires and government leaders were the next thing to be expected. The secret formula was now a coveted item rather than some scribbles on a sheet of paper. They of course would do another complete set of tests but at this juncture in time, the new formula worked. They knew the likes of Elon Musk would soon be calling, trying to woo them into the Tesla family of fine automobiles.

Gary's father Clyde had spoken to his old friend Walter Hofmann about some seed money, just in case his son decided to leave Ballard Power Company and head out on his own. Between Gary, Clyde, and Walter they were spit balling around an idea that they could open a new company, Eternal Energy Ltd., (E.E.L.) and focus on batteries only. What Clyde and Walter didn't know is that Gary had already agreed to stay on even after he created the battery and that they would have nothing to sell to anybody because Gary had signed a new non-compete clause to make sure he didn't recreate the battery for someone else's benefit. Ballard Power owned those rights, and they planned on keeping them. This battery was about to change the world.

Within a day Walter had tried to contact Randall to set up a meeting. Walter never detailed what the meeting was about, but Randall knew that Clyde might have jumped the gun in an overzealous manner and leaked some facts about a revolutionary new product, the new Super Long-Life Battery. Randall knew all too well that many people were going to come forward and promise the moon, however; Geoffrey Ballard was rich enough that he wouldn't require the financial assistance of somebody at Walter's financial level. He was too far down the picking list to be noticed at this level of money. The richest people in the world were going to want this product along with every single consumer all over the planet. This battery was the future of electric cars and countless other uses yet to be discovered. Randall returned the call to Walter and as expected, he wanted to talk dollars and cents. He did mention that his partner was none other than Guy Tremblay, currently the richest man in Canada and one the wealthiest men on the planet. It's all a big blur at the top but the New York Times said he was in the top twenty in the world. Randall did agree to take a meeting with Guy when he arrived from Quebec City on his private jet at Vancouver International Airport. Guy came into the Burnaby office like he owned the place and sat down in the boardroom with Randall MacEwen and began to spin his yarn as to why they were a match made in heaven, but little did he know that Scarlet Larsen was sitting in Randall's personal waiting room to discuss some kind of arrangement with her boss, who had an "arm's length" type approach to ownership. Let your stars shine - she was always taught. Needless to say, the last thing in the world that Serge Bouchard wanted was a bidding war with Guy Tremblay, who was just as rich as him. It was hopeless already, and Elon Musk and other rich entrepreneurs would soon be making their appearances. He needed this stopped at once, no matter what it took. Whom ever took this to market was rich beyond all measure, for life. So far, the only people that knew about the invention were Randall, Clyde, Walter, and the inventor, Gary. It was still a controllable list. Scarlet knew she needed to reconvene with Jimmy and see how he wanted to deal with this new competition. "Jimmy, it's Scarlet. I'm here with Randall MacEwen, the current

President, but I know there are four other people that are aware of the existence of the batteries. Only two of them know for sure about the test results from the last battery field test but our contact has confirmed that they were green lighted. Within a couple days from now many other souls will know about this potential product. If we wanted to end that cycle, we could take down the operation in the next couple of nights and set up the entire group to be at the site together for one night. Bim-bam, take out the whole shebang. I will stay in town until you make your decision." Scarlet said and disconnected the call. Now she had to play the waiting game. If she was instructed to move ahead, she was going to recruit Diane Fletcher and Cindy Denton to sanction as many people at the plant as possible, so the company has a harder time rebuilding if all of the key staffing positions are expired. It definitely put up some tremendously difficult roadblocks for any business owner to overcome. Jim knew that they would have to act quickly in order to control the potential buzz that would follow up the positive results from the last battery testing and be sure to squelch any and all talk about the revitalized product, for good. The less people to find out about it at the front end could help tremendously in keeping the competition away for as long as possible. The RRA needed to act quickly to keep this information under wraps.

Chapter Fifteen

Jimmy was in communication with Scarlet and Dr. Cook to discuss the next steps and create an action plan. It was believed, at this point, that only four people were aware of the new battery and the recent test results, however; they didn't know for sure. If that were the case, they could approach the next steps in a different manner. Less people to evaporate, however, also less time to do it in. Jim, Scarlet, Laurent, and Thomas Cook decided to meet in person to go over the details of the plan. They met at Scarlet's apartment at the Queens Quay to cover the details and be sure they were prepared to meet with the ladies. Scarlet would work with Diane Fletcher from Toronto and Thomas Cook was to be Vancouverite Cindy Denton's handler. Laurent came along for any logistical input.

"We need to contain this information as quickly as possible. If the current number of people is four, then it could be ten by the break of dawn. We could simply invite the four to the main boardroom under false pretenses and just blast them all right there on the spot. Quick and easy, and then we sneak down the back staircase and disappear for good." Dr. Cook suggested.

"I don't think Serge is interested in the entire staff of Ballard Power being gunned down one-by-one in a huge hit, the likes of which Vancouver has never seen before." Jim responded.

"We could just pose as a cleaning crew tomorrow night and spray the people of interest workspace's with something horrible and lethal and let chemistry do the rest. The four of them would perish and possibly a couple more from touching things around the crime scene but the overall loss of life would be negligible compared to blowing up the entire building. Besides, there are two different buildings that they operate out of, so who knows where they may all be at the same time. We would still require some recon to understand the area and the buildings. What do you think Jimmy?" She asked.

"I am certainly more inclined to the clandestine approach rather than the "let's shoot everyone in the place" approach, however, the one thing about a bullet to the temple is that it is final. No more worries. So, we need to activate the two ladies immediately. Let's get the two of you, pointing to Scarlet and the doctor, out to Vancouver and get started on the recon on the Ballard Power buildings within the next twenty-four hours. How quickly can the two of you leave," He asked, already knowing the answer.

"We're both good sir. We can leave for YVR right now and contact you once we've established a home base. Should we use Vancouver Hotel?" She suggested.

"Yes. Book suites for the ladies and get them into position as soon as you make contact. Get a room for the team to use. I'll get there soon. I can brief the ladies of the assignment at that time" he instructed. "Stay with them at all times and pump them up as much as they can take. Make sure you explain to them that these people are the ones making illegal drugs right here in Vancouver and then shipping them all over the world to innocent women and children. Let them know they are really contributing, and it truly helps fight the war on drugs."

"Yes, of course sir. Flattery and nothing but the truth, so help me God." Scarlet said.

"So, help you God." Jimmy said.

***

On their way to the YYZ – Toronto Airport, Scarlet reached out to Cindy Denton and Dianne Fletcher to let them know they needed to pack a bag as quickly as possible and be ready to meet in Vancouver within twenty-four hours. The ladies all knew that the stingiest of information would be provided on the phone, so they were best to just wait and see what happens. No sense getting all wound up about something that might not even happen, or at least the way they thought it would.

Scarlet first reached out to Dianne because she would need to travel to Vancouver from Toronto within the next day, which left no time to waste. She answered and stated smartly, "This is Dianne Fletcher, reporting for duty."

"Hello Dianne, this is your handler from the Ministry. This is Scarlet Larsen. I wanted to let you know that you are needed in Vancouver, BC and there is a first-class ticket waiting for you at the Air Canada ticket counter. Once you check in you can wait in the First-Class lounge until it is time to board your flight. Once you land there will be a car and driver waiting for you at the airport to escort you to the hotel. He will have a sign with your name on it. I will contact you once you are settled in. See you sometime tomorrow in Vancouver, Dianne. Safe travels." Her mind took off to somewhere else and she liked the scenery, so she allowed herself to keep reminiscing. A happy smile perched itself on her lips for a moment when she thought of the first night, she had met Tom, just off Avenue Road in front of the Scaramouche Restaurant in the winter of 1974 when he was out for a walk, and she was at her friend's wedding. When she stepped outside, she lost her footing and was about to fall onto the wet, frozen tundra when he scooped her up like "Tarzan of the Apes" did when he swung down and rescued Jane in the nick of time to place her back onto terra firma. He stood her up and made sure she had regained her footing and he let her go and no sooner than he released his grasp of her she was in peril again. He walked her back into the restaurant where it was warm and dry and would allow Dianne to dry off a bit before facing the elements again. During that time waiting Tom took a fancy to Dianne and decided to ask her out on a date that he thought would be fantastic. He mentioned the idea of a simple local walk to look at the hundreds of species of birds that surrounded the local area. It was a splendorous sight. The great news for Tom was that she too was a bird person and actually owned a cockatiel named Fred Flintstone, for over twenty years. The two found common ground on almost every subject they would encounter for the rest of their lives. It was instant love and devotion for each of them. Weeks later the two were married. They moved into a house that Tom's parents owned and willed to him back in 1964 when they had both died in a tragic car accident. Soon after their passing Tom decided to hide from the world as much as possible and got a job as letter carrier for Canada Post. Tom was a steady reliable type who seldom took holidays or spend money he didn't have which meant that over the years, he stocked away a fair amount of savings and his house was mortgage free; so, needless to say, Tom was a catch. He stilled lived in this house on Russel Hill Road just off Avenue Road. He loved long walks on the beach…or anywhere else you could think of. Two years later they had their first child, Mike, and then a year later they had Rick. Both boys were good kids and never caused Dianne or Tom any real trouble over the years and both have since moved on with their lives, so Dianne has no one to fuss over unless the grandkids were in town which was seldom since they were born. She walked into the TV room and sat down beside Tom to get his attention. "Sweetheart, I have to fly off to Vancouver for the Ministry of Special Projects. I will be gone for two days. They'll pick me up here and bring me back home once I have completed my assignment. Are you going to be okay on your own or do you want me to ask one of the boys to come and stay here at the house with you?" Dianne asked.

"Not to worry love. I'll be fine for two days. If it looks like it will be longer than that then we can talk about getting a bit of help for me, okay?" Tom said.

"Just eat all the frozen stuff in the freezer. Stick it in the microwave to warm everything up and presto, hot delicious meals. I will be back here in three days. Call me if you need anything Tom. I'll head upstairs now and pack." She explained to him.

She went to the bedroom, packed a light bag, and fetched some toiletries. Within the hour she was ready to leave and began watching out the front door waiting for her ride to arrive. Before she knew it, she was saying goodbye and kissing Tom's cheek. Off to Vancouver for her turn at the government attaché life.

Scarlet's next call was to Cindy Denton in West Vancouver. She answered the call with her strong Londoner accent, as fresh as the day she arrived with it. The two exchanged pleasantries and then planned when to meet. They were going to meet at the Vancouver Hotel in one of the suites the following day. Cindy acknowledged the call and then instantly set to packing for her downtown excursion. She had absolutely no idea what was going to be asked of her, but she had committed to doing whatever was necessary. She had given this a lot of thought, and she definitely wanted her kids, Kim, and Rachel, to live privileged lives. What parent wouldn't want that for their family. She had also come to grips with the fact that she was going to expire within the year unless a new medical breakthrough took place. Stage #4 cancer is pretty serious stuff. Cindy got herself fully organized and waited for the transportation to arrive to take her to the hotel. She stared out the front window of her West Vancouver house that she and Len moved into when they immigrated to Canada in 1975. Len and Cindy were both twenty-five years old at that time, when they put all of their hard-earned money into a house in the British Properties. Len was born and raised in London, England so it just made perfect sense that he would live in the British properties in Vancouver BC. It was all coming together. Len was born in same year as Cindy, in 1950. The two knew each other from around the neighbourhood but they had never really met officially before. At a dance at school in 1966, the boys from an all-boys school had a dance with an all-girls school from the next county and of course, it took half the night for the kids to get up enough courage to go over and ask each other to dance, but once they did the boys never stopped asking for dances; making all of the girls as happy as young girls could possibly be. At the end of the night Len had conjured up the guts to ask Cindy to dance and she said yes. He had never danced with a girl before, but he was ready just to stand close enough to smell her breath. The two epically walked onto the dance floor and leaned into each other, touching forehead's, and rocking back and forth for the next two straight hours, at which time the adults announced that the girls had to leave to go catch their bus. Len was in a trance, but so was Cindy. Len decided that night that he was going to date that girl once he graduated from high school. Some way…somehow…Len continued on with his tennis career and played at a prominent level in men's and mixed doubles for many years earning him all kinds of notoriety, but he was never ranked in the top one hundred in men's singles, so he was quite unheard of amongst tennis fans that like only the top-level players. Len still earned a six-figure income just playing men's doubles in the satellite tennis circuit throughout the USA. When Len finally moved to Vancouver to live full time, he became a full-time tennis instructor and earned his Level Five teaching certification, which is the highest in the world. From then on, he worked full time at the Capilano Golf and Country Club and enjoyed playing and teaching tennis with kids and seniors. His life was full and after the birth of the twins in 1980 he couldn't be happier. Kim married a pediatric surgeon who worked at VGH, and Rachel married a tug boat captain who worked for Seaspan. Cindy was the type of woman everybody liked. She was kind, friendly, and full of life. Just being around her made you feel better. If you were ever sick, she would be the kind of person that you would love to come and have check in on you. Cindy knew that her Stage #4 cancer, slowly creeping into her brain, was clouding her thoughts and that soon she would no longer be who she was currently. She gathered her thoughts and brought herself back to reality. She had to move along to the Vancouver Hotel and meet up with the rest of the team. This was it. She was really going to go through with this. Her mind wandered aimlessly trying to imagine what she was going to get up to. She glanced out the front window of her home and saw the big, black car waiting for her. Cindy gave her husband a kiss on the lips and headed out the door. She was excited to find out what lay in store for her.

The team was heading to the Vancouver Hotel to meet and strategize. Cindy and Dianne had both checked into their suites at the hotel and were in their rooms awaiting instructions. Dr. Cook and Scarlet were on their way up the elevator to the room when Laurent pulled in front of Dynamic Cleaning Services. He surveyed the interior of the cleaning truck on the street in front of the business. He contemplated what keys could be hanging from the driver's side visor and slid open the step van door to take a closer look. On closer inspection he could clearly see that the keys were the ignition keys to start the truck. He plopped himself into the driver seat, plugged the key into the ignition, turned it and started the vehicle. He headed off down the street looking to find a place to meet with Dr. Cook where they could beef up the contents of the onboard chemicals and see about adding more of a lethal ingredient for the onsite cleaning crew that needed to treat the surfaces of some key personnel at the Ballard Power Company who needed to be silenced. Once the cleaning cart could be retrofitted with the modified products, the ladies were ready to carry out the assignment. They simply had to apply the anthrax liberally on every surface where the four key individuals worked during the day. They wanted to be certain that these people never had a chance to speak to another living soul about the battery discovery and its newfound riches that were to follow. It had to go the way of the dodo bird, gone, and forgotten. Laurent personally organized the cleaning company truck, so it was set up and ready for the work they needed to do inside the Ballard Power offices. He checked the work schedule that was left in the truck cab, connected to a clip board that allowed him to see that the next scheduled visit to Ballard Power was not until next week on a Friday but that was not going to work for the RRA. They needed to be in the building tomorrow night to distribute the lethal chemicals and stop any further chatter amongst the key personnel. Laurent decided he would just go for it and show up at the end of the work day and attempt to walk right in the front door and see if anybody would stop them or just allow them to go about their cleaning duties. It had been his experience that jobs that nobody wants to do are easy to avoid and hopefully get someone else to do them, so the possibility of the cleaning crew being stopped or dismissed was highly unlikely. He assumed it would be business as usual and they could get inside and set the stage. He then had to head to Brentwood Mall in Burnaby so he could get matching T-shirts for the "pretend" staff so they would appear to be part of the same cleaning crew when they arrived on site. Once he had the shirts and the cleaning truck, Laurent had also purchased rubber gloves and protective breathing masks, so they didn't end up killing themselves with the toxic material while they were working with the product. Laurent knew he wouldn't be part of the task force entering the building, but he was well aware of the hazards involved with such a lethal product as Anthrax. He drove the step-van to an alley and parked not far from the Vancouver Hotel so the vehicle would be close by when they were ready to move to the location. The regular cleaning crew would usually arrive at Ballard Power at approximately 7:00 pm, start on the second floor, move through the building and finish in the lunchroom by ten o'clock. They would need to complete the entire routine to be sure that the ruse wasn't detected by them finishing their duties too early. Everything had to appear as normal as possible. He locked the vehicle and headed to the hotel suite of Dianne Fletcher to deliver the keys to her and Cindy Denton.

***

Cindy and Dianne were in their own rooms when Scarlet and Dr. Cook arrived at the hotel. They headed up the elevator to the suites and Scarlet went to Cindy's room to have her join the others in Dianne's room and go over the plans. Once they had the group together it was merely minutes before Laurent rapped on the door to Dianne's room. When he entered, the team instantly got to planning out the evening, getting inside the building, and spreading the lethal powder around the desk areas of the targeted employees. The second trick was to find out where every person's desk was situated because it wasn't initially obvious, and they would have to figure it out once they were inside the office. It was going to be difficult at best to find a personnel map of the building that showed where every person was situated throughout the office space. They knew they may have to look around people's desk to find name plates or identifying objects that would make it clear as to who sat where in the office. This also meant that they may have to spread the powder on some unsuspecting individuals because they might not be able to correctly find the desks for the correct people. It wasn't a pleasant thing to do to people, but the Ministry had a job to do, and they were going to do it. Laurent had already made some wonderful looking fake identifications for the cleaning crew to present to the night security guards upon their arrival to site that evening. When they had gained access to the building past the night guards, they should be home free because nobody really ever tries to chat up the night cleaning staff. They went down the list twice to be confident that they knew who it was that they wanted to dust with Anthrax, but they knew entirely well that many people do not wash their hands efficiently at work, so the chance of the Anthrax making its way through much of the building was no surprise to the team, with the exception of Cindy and Dianne. Of course, the ladies had never been exposed to a lethal powder like this before in their lives and had no idea of the widespread lingering power of the chemical. It was a deadly force, and many Ballard Power employees were most likely going to die. This was always the trouble with espionage - all of the collateral damage it caused. The four donned their outfits and made sure they had the critical ingredients with them to complete the assigned chore. They all looked at each other standing in the suite at the hotel and burst out laughing. They really did appear to be a cleaning crew trying to eke out a living in the big city of Vancouver. They all had overcoats to disguise the working man appearance so that people in the hotel wouldn't suspect the group of being homeless bums that had somehow made it into the hotel elevator and were just hanging around the building. They took the lift down to the parking garage and covered their faces until they had exited the building to avoid being seen by CCTV cameras and then made their way down the alleys of Vancouver to collect the cleaning truck and head off to their destination in the Burnaby suburbs. Although the drive would only take thirty minutes or so they had to get moving along so they wouldn't be late for their shift. When they drove down Glenlyon Parkway, they entered the parking lot from the main entrance and made their way over to the loading dock area and backed the truck into one of the empty stalls. From there Thomas and Scarlet took the lead and acted as if they had done this a thousand times before. They made sure they had all of the supplies they would need, removed the cleaning carts from the back of the truck and rolled them onto the flat loading dock. To be expected, Dianne and Cindy were having heart palpitations because they were so nervous to be taking part in anything like this.

"When we get inside and pull up to the security guard desk, please stay quiet unless spoken to, then present your ID cards to me, and I will pass the cards to the security for inspection. If it looks like something is going to go sideways you will know instantly because I'll have to kill them on the spot, and then we'll need to do the job a little faster than expected. We've never had trouble in any past jobs but that was then, and this is now. Keep your eyes down at all times and don't lift your heads and look around like you've never seen this place before. It must appear that you hate being here and that you can't wait to be done and heading to your next place to clean. Slow and steady with your eyes on your work. Once we are in the office area, we will work together but we will have to actually clean most of the building, so they don't suspect anything is wrong or out of place. We're just a miserable group of people who hate their jobs doing whatever it takes. Everybody stay calm and we will be fine, I promise." Thomas said as he looked at each person and made eye contact to be clear that he was understood. They pressed the night buzzer which was a direct line to the security guards work station at the front of the building, "How can I help you?" A male voice gruffly answered.

"Hello there, it's Dynamic Cleaning here." Thomas announced into the speaker box.

"Hey there. I will buzz you in. It's only me on tonight so I won't be doing rounds all night like usual. I will do just a couple walk throughs later on in my shift. Talk to you later." He replied and disconnected.

The buzzing sound of the door latch released and allowed them to pull open the locked door and enter the building. Step one was done without any troubles. "What a fabulous start to the night," Thomas thought to himself as he made his way over to the elevator core. The four of them huddled together and climbed into the elevator when the doors opened to take them to the second floor. They exited and headed to the large open area that had over fifty work stations and began to make their preparations. The fact was it couldn't have been any more ideal because the security company only had one man on shift that evening, so it gave them free access to the building without having to look over their shoulders the entire time. Dr. Cook was grinning from ear-to-ear with all the good luck they had so far, and he hoped it would continue until they had finished the task. However, so often the best made plans seem to fall apart sometimes. The plan was to take some of the Anthrax powder and to lightly dust it over all of the surfaces of the four people's work space's but not so thick that it was obvious to the naked eye. When Anthrax is inhaled is when the chemical does the most amount of damage to humans. If it gets on the skin, it can cause rashes but typically couldn't kill somebody. The group knew they needed to be extremely cautious when dealing with this product, however; they still needed to do all of the cleaning responsibilities to keep up the ruse and have the Ballard Power staff believe the cleaners came in last night and did their job. The group got to work and out came the vacuum and the feather dusters, and they began doing the laborious chore. Thomas was rushing around from desk to desk trying to find the names of the four people that needed to be silenced so they could apply the deadly dust to their workstations. Within a few minutes Thomas had located the desired work spaces and he and

Cindy Denton headed to the first office to cast their evil spell. Thomas had transported the powder in Dutch Cleanser bottles so it would appear as a regular cleaning product and would not catch the attention of any on-lookers. The idea was to sprinkle the surfaces with the powder and then wipe off the excess residue just leaving a thin but lethal coating. Cindy and Thomas got on their protective gloves and breathing gear and began spreading the powder throughout the required offices methodically. Two large offices and two workstations and they would be done the deadly part of the evening. They still had to clean the entire two floors of the office, but they had all cleaned stuff before in their lives, so this wasn't a job that was beyond them. A few hours later the crew were all on the main floor now finishing up the work and repacking their cleaning carts to prepare to leave the premises when Cindy tripped on a chair floor mat and toppled over and knocked a container of Dutch Cleanser off the cleaning cart and onto the floor which erupted into a large poof of a white chalky substance that landed inches away from her face. She squiggled backwards on the floor as quickly as she could, but it was all too late. Cindy had inhaled a large amount of the Anthrax, and she knew instantly that she was in trouble. The four of them all looked at each other but said nothing. The group gathered up their equipment and headed to the back loading bay exit and loaded their materials into the step van and drove away. A brief time later Dr. Cook told her, “You’re a goner Cindy. This stuff works one hundred percent of the time so it will only be a while before it begins to consume your soul. I will drive us back to the hotel and then dump the vehicle. I am going say something I never thought I would say however, I think you should call a cab from the hotel and head home to be with Len because you won’t make it through the night. You took a heavy dose of the powder and I know that it kills people, and it always works so, I’m sorry Cindy but you only have tonight left in your life. I think you might want to spend it with your husband. As long as you don’t kiss or breathe into each other's faces, he will be okay. He can call an ambulance once you have expired, and the hospital will not do an autopsy on a seventy plus year old woman with Stage #4 cancer. Well, at least I don’t think they will. If they do, Len will have some explaining to do, but he will have no idea how you became polluted with Anthrax. I know that Jimmy is our boss, and he calls the shots, but I would just tell him that you had the mishap and then when we got back to the hotel you left without saying a word to anyone. I am deeply sorry Cindy. This is not a good thing. In the next few hours, your lungs will begin to swell and then you will be fighting to breathe and then asphyxiation will occur. At least if you are at home, he can comfort you through the process. He stopped the truck in the alley a block away from the hotel. “I need to lose this truck right now. All of you need to head back inside. Cindy you will make the call for a taxi cab. Grab all of your belongings and leave. Scarlet, you go to her room and stay the night, so it appears that someone was there in the morning. Dianne, you head back to Toronto on your scheduled flight from YVR tomorrow. We will contact you on your special phone and give you further instructions. I will meet up with Laurent and we will make our way back to Toronto in a few days. Thomas released the buckle on his safety belt and slid the step van door open and jumped onto the pavement and put his protective mask back on and walked over to Cindy and gave her a big bear hug and said, "I pray your soul finds peace with God. Goodbye Cindy Denton."

He stepped back up into the step van and slid the door shut and drove away. Two blocks away in an alley off Granville Street he pulled the truck over to one side, shut off the motor, pulled the door open, stepped out and continued to walk down the street into the darkness of the night.

Chapter Sixteen

The following morning at Ballard Power was chaos, as to be expected. Within a couple of hours of the staff arriving, many people in the office were becoming sick and soon the building had to be evacuated. The police were notified and arrived on the scene with the hazmat team to sterilize the office interior. Some of the staff had shortness of breath while others had swelling in their ankles and hands and an itchy sensation all over their skin, so the ownership sent all staff away until the Hazmat could clean the hazardous materials and get the premises back under control. In a short period of time, they discovered that the deadly powder was indeed Anthrax; so at least they knew how to treat the people that had been affected that morning. Although the authorities had the situation under control quickly, which allowed the police to begin to investigate the crime scene: it was still going to take a lengthy time to figure out what took place at Ballard Power last night. The toxic powder was brought to the office to do one thing, and that was stop the four key people from ever revealing the results of the newest battery test to another living person. The chemical had been effective on three of the four people because they all started to choke and cough once they arrived at work that morning and were rushed to the hospital with no idea what they were dealing with however, the Anthrax was a dangerous product and by midday it summarily extinguished three of the four lives that the Ministry had been targeting. Unfortunately, Gary Blin had a dentist appointment in the morning, which delayed his arrival at the office until after lunch. This created some difficulties for the Ministry because Gary was to be one of the staff members that was supposed to be in contact with the deadly chemical that morning and should have been dead by noon. When Gary showed up to the office after lunch and saw all of the cop cars and Hazmat Teams swarming around the building he was apprised of the situation and removed from the site immediately for his protection. He couldn't believe that his discovery was this volatile after just a couple of days since the new battery was tested with amazing results. He sat in shock that his colleagues were in peril for simply doing their jobs but had managed to get caught in the crossfire. So many lives at risk over a stupid battery. Progress is a monster that consumes the past and disregards the devastating effects it may be causing in the future. Some days Gary hated being smart and believed that he was going to help the world. He had never created the battery to generate money, he did it to help the human race. His bosses on the other hand had alternate plans for the discovery. The police had to whisk Gary away to a covert location while they ran tests and cleaned up the infected building so the staff would be able to return to work sooner than later. The biggest disappointment for Gary was not having his laboratory available to work in while the police were performing their investigation. He couldn't stand being idle at any time, especially for long stretches of time. Indolence was the bane of his existence. Geoffrey and Randall were both delighted that their star employee was not harmed during this act of terrorism and were relieved that only a couple of staff members were harmed by this horrible crime. Every life mattered to ownership, and they would move mountains if they had to bring these deplorable people to justice. Geoffrey had a little place in a quiet area called Bedwell Bay near Belcarra, an extremely isolated place on the outskirts of Port Moody, which would make for a wonderful place to hide Gary until the police and investigators had an opportunity to figure out what took place at the Ballard Power offices. The important thing now was to keep Gary out of harm's way until more information surfaced. Randall was filled with dread having to communicate with the victims' families and try to rationalize what had happened. It could be years before they had the answers to all of the unresolved questions.

***

Laurent contacted Dianne Fletcher to tell her to not get on the plane returning to Toronto that evening, rather, he told her to head to the Sutton Place Hotel on Burrard Street in Vancouver and stay there until he or Scarlet contacted her with new instructions. The team knew that Gary Blin was going to have tight security surrounding him for some time and they were going to have to find out where he was hiding. This was going to take time which, at this very moment, they had none of because every day that went by had the chance for somebody else to be told about the new battery discovery. This was of course a huge problem for the Ministry. They needed to find Gary Blin right away and silence him from spreading the positive news results of the battery. When Jimmy Smits learned of the problem of the disappearing genius from Ballard Power he contacted Tim Dixon, the Ministries IT expert, and had him start a search for the whereabouts of Gary Blin. They needed to find him quickly and stifle those loose lips. As Tim did his research, he was able to find that Geoffrey and Randall both had substantial real estate holdings across the country and a couple other residences offshore, which wasn't uncommon for multi-millionaires to have in their portfolios. The question was going to be - where they moved Gary to after the Anthrax fiasco. As Tim scoured the information, he found that Randall's wife had a house in Bedwell Bay listed under her maiden name Verporte, which had been willed to her years before. Tim easily referenced a map and saw that the house would be ideal for hiding someone with a need for total privacy from the outside world, especially if people are trying to kill you. Tim looked the address up on Map Quest and realized that the house was merely an hour away from where the Ballard Power offices were located in Burnaby, which of course made him think that it would be an excellent place to take Gary and have him lay low for a while. Once Tim had found the potential hiding place of Gary Blin, he contacted Jimmy with the information so he could formulate a plan. They needed to have eyes on the house at once! Jimmy asked Thomas to go acquire a boat and check the house out from the water front and, he also had Scarlet do some recon on foot in the neighbourhood. She would be able to walk about the area without drawing suspicion to herself and Thomas would have no worries buzzing around the bay in a boat aimlessly for hours, because people did that kind of thing in Bedwell Bay on a daily basis. Once the team was able to survey the land and surroundings, they would have a better idea if Gary were there and who else was there with him. There was no doubt that the Ballard Power executive team knew that someone was out to get Gary and ownership was not about to let somebody waltz through the front door and fire a couple of bullets into him. If he was at the Belcarra home, he was going to have a security detail with him at all times. Jimmy knew that Dianne was the only one that was going to have a chance to get close enough to sanction this individual while he was in a guarded house. Within a couple of hours Thomas was standing on the deck of a small twenty-four-foot-long twin screw Donzi hull boat staring up at 3905 Bedwell Bay Road taking pictures with his high-powered telephoto lens of the house and looking for any sign of life that could see from the water. He did happen to catch a few glimpses of what seemed to be more than just one person in the house, but he could not tell how many. Thomas thought he would just come back around at nightfall and see if the occupants lowered the blinds down for privacy or if they possibly left them open so he could see inside and do the head count. At the same time that Thomas was checking the home from the water Scarlet had donned an active walker's outfit with her two ski poles and runners and was steadily making her way down the street in front of the house looking for clues, when she happened to get lucky and noticed Gary standing on one of the outside sun decks off the side of the house drinking a Pepsi and making notes. She stood for only a moment to confirm the face until she was convinced that it was him. They had found their man. Scarlet called Jimmy back to share her findings with him and wait for his next decision. They had to act fast. Jimmy asked Dr. Cook and Scarlet to meet at Dianne's hotel suite that night to plan their next move. By seven o'clock that night Dianne, Scarlet, and Dr. Cook were in Dianne's room going over the recon gathered by the team and trying to figure out the best way into the building and the best way out.

"We could arrive by water, dock a boat at the waterfront and walk up the hill to the house and gain entry and do what we came here to do. There is a dock about a block away from the house and then after we finish our work we could simply jump into the boat and motor away without drawing attention to ourselves. Once we get out of Bedwell Bay, we'll zip around to Reed Point Marina in Port Moody and leave the boat at the gas barge, walk up to the parking lot, and borrow a car to drive back downtown to the Sutton Place. Hell, we could motor the boat all the way to the foot of Nicola Street and just leave the boat there at a private dock and walk back up the street to the hotel. Both ways could work." Thomas said.

"That might be a better idea than using the road because the place is so isolated that if for any reason the police were contacted, they could easily block off all of the routes in or out of the Belcarra area, which would mean that we would have to walk out on foot while avoiding the authorities until we were back to an area with more people and available roads to drive away on. Not impossible, but the boat idea seems good. Can you get your hands on a boat that does high speeds in case of a chase situation? We would need something that could outrun local Harbour Patrol watercraft and still be able to take a wave in case the water gets rough in the inner harbour." Scarlet said.

"How are we going to do it? Just knock on the door and when they answer we shoot them in the heart?" Dianne queried.

"No, it will be a little more humane than that. We will arrive by water and tie up to the dock. The three of us will then head up the hill to the house, we will apply fake blood to your knees and hands, and you will explain to them that you've fallen, hurt yourself badly and are in need of help. Automatically they will open the door and let you in, as you cry and shake in pain and the house occupants will all be trying to help you in your hour of need. Then, while you have their attention, we will take the opportunity to position ourselves outside so that when the time is right, we can whisk you away back to the boat and zip down the harbour and make our way back to the Sutton Place. We will provide you with one of our poisonous rings and all you need to do is touch the pin head on the ring to any spot-on Gary's body and the poison will look after the rest. The poison is highly lethal and the dosage that you will inject him with will be sufficient to do the job in under ten minutes. It will look like any other ring you may be wearing on your fingers. Once you have delivered the deadly dose you need keep the ring with you until you are back on the boat and then, and only then, can you toss it overboard so that no traces of us are left behind." Thomas said.

"Well, there is a bit of a problem with this plan. I can't swim!" Dianne exclaimed with panic in her voice.

"You won't need to, but to error on the side of caution you could wear a life jacket while we are motoring and then just take it off when we reach the dock and put it back on when we have finished our task on shore. No worries about being in the water. How does that sound?" He asked.

"Okay, you've convinced me. When are we doing this?" Dianne asked.

"Tomorrow morning Dianne. I will go borrow a boat for the trip and I will be in touch once I have the equipment ready and I am sitting in the water ready to head down the harbour to Bedwell Bay. We should be able to power down there in about thirty minutes and that should still put us there before noon which will work perfectly for you to be going for your health walk when you fell and hurt yourself. Most certainly they will open the door and offer help to you. It is what nice people do." Thomas surmised.

"Sounds good to me. I need to eat something, and you should eat before you leave because it could be hours before you get a chance to nosh down some dinner. If you are going to go and get a boat for us to use tonight, you won't have an opportunity so let's get some room service right now." Scarlet said as she picked up the room service menu and began perusing the selections.

The three ate dinner and watched a rerun of the "Big Bang Theory" as they chatted about what's next for Dianne once she got back home to her husband and family.

"My life will all seem a little milk toast compared with all this action, being with you two. You both seem so calm and at ease with all this stuff where I am just freaking out on the inside all the time. No offence to you two but, I can't wait to never see you again. My heart can't take the excitement. Too much adrenaline at one time for seniors like me is a dangerous thing now days." Dianne declared.

"Dianne, we fully understand. This life is not for everyone. Most of the time we can't believe what we do but then we get another phone call from the Ministry, and we feel compelled to serve our country the only way we know how." Scarlet said.

Dr. Cook stood up and held his belly with his hands and announced, "Holy cow…I feel like I've eaten a cow. That was some of the best room service food I have ever had. Ladies, I must go shopping for a luxury speed boat for tomorrow." He pulled on his coat and headed for the door. "I will see you both in the morning."

"Dianne I am going to stay here with you tonight so we can be efficient in the morning when it's time to leave. I can sleep on the sofa bed in the living room. I will set a wake-up call for 7:00 am so we can be showered and ready to go once we hear back from Thomas." Scarlet said.

The pair went about their nightly routines and headed to bed for the night.

***

The following day Scarlet's cell phone lit up and she answered. It was Thomas and he had gotten a boat that would be perfect for the assignment at hand. The two ladies were going to take a cab over to the Bayshore Inn which had a huge dock on the waterfront, and they were to meet Thomas at the wharf where he would pull his bow up to the dock and the two women would just jump in and get underway. As they pulled away from the dock Thomas made sure that Dianne had her life jacket on securely. With that, Thomas cleared past all the moored boats and when he was clear of the 5 MPH section of water, so that the boats wouldn't create a wake, he threw the motors into high speed, and they raced off down the harbour at high speed. Thomas had to be careful to not go too fast and risk being detained by Harbour Police for speeding and issuing him a ticket. He set the trims, so the boat planed along the surface at a comfortable 40 MPH, but it did seem like all other watercrafts were standing still. They continued under the Iron Workers Memorial Bridge and Thomas applied more throttle and the boat began to skim across the surface by what seemed was just the two legs of the V-8 engines and their propellers barely touching the water. They angled off to the west, flew past Belcarra Park, arced around Jug Island, cut the throttle, and dropped the hull down into the water and began cruising at 10 MPH to the dock that they had selected the day before. They pulled up and Thomas cut the power and Scarlet leapt onto the dock and secured the bow line. Thomas climbed to the back and tied off the stern line and they were ready to go. The water was flat and reflected like a mirror over the bathroom sink. There wasn't a sound and there was no sign of any other people. No witnesses were always a fantastic way to start the morning. The trio grabbed their necessary items and began to head up the hill to Bedwell Bay Road. Once they got to the top Marine Avenue it was a short walk down the street to the target location. When the three were on the flat grade of Bedwell Bay Road Scarlet and Thomas stayed off to the sides of the road and wanted Dianne to continue down the road, walk past the house, and see if there was any activity or if she could spot other people in the house through an open window covering or somebody walking around the yard. On her first pass she was walking with purpose and swinging her walking poles to create the illusion of her being a true outdoorsy type of person, however; Dianne did not see any sign of people when she walked by. There were a couple of lights on in the interior, but she could see nothing. She continued her pace down to the end of the road till she got to Main Avenue where she collected herself and turned around and walked back down the street to meet back up with Scarlet and Thomas. The plan was being developed as they moved their way through the scenario because they knew they had to get the front door of the house open and get close enough to Gary to tap his skin with a lethal dose from the ring that Dianne was wearing on her left hand. The real problem that the three currently had was that they were standing on the side of a road in Belcarra with no reasonable excuse for why they were there. They began walking down the deserted road and got to a stand of public mailboxes and slipped in behind them just so they weren't completely exposed to any potential passing by traffic. They decided to apply the fake blood to Dianne's knees of her workout attire and some on her elbows and hands to create the look of a fallen hiker out for the day. She was going to pretend that she was stunned from her fall on the road, and she thought that her good friend lived at this address and stopped to see if they could give any comfort and assistance to an old lady who was badly hurt from her fall. They assumed the best thing was to walk down the driveway and knock on the door and see who came to answer. If their plan worked, Gary and the other occupants would let her inside the house to clean her up and help this suffering old woman. The plan was set. Once Dianne had gained access to the house Thomas and Scarlet would position themselves strategically outside the house so they could force their way into the home and be sure that lethal dose was administered correctly. When the victim was drugged, the trio were to head back down the hill to their waiting boat and head back down to the dock at the Bayshore Inn and they could fade to black and get Dianne onto a plane heading for Toronto. They got Dianne organized and applied the faux blood until she appeared like a lady who had fallen and was in rough shape from her imaginary tumble. Now she had to walk a one hundred meters down the road to the down slopping driveway that arrived at the upper-level back door of the house that faced onto the roadway. The west facing front side of the home looked out onto the water and overlooked Bedwell Bay which was a wonderful cover from the outside world.

"My heart is pounding so hard it feels like it's going to explode out of my chest. I am so nervous right now I don't know if I can do this. What if they don't open the door and let me in like we have planned for. What if they tell me to get lost. What then?" Dianne conjectured.

"We are trying to perform this deed in a clandestine way, however; if you are not able to gain access to the house we are going to come up with an alternative plan. We would prefer to not bash down the door and shoot everybody in sight, but we are hired to complete these tasks and we will do what is expected of us, do you understand Dianne?" Thomas said.

"So why bother having me do this silly cloak and dagger scene? Why not just go in the front door with guns a blazing and finish the job? Dianne asked.

"The concept of having seniors helping fellow Canadians infiltrate these horrible people's organizations that disguise themselves as hard working tax paying

Canadians is what the Ministry is all about but, we are trying to do the messy chores in a clandestine way, so that we do not attract National attention to ourselves every time we take down a bad guy. This is the reason Dianne, that we only have you do one assignment and then go back to your regular routine to enjoy the last part of your life as a Canadian Hero. A person who fought back against the tyranny of millionaires who think they are above the law and can do whatever they want to whenever they want. These are the steps we need to take to stop this way of thinking. We need you to be brave and to go down there and knock on that door and let this scenario play out. Once we are in, we will be heading back to the boat before you know it." Thomas said in a reassuring way.

"Okay…I'm ready. Let's get this done." She blurted out and she began walking at a pace down the road to the house.

Dianne kept a strong pace down the road towards the target address trying to keep her courage up until she came to the slopping driveway where Gary was hiding out inside. She paused at the apex, and then pushed herself to walk down the driveway to the double red entryway doors and rang the doorbell. She quickly glanced back over her shoulder to confirm if Scarlet and Thomas were still in tow and taking their positions outside the house. The door swung open, and it was a young handsome man that sported the haircut of a cop and he said, "Hello there, how can I help you today?"

While all the thoughts were swirling around in her head, she had already forgot the name of her pretend friend that she thought lived there. She went blank. Before Dianne could mutter a word, the young man noticed, "Oh my goodness, you've been hurt. Did you fall down somewhere?" He asked.

"Yes. I was out for a walk, and I thought I heard a bear rustling around behind me, so I tried to speed up my pace a bit and before you know it, I was down in a heap on the pavement. I thought my friend Sally Miller lived here so I thought I could ask her for a drink of water and a bandage, or two." Dianne came out with, hoping for the house entry invitation.

"Oh, my goodness," the young man proclaimed and instantly opened the door to Dianne to enter the house, "Please come in and we can get you patched up in no time."

Dianne began to panic because she knew all her wounds were pretend and it would not take long before someone offering up aid would realize that she was making this injury report up. Her head swiveled to behind her to see if she could spot the whereabouts of Thomas or Scarlet but at quick glance, she could not see them anywhere. She had no choice but to enter the house and see what played out next. She followed the man into the kitchen where he began to look through kitchen drawers trying to find a towel to aid in cleaning up her injuries which lead her to believe that this man didn't live here full time, which meant he was potentially a cop. The young man pulled open several doors and drawers and still hadn't found what he was looking for and then he yelled out to the rest of the house, "Hey Gary, do you know where these guys keep their kitchen towels and first aid kit?"

A moment later a man matching the picture she had been showed walked into the kitchen and said, "They may be over the oven," and he reached up and looked in the cupboard. He walked across the room, opened a cupboard over the microwave, and pulled a small white plastic box first aid kit and brought it over to the other man and placed it on the table beside Dianne. She was astounded, he was here in the house with her, how could this get any easier. Her fingertips began running over the pin-cover that concealed the lethal poison. She knew she had to remove it before touching Gary with the ring to make sure he received a full dosage of the toxic material. She began to wipe her hands and her knees to remove the imaginary blood and decided to try and get Gary to come over and help her stand up. She acted shaky and confused and made it to her feet and tried to steady herself and by this time she had removed the protective cap covering the head of the pin and she reached out and grabbed Gary's arm and she pretended to temporarily lose her balance.

Dianne was staring right into his face when she made contact with his arm, but he didn't make a sound. She began to wonder whether or not she administered the poison properly or had she failed to get it to make contact with his arm. Gary steadied Dianne and helped her to sit back down because he was concerned that she may fall down due to the fact that she seemed so out-of-it. The young man had returned to the kitchen and was rinsing a small hand towel under the tap to create a cold compress for Dianne's forehead when unexpectedly she announced, "Thank you so much for your help today. You have both been so kind, but I must be heading off to get back home. My husband is going to be worried sick about me being gone for so long. I will think twice before I decide to take a wilderness walk in Bedwell Bay without making sure I have a can of bear spray." She said and stood up and headed straight for the double entry doors.

"Are you sure you're, okay? We don't want you to hurry out of here and then have another fall five minutes down the street." Gary said.

"No. You have both been so kind, but I must get out of your hair and let you get back to your lives. Again, many thanks for your kindness." She said and stepped out of the door and headed up the driveway to the road.

As the two men closed the door and watched Dianne through the window when Gary turned to the cop and said,

"I feel like I'm coming down with a cold. Starting to feel all achy and I have a headache brewing. Think I will go lay down for a bit. I'll be in the bedroom if you need me, Zack." And Gary headed down the hall to the bedroom he was occupying to lay down.

***

As Dianne pushed her walking pace down the pavement away from the house, she suddenly realized that Thomas and Scarlet were trudging along right behind her. "Where did you two come from? I didn't see you at all when I was in the house with the men." Dianne said.

"We were hanging around outside peeking in through the windows trying to make sure you were safe. We could see you, but we couldn't hear you. Thomas saw you give the dose when you grabbed his arm so we knew we could just hold back and wait for you to appear from the building. If you hadn't, we would have kicked the door down and come in with our guns a blazing for you Dianne." Scarlet said.

They kept up their walking pace and got back down the dock where their boat was still tied to the dock. No sooner that they were climbing aboard the boat a woman appeared and marched over and stood looking at the trio as if she had caught the criminals in the act and said, "Excuse me. This is a private dock and not open to anyone that just wants to show up uninvited and take up space at our dock. You need to check with the owners before you just start using other people's things."

Dr. Cook reached inside his jacket and pulled out a 9 mm pistol and waved it at her and said, "Is this the permission slip you are speaking of crazy lady? How about you get your fat ass off this dock and out of my sight before I start feeling less charitable." Thomas sniped at her.

The dock guard turned and quickly made her exit off the wharf and back up the hill to terra firma and watched them from a distance not wanting to provoke Dr. Cook any more than she had to.

Thomas fired up the twins and Scarlet dropped the lines. In one quick motion the boat raced backwards from the dock, and he slid the engines in neutral and allowed his bow to come around at which time he hammered the engines into full throttle and off like a bullet they went racing down the bay to Jug Island where they came around and headed back towards the city of Vancouver. Thomas kept a high rate of speed until they were well clear of the area and heading in a direct path of the inner Vancouver harbour. The boat was smooth and powerful and was doing about 50 MPH when Thomas didn't spot a large deadhead log just hiding beneath the surface of the water when he hit it and the boat shifted onto its starboard side, but the impact was a hard enough jolt that the boat actually rose several feet into the air and everything and everyone inside defied gravity for a second or two, including Dianne. The boat soared through the air for twenty plus feet and when the hull contacted the water again it hit with a mighty crash that Dianne was not prepared for at all, and over the edge of the craft she fell. Because they were in a rush to leave the dock back in Bedwell Bay Dianne had not had the chance to put her life preserver back on and so when she hit the water, she had nothing to keep her buoyant. The waters under the Iron Workers Memorial Bridge are very treacherous and on a heavy tide change of thirteen feet the waters rip through this gap at a high rate of speed, but the lethal part is all the under currents and eddies which were the death of many people over the years and today was no exception. Once Dianne's body hit the water, she slid under its dark murkiness and never returned to the surface. Thomas stopped the engines at once and the two began scanning the water to see if there was any sign of Dianne, but she was gone. The two putted around in circles for a few minutes hoping that she was going to pop up, but this was not the case. She was swallowed by the ocean never to be seen again. Scarlet stepped across the boat interior and placed her hand on Thomas's hand and said, "I don't think she is coming with us today, Thomas."

He threw the engines into gear and pressed hard on the controls as the powerful boat rose out of the water and resumed its skimming across the tops of the inner harbour waves. Within ten minutes the two pulled up to an old, abandoned fish wharf and tied off the lines, shut off the engines, and made their way back up to the Sutton Place Hotel to collect their things and get instructions from Jimmy Smits. As the they stood at the top of the gang plank connected to the dock Thomas looked at the cold dark water and felt sadness over the loss of Dianne Fletcher. She had completed her task and wouldn't have the chance to celebrate her victory. He turned away and continued his walk back into the downtown core of the city.

Chapter Seventeen

Marie-Jose Cote was born in Montreal in April of 1945. She had lived with her parents, Gilles, and Francine, on Avenue Rosemount her entire life and enjoyed an affluent lifestyle and was treated like a little princess as an only child. Her father Gilles had got into textiles as a young man growing up in Quebec City, but his parents moved to Montreal years later and he found himself needing a job which, at that time, was still exceptionally difficult to get. He decided to take a chance and open his own sock factory with a couple of used machines and a few friends to help manufacture and package all his products. For the first couple of years, he could barely afford to pay for his business and find enough money to eat and pay for a place to sleep. The rules were extremely strict about sleeping in one's own factory at night. There were too many laws surrounding it so Gilles continued to find places to sleep while trying to keep his cost to a minimum so he could funnel all his excess cash back into the business to keep his employees and grow sales. Within a few years of constant struggling, he met with the head buyer from The Hudson Bay Company, and he was awarded an opportunity to supply them with one of his latest creations of cotton and poly combination that helped keep your socks from falling down and they came in a wide variety of colours. The initial order was only for one hundred pairs per month for the downtown Montreal flagship Hudson

Bay store for one year to evaluate the market for sales and customer satisfaction. It took a few months for the socks to catch on but soon the Bay was not able to keep the socks in stock and would deplete their monthly order of one hundred pairs within a week. The popularity continued to grow as did the sales and, after one short year, he was awarded an opportunity to sell his product nationwide to all Bay stores. By this point Gilles was ready because he had already had the chance to reinforce his infrastructure to manage the kind of volume he would be expected to deliver to this customer. With the one national order his company was launched into the stratosphere of insane money deals, and he was now making the kind of money that he could have only dreamt about. In less than two years “Bonheur Pieds Ltd.” was the number one supplier to the Hudson Bay stores and his tiny little factory was now employing over one hundred people full time, which years before he couldn’t even imagine this level of success. With having surplus funds available to him for the first time in his life he decided he was going to try and get a girlfriend, and he did. He began attending musicals, art shows, opera, symphony engagements, and had decided to find a woman of substance with education, beauty, and skills. He wanted to find the complete package even though he always felt he wasn’t worthy of the fortune he was amassing because he was told, money isn’t everything. Gilles met Francine at a ballroom dance class he was attending in his personal pursuit to become a true Renaissance Man who was more than just a big wallet. Francine was beautiful and dressed to the nines which meant that she was from a wealthy family, or she had an amazing job which was difficult to swallow because she was still an incredibly young lady. One class turned to six classes, which turned to twenty dance classes, until they had become proficient at all the dances and had grown fond enough of each other and simply didn't want to spend time with other people. Gilles asked Francine's father for the privilege of his daughter's hand in marriage, and he gave Gilles his blessing. The wedding was soon after and Gilles and Francine began their happy, married lives together.

After the arrival of baby Marie-Jose the couple couldn't have been happier and for the next eighteen years of their lives Gilles continued to run the business and Francine brought Marie-Jose up to be a debutante. She had it all. Smart, alarmingly attractive, gifted in sports, and swift to put unruly men in their place should the need arise. Francine could not have been any prouder of her little girl until her final year of high school when she met a boy playing pool across the street from the high school. He was a young man only looking to put notches on his belt and had no interest in love or relationships, and she was head-over-heels. He had graduated from school years before, but he was impressed only with her beauty and not her mind or accomplishments.

His goal, like many young men, was to have sex with her and dump her. Marie-Jose had never even spoken to a man that had this type of attitude towards the female gender. He seemed filled with disdain with the female race, yet she felt herself falling for this horrible man. Her parents continued to tell her that this man was after one thing and once he had it, he would move along to other women. Francine was beside herself because of all the nurturing she had provided to Marie-Jose and even with her strong advice, her daughter, for some reason, she would not give up on this man. Before long it was time for Marie-Jose to graduate from high school and head off to McGill University to pursue her dreams of becoming an opera singer. She knew it would suit her lifestyle and she always had enough of an ego to anticipate that she could be a little bit famous one day. With graduation day looming a couple weeks away she went with her mom to pick out a grad dress for the ceremonies for the big gala. Francine and Gilles shed tears of joy when their little girl entered the try-on area in the dress shop as they both tried to take in what they had created. The perfect angel. On Grad night the so-called boyfriend didn't show up. 7:00pm, 8:00pm…9:00pm, where was her grad date? By ten o'clock the waterworks had begun, and their daughter was going through her first bout of rejection and being seriously hurt by a man. All the men in her life had worshipped her so what the heck was happening with this one. Her female dominance was ineffective on this boy as if he didn't give a crap about anyone except himself. Marie-Jose missed her graduation night and cried herself to sleep that night. Gilles was so angry he was ready to go kill this young man for his impertinence and for hurting his daughter's feelings. Francine had to hold him back from leaving the house in a rage. His only consolation was that Marie-Jose was eighteen years old and she would soon forget this guy ever existed. So, he thought. Five days later the scoundrel phoned Marie-Jose and said he had simply forgot the big night because he had graduated years before and it was no longer something that he would covet. He asked Marie-Jose if she wanted to go to a local party happening at a friend's house close to her home and she forgave him and gave him a second chance. Gilles and Francine pleaded with their daughter to not give this idiot the time of day but, as all parents know, love is blind, and you can't stop young people from getting together, no matter how hard you may try. He came to the house and pulled up out front and honked the horn several times to show that he had arrived. Gilles was ready to go out to his car and beat him senseless; to have the nerve to come and collect a lady and not walk to the door was too much for Gilles. However, Marie-Jose begged her dad to understand and simply give the man another chance. Gilles had to concede to keep the peace in the household. She headed out the door looking stunning, like always, and went to the party in the city. Gilles was sitting on the living room sofa waiting for Marie-Jose to return home from her date at 4:00am when he heard a car pull up out front. He leapt to his feet to look out the window at the belligerent man who was bringing his daughter home four hours late. As Gilles stood looking out, he could see someone untangle themselves from the driver's seat and go around the car to assist Marie-Jose out of the automobile and up the pathway to front door of the house. She wasn't quite right; he could see it in her movements. When they arrived at the door Gilles could see it was another woman who was helping his child get to the front door. He swung the door open and clearly Marie-Jose was upset and was still sobbing uncontrollably, and he helped her inside the house. While he was guiding her up the stairs to her room, Francine appeared and began hugging and consoling her and took her to the bathroom to clean up and calm down. Gilles walked back down the staircase with hate seething out of every pore on his body, but his daughter had pleaded with him to not get involved and just leave her and her friend alone. He conceded. Her mother stayed with her that night and continued to comfort her as much as she could but there was something wrong. The next school day came, and Marie-Jose refused to go. She had stayed in her room at the house since the night of the party. Two weeks later he came home to find Francine and Marie-Jose sitting at the kitchen table when she announced to her dad that she had missed her period, and she was possibly pregnant. The three climbed into the family car and went to the hospital to have a test done. A week later the doctor's office called with the news, she was going to be a mother. Gilles' blood ran cold. This was nothing like he had planned for his amazingly talented daughter. The good news was they had money and the two of them could help Marie-Jose with everything there was to raise a child. What Gilles wasn't prepared for is the deep depression into which she had fallen. She was no longer like the little angel they nurtured. She now would stay in her room for days at time and wouldn't eat properly or wash herself or even speak with any of her school friends. Marie-Jose was convinced she was looked upon as the school slut and everybody was talking about her, and they all were. Parents, teachers, and all the high school attendees. This was a big-time story for these days. Local millionaire's daughter gets knocked up at high school dance. The local papers had a field day. It even made it to the Montreal Gazette, which was the city's biggest newspaper. Gilles couldn't believe that this nothing of a story would not die. Marie-Jose began showing the baby bump after about five months of pregnancy and wouldn't be long before her belly was massive. He knew that she was not going to leave the house while she was so noticeably bulging because she couldn't take the finger pointing and the criticism. Since that fateful night she had never seen or heard from the boy again. He had vanished. After nine months, his child produced a child. Born into the world a healthy baby girl, Marie-Jose held the child and couldn't feel an attachment to this baby girl in any way. It came from her body - it hadn't come from her heart. This baby instantly reminded her of all the mistakes she ever made in her life and now this child was the biggest mistake of her life. She couldn't send it back to where it had come from. It was now her responsibility and she wanted nothing to do with it. She looked at the baby and saw a tiny bright red birthmark on her shoulder and said to her mother, "Her name is Scarlet." From that moment forward she had a name.

Gilles passed from an unexpected heart attack five years later and left Francine alone to face the world; and her daughter and granddaughter clung to her apron strings for support financially and for mental support. Marie-Jose was never the same after that night. She never went to university or continued her studies in music or anything else in her life. She began drinking more alcohol after her father's death and his watchful eye to keep her in line and stop her from destroying herself, but it was all too late. Marie-Jose was an alcoholic, and she would need many hours of counselling to bring her back from the dark hole she had fallen into. Francine couldn't spend too much time trying to work on Marie-Jose because she was basically a mother to Scarlet now. It wasn't a job she asked for, but she loved her daughter, and she adored little Scarlet. It was never work for her; it was about raising responsible children. By the time Scarlet was in middle school her mother was a full time drunk. One day on a booze run to get more of the almighty elixir, she bumped into a woman who said to her, "I can work with you to remove your pain."

Intrigued Marie-Jose said to her, "Really. What is my pain?"

"Your loss. Something was taken from you. You need to fight to get it back or you will fade into oblivion. I am a therapist. I can lead you on a path to salvation. Only you can decide to take the necessary steps to regaining your vitality. Your soul called out to me." She professed and passed a card to Marie-Jose. "You know she's still in there. Let her back out. It's time." And she walked away.

She sat on the sofa in the living room feeling angry with this woman. How the hell does she know what I need or what I want. She was feeling rage come over her like walking into a sauna fully clothed. She picked up the house telephone and dialed the number of Clara Humboldt as shown on the card. The number began to ring and then a voice answered, "Hello, this is Clara, how can I help you." She spoke.

"Hello. You saw me at the liquor store today and gave me your card. You said I am broken; how can you tell?" Marie-Jose asked.

"Because you called me." She replied.

That was the last drink that Marie-Jose ever had. She started meeting with Clara on a weekly basis and began climbing out of the rut she had allowed herself to fall into. She started spending more time with Scarlet and her mother and began singing opera again. Week by week she fought to regain her life as a free spirit filled with hope and gratitude and put her past behind her. She had decided to be the champion her parents had raised her to be. Marie-Jose was empowered once again to take on the world and all its challenges. She was a human being again and no longer just a victim. Those days were behind her now. Scarlet noticed the turnaround in her mother, but she dared not say anything to draw attention to it in fear that she would relapse and fall back into despair. She was more than happy to have her mother acting so positive and Grandma Francine was delighted to have the help and the conversations back in the house. Things were slowly turning around, and Scarlet wanted to be a member of a functioning family again.

***

When Jimmy Smits was on the phone with Serge explaining the details of the Bedwell Bay situation, he could hear the delight in his voice about the team's accomplishments. He could not believe his luck vis-à-vis Dianne Fletcher falling into the ocean and drowning and, Cindy Denton accidently breathing in some Anthrax and passing later that night was music to his ears. None of the staff ever actually knew if anyone would ever be paid the million dollars but none of them ever asked Jimmy what ever happened with any of the candidates. The group enjoyed the lifestyle and they all still especially liked killing people. If anything, the ladies were cutting into their fun by taking the lethal part of their jobs away. They knew it was temporary, but they were all in no rush to seek employment elsewhere. Possibly the future of their business was to continue to have old ladies do their bidding, but it could become so much more. The real mystery was - could old ladies remain invisible in public long enough to commit murders, without ever being noticed, and as it turns out they could. This idea could grow into so much more in the years to come. So far Serge had only sent the million dollars to Louise Gagnon and then they had to relieve her of her duties because she was becoming too public when the Montreal Police continued to show her blurred image on the local TV stations asking the public for help in finding this old lady. Her disappearance was necessary, and she managed to not get killed when she performed her assignment. Serge had truly decided to not pay any of the women but when Willow and Louise knocked off Benoit Dupuis, who was Guy Tremblay's right-hand man, he was so delighted he couldn't help himself. He knew that Benoit taking political office was going to be an obstacle he didn't want to live with, and those two women had made his life a lot easier that day. Serge was pleased with his team for all the splendid work they had done with this new senior assailants idea and wanted to demonstrate some kind of show of gratitude to the Juste Droite Armee, but he really didn't know what he should do to show them his appreciation. In the past he kept it simple by giving them all lots of money. Pats on the back were Jimmy's thing. He always wanted to stay in the background and just make money and try his hardest to destroy other peoples' lives. Jimmy piped up with a suggestion, "How about if the team all meets at your place in the Muskoka's in Ontario. It is a beautiful place, and it's well hidden from the outside world Serge, so you can maintain your privacy. The team would love the place and you only need to bring along one of your chefs to keep the group fed for a few days. Most of them barely drink and they all exercise themselves to death, so they won't be eating a ton of your food. What do you think of that idea Serge?" Jimmy asked.

"There is a lot of merit to what you have proposed, Jimmy. You said we have exhausted our supply of seniors for the moment, and we have not discussed our next round of sanctions that need to occur so we do have a bit of a lull currently and it would be nice to actually meet these people face-to-face finally. I do have some other engagements that I could change around so yes, I like your plan, Jimmy. We could all meet at the cottage for a few days of R & R. There are plenty of rooms and we'll have a housekeeper head there ahead of time to get everything tidied up and ready for us. It could be just what the doctor ordered. I don't think I've taken a day off to do anything this year. It sounds like a terrific plan Jimmy. Can I leave it with you to contact the team and give them an address and a map?" Serge said.

"Yes, of course sir. I would be honoured to look after this for you. I will contact the team and make all the necessary arrangements. This will be an excellent lift for the team Serge because they were a bit down that all the ladies except Louise perished. It wasn't their fault, but they do get a bit attached to these people only to watch them die in some bizarre set of circumstances." Jim said.

"Jimmy they all knew what they were signing up for. The tasks didn't come as a major surprise. They knew on day one there was always a chance for things to wrong and when they do, people die. A side effect of the business we're in." Serge explained.

"You are absolutely correct sir. They all had knowledge of the risks involved and made their own decisions to move ahead or walk away. But you have admitted that one million dollars is still a nice piece of money." Jimmy smiled and rubbed his fingers together.

Jim contacted the team and passed along instructions as to where and when this gets together would take place. The only people among the group that had not ever seen Serge face-to-face were Scarlet Larsen and Tim Dixon. The rest of the team had never been in the same room at one time with Serge. Jim was excited to have a few days with his colleagues when they were just acting like normal human beings. Maybe they could play a game of Monopoly?

***

A year ago, Scarlet was at her grandmother's house helping to organize some old boxes filled with aged documents and other useless items when she became intrigued with some papers that looked very official like they had been created by the Government of Canada. She shifted through page after page of some of her father's business contacts, company documents and forms that had not found their way to the dumpster. She glanced at the top of one page, and it was a birth certificate. Scarlet pulled it out and away from the other papers and read this one carefully. It was her proof of birth in Quebec. She noticed that her father had signed as the Power of Attorney of her and not her natural father, who she had never met or ever heard anything said about him. He was a complete mystery to Scarlet for her entire life and she was the type of kid that didn't ask a lot of questions. When she was told to mind her place, she did. She continued to scan through the heap of papers looking for anything further, but it seemed she had come to the end of the trail on this information. Scarlet picked up the birth certificate and walked into the kitchen where her grandmother was preparing some food and held the document out in front of her and said, "Did you ever meet my real dad, Nana? This form says that grandpa is my legal guardian, and my father never signed the certificate. Did you actually know this man?" She quizzed her Nana.

Once she got over the shock, Francine pulled herself together and admitted "Yes, I did. I saw him once about a week after your mother's high school graduation. He came by the house to pick up your mother to go on a date. Grandpa was so angry because he didn't get out of the car and come inside to meet us and say hello and honking for a woman to come out for a date was just not okay with Gilles. After that we never saw or heard from him again." Francine replied.

"So do you know who he is?" She continued.

"I have no idea at all. I am embarrassed to tell you that I can't remember his name. It was a French name, but it escapes me now. Why don't you just ask your mother?" Francine suggested.

"She has never talked to me about it. She has forever kept all that part of her life totally clandestine. I always assumed that one day she may feel like sharing but I was okay with not knowing. You and grandpa never brought up the topic, so I figured I better not fan the flames, if you know what I mean." She spoke.

Just then her cell phone lit up and she excused herself from the room and took the call from Jimmy. He explained to her that the team was going to take some R & R time and meet at Serge's summer cottage in the Muskoka's in Gravenhurst and just hang out, drink beer, play games, and try to act like normal people. When she found out the entire team from across the country would be joining them for the festivities, she became excited. She could finally put a face to the name that she had been speaking with for the last couple of years. Besides, she loved Gravenhurst and seeing all the leaves changing colour. It could be lots of fun. Jim promised to text the details and hung up the phone.

She walked back into the kitchen and sat down at the kitchen table and took a sip of her black coffee. Marie-Jose had entered the room and was pouring some hot water into the teapot to steep the brew for a minute.

"Who was that on the phone dear?" Her mother asked her.

"It was one of the men I work with. We are all going to Gravenhurst Ontario for a company retreat. Should be a fun thing and I will finally get to meet my employer face to face. Can't wait." Scarlet said.

Her mother picked up the teapot and began carrying it to the table when Scarlet said, "I will finally meet the secretive and illusive Serge Bouchard." The teapot dropped from her hand and crashed onto the floor breaking into a million pieces.

Marie-Jose snapped her head to face Scarlet and blurted in a panicked voice, "Why did you say that name?" She had turned white, and her hands were trembling. She reached out to get some balance from the back of a kitchen chair as she wobbled like a boxer who had just been punched by his opponent.

"What are you talking about, Mom. That's my boss. Serge Bouchard is the man that pays me to do my job every month. Why are you freaking out?" Scarlet said. She looked over at her grandmother and could see the look of shock on her face.

"That's the name Scarlet. Remember I told you I couldn't remember it anymore. That's the name I couldn't recall. Did she tell you the name today, Scarlet?" Francine asked.

"No Nana, that is the man I currently work for. My immediate boss is Jimmy Smits, and his boss is Serge Bouchard. What are you saying Nana? My boss is my real father. How can this be? It sounds completely impossible." She turned to face her mother who had begun to tend to the broken teapot on the floor. "Mom, what's my father's real name? I have a right to know." She snapped.

"I cannot tell you how this has happened, but your boss is the man that raped me a week after high school prom at a frat party. The only person I have ever told that name to, was Nana. I never even told my dad because I knew he would go and kill him and would then spend the rest of his life in prison and that wasn't going to work for me. He is the reason

I went to therapy for ten years. I still have never trusted a man again in my life because of that night. How the HELL are you working for this bastard. Does he know you are his daughter? Does he?" Marie-Jose yelled.

"There is no way he knows. Remember when you legally changed your last name all those years ago to Larsen so there is no chance that he knows who I really am. Are we sure it's the same guy. Maybe it's just the same name and not the same guy…maybe." She said recognizing the look on her mother's face. It was the right guy.

"Oh my God. How has this man found me after all these years?" Marie-Jose burst out!

"He hasn't sweetie. This is just a coincidence. A fluke. He has not been looking for you, ever. He never showed back up to take responsibility for his actions and he still has no idea where or who you are. It is amazing that in all of Canada you managed to find your real father, without even trying." Francine said.

The three generations of women chatted about the past and Marie-Jose was able to release more of her pent-up emotions. She was finally able to rid herself at last of that horrible man that took advantage of her all those years ago. They all had an opportunity to share what impact Serge Bouchard had on each of their lives, but they were stronger and better equipped to handle so much more now. With age comes maturity and the ability to sweep all your problems under the rug. Sometimes however, it's better to throw out the old rug and just get a new one. As they say, a new rug sweeps clean?

Chapter Eighteen

Serge Bouchard was driven to the cottage on the Friday so his staff would have the opportunity to tidy the house, change the linens, and add fresh towels. It would also give a chance for Chloe, the chef, to do some food preparation before all the guests arrived for their stay. Serge never traveled alone anymore so he was accompanied by his personal bodyguards Simone Baston and Claude Durand who had been under his employ for over five years. They were both massive in size, tough as leather and loyal to their boss and they were both ready to do whatever had to be done to protect him. They both grew up in northern Quebec and learned from an early age how to handle a wide variety of firearms. They then became proficient with explosives when they helped remove stubborn tree stumps and other obstructions that needed a little extra help to eradicate. Neither man had ever worn a suit in their lives before coming on board to work for Serge, but it was part of the job and they both desired to change their location and lifestyle because they had both been in the bush for most of their lives. Once they arrived at the cottage, the two men checked the grounds perimeter to be sure there was no unwanted guests hanging about. He had an independent power station on the property to supply electrical power to the house and the ground's that had the ability to light up like a Christmas tree. The cottage was your run-of-the-mill ten thousand square foot summer cabin with all the amenities that you'd expect at a luxury hotel in downtown Toronto. The driveway was a long, sweeping road that was almost a mile long so once you were at the cottage, you'd think of any excuse to not walk down to the end of it unless it was necessary. The property had a main house and then another large building that housed the guest bedrooms because Serge did not like his guests to sleep in the same house as himself. The one level bedroom building had ten identical bedroom suites with a king size bed, a small sitting area, an ensuite washroom, and glass sliding doors that walked out to a massive wooden plank ground level deck that ran the length of the structure. All the finishes were top quality and done in fashionable fabrics, colours, and furnishings. The main house had an enormous living room, great room, and a dining room that could sit sixteen people comfortably. The kitchen was open and inviting and the main feature of the cottage was an island that had ten counter stools across the front for guest to gather. Off to one side it had a smaller eating table that sat ten people and a couple of spare matching chairs in case the group was larger. The interior was right out of the pages of Architectural Digest and Serge's design team had entered the project into the Canadian Design Awards and had won a Gold Medal for their work. The cottage had the best of everything and yet he only came to the place once or twice a year. Serge stayed mostly in his downtown Toronto apartment or in his Westmount house in Montreal. Traveling was no longer something that he wished because it took him away from his businesses and from sleeping in familiar beds. He loved getting a good night's rest but found it virtually impossible to get quality sleep time when he was away from his own creature comforts. Serge had arranged for Chef Chloe and housekeeper/house cleaner Jeanette to arrive on the Thursday evening so they could prep the house and the food before all the team arrived and he always wanted to impress his guests like they were in a Five Star Hotel. He entered the cottage, went straight to his office, sat down in front of his computer and started working, while Simone and Claude continued their sweep of the building and property. About forty minutes later the two returned to his office to report that the property was secure. He smiled and leaned back in his chair and was actually intrigued with the thought that he was finally going to meet his so-called Ministry of Special Projects team in person. Serge loved to show off his fortune to others, so having the group to his cottage was a wonderful opportunity to put the unfamiliar faces to the names.

The following morning the team was to arrive around noon and weather permitting, they would have cocktails and appetizers on the patio by the swimming pool. Later that night, they would feast on rack of lamb with all the trimmings. He asked the chef to select a few vintage

Amarone wines to compliment the meal followed by one of his favourite desserts, Crepes Suzette. The cottage was warm and cozy with the two massive fireplaces roaring and filled with the wonderful aromas of the chef's divine cooking techniques and scented candles throughout the interior. At eleven o'clock Jimmy showed up first and knocked on the front door. Instantly it swung open, and Simone was standing in the doorway. "Jim how are you doing my friend," he said as he wrapped his arms around Jimmy and gave him a big hug. "I haven't seen you in a bit. Hope all is good with you."

"Hello Simone, so nice to see you. I was hoping that you would be here for this get together. Where is Claude?" Jim asked.

"He's here somewhere," Simone said as Claude was coming out of the great room and walked over and embraced Jimmy with lots of back slapping and smiles.

"I am so glad to see the both of you. It has been too long between visits. We should be doing this far more often. I assume that Serge is here somewhere, in his office no doubt." Jim said.

Jim stepped inside and the door closed behind him. He went down the hall to Serge's office to greet him. No sooner had Jim gone around the corner, someone else had arrived at the home. Simone opened the door to find Luc, Tim, and Laurent all standing at the front door with their overnight bags in tow. As everyone began chatting and raising the volume level, Thomas pulled up in his car and scooted into the house while the door was still ajar with guests. The group of men all congregated in the entrance hall shaking hands and saying their hellos when Jimmy returned to the foyer and began back slapping and reveling in the positive vibes taking place.

"I've got an idea gents. Let's get these bags stowed in your rooms and then we can get to relaxing, and possibly a few drinks." He laughed and picked up his travel suitcase.

Jeanette suddenly appeared from somewhere in the cottage and escorted the group of men to the guest building to assign them rooms and to drop off their grips. Ten minutes later they all met in the kitchen and started mixing drinks and telling stories. The room was filled with laughter and joy.

***

The drive was pleasant for Scarlet and Marie-Jose up Hwy 11 to the Marriott Gravenhurst. They pulled into the drive through at the front of the hotel and went inside to collect the room key for Marie-Jose. Scarlet picked up the room key and drove her around the parking lot and pulled up near the room. Once her mother was settled Scarlet had to be off to meet with the others at Serge's cottage. The Marriot was not far from Serge's place, so she didn't bother stopping for gas at the Petro Canada located a block away. The drive up had given the women a chance to discuss so many unspoken things that had been building up over the years and it was an opportunity for Marie-Jose to tell her daughter what she had been through as a young woman and how the one event had truly ruined her life. She was happy that she had Scarlet as the years went by but in the beginning of her life Marie-Jose was upset and depressed and it took several years until she felt like she could actually love Scarlet. So many emotions were released, and the two women felt a bond stronger than it had ever been. The time in the car allowed Scarlet to come clean and tell her mother what she did for paycheques. She had never really told her mom anything about it but with this newfound information, the two wanted to express themselves openly. She tried to explain to Marie-Jose that she, from an early age, lacked empathy. She wasn't sure what had happened to her to make her this way, but she didn't really feel anything towards her victims over the years she had been doing this work. Marie-Jose blamed herself saying, "I should have hugged you more and spent more time with you, but I just couldn't." Whenever she was with Scarlet, it reminded her of Serge, and she went back ten more steps. Marie-Jose didn't ever say to Scarlet that she didn't approve of what she was doing for work because her heart had also grown cold and hard over a lifetime of trying to climb out of the hole that she felt Serge had pushed her into. She instantly forgave her and only hoped that the two would now have a better understanding of who each other was.

“I must head off to Serge’s cottage now, but I will come by and pick you up tomorrow at some point so please leave your cell phone on and be sure to answer when I call. If you need me Mom, just give me a ring, okay.” Scarlet said.

“I am looking forward to a hot bath and some room service and good night's sleep. See you tomorrow sweetheart.” Marie-Jose said as she hugged and kissed her daughter goodbye.

Scarlet walked back out to her car and slid into the driver's seat and opened the glove box to see two of her favorite guns waiting to be deployed. She pulled them out and checked the magazines to make sure they were both loaded and ready. She put her 9mm into her purse, left the Baretta in the glove box, started the engine, and headed off down the highway to Serge Bouchard’s fine country home.

About thirty minutes later she arrived at the property and drove down the extensive driveway to the cottage. Scarlet was absolutely impressed with the home as she knocked on the door. The door opened and Jim was standing inside with his arms open to give her a friendly hug and greeting. She left her grip and followed Jim into the kitchen area where all the men were sitting and drinking a variety of alcohol concoctions making more noise than one could possibly believe and jumped right into the mix. She grabbed a drink and got right into the conversation without missing a beat. The group had seen each other recently but they all still liked each other and were looking forward to having a forum where they could just chat casually about the ups and downs of the job. Simone and Claude appeared and introduced themselves to the people they hadn't met before and no sooner had they arrived, they were gone. They took the protection of their boss seriously and were forever vigilant. Chloe continued to bring tasty treats out of the oven and brought them over to the group to nosh on. The temperature outside was a smidge cool so the group decided not to venture into the swimming pool that day and thought that perhaps tomorrow would be warmer for that activity. The room decibel level was on the rise and the group was having a terrific time when Chef Chloe announced, "Dinner will be served in the dining room in ten minutes so please allow yourselves enough time to get freshened up before we eat. Mr. Bouchard will join us in the dining room. Please be prompt." Chloe said and continued with her preparations.

Ten minutes later the group gathered in the dining room and noticed that there were name tags for the seating arrangements. Everyone took a seat at the beautifully decorated table and waited. Soon after Serge made his grand entrance into the room wearing a bright smile with white teeth showing in a sincere look of happiness. He walked around the table and shook each persons' hand and poised himself at the head of the table.

“Shall we?” Serge said as the group all settled into their chairs and Jeanette came into the room and began pouring the wine that had already been decanted.

Serge was not an ugly man, but he wasn’t attractive. He was smart and he knew how to be suave and win over people quickly. Always full of poignant questions and with some knowledge on a huge set of topics and interests that made him so engaging. The group chatted and dined on the succulent food that Chloe had prepared and enjoyed the company with the warm feeling one gets from long-time friends when you get into a room with them, and it seems like you just saw them all yesterday. Serge projected a confident man that was clear with what he was after and somehow seemed to know how to achieve it. Scarlet was filled with rage to know that this is the man that caused so much heartache and pain in her mother’s and grandparents lives but she had to control her attitude and her temper and see where this weekend was heading. The dinner plates were cleared from the table and then Jeanette brought in the bar cart filled with all the best brandies and cognacs from around the globe and offered everyone an after-dinner drink. Chloe reappeared and brought in a mobile cooking station and wheeled the unit over to stand beside Serge at the head of the table. With a flick of switch the burner came to life and she began to prepare the Crepes Suzette for dessert. She put on a show for the table and demonstrated her skills to the group as they all stared in awe of the spectacle as she served it up to each person. The result was glorious. She then vanished with her cooking tools as quickly as she had appeared. The food was as good as any restaurant they had ever eaten in before and Scarlet began to wonder if Serge ate like this every night at home seeing that he had a live-in chef. She wondered how fat she would become having this wonderful problem to bear every night of the week. Scarlet stared hard at Serge every chance she could to try and spot any family resemblance with her, but it just wasn't there. She wondered if her mom had the right guy. Maybe it was a different Serge Bouchard. When the table had completed their desserts and were relaxing around the table Serge finally spoke up and said, "I think we all need to discuss our success with the seniors and where do we go from here." He looked down the table to Jimmy and winked and gave a nod. Jim got up and reached into his inside suit jacket pocket and pulled out a bunch of white envelopes and passed one out to each member of the team. Scarlet took her envelope and opened it to reveal its contents of one hundred thousand dollars in cash. The dinner party guests were taken aback however, they had all been paid handsomely for the work they had performed for Serge previously, so it was not a shock, but it certainly was nice to receive.

"I have been considering keeping the "Ministry" together and expanding our services to other countries that might want the same type of work done. This could be an opportunity for us to take this concept to the next level and would obviously generate millions of dollars in cash for all of us. All the seniors that had participated in the program perished except one, so it was a highly affordable decisive test for the idea. It was never the plan to have these fine women die while performing the jobs that they volunteered for but, when you play with fire...you are going to get burned. I formed this group to help rid this country of parasites and you all did a fantastic job. So, the question to the team is simple, do we keep it going? I wanted to meet all of you because of your dedication and perseverance and to celebrate your accomplishments but I ask you, should we keep moving ahead or do we keep it on Canadian soil?" Serge asked the group.

Jimmy immediately piped up and said, "You have been my friend for a long time, but I got to be honest, I couldn't imagine doing anything else. I do not see myself as a killer, but I know that this is how I make my money to live my life, so for me it's easy, I'm in for whatever comes next."

The group at the table all began nodding positive affirmations in response to Jim's statement. They all enjoyed having lots of spending money and they all got to quench their bizarre appetite for killing people. The conversation flourished into all kinds of current ideas and positive feedback about the program and next steps. They were definitely all in. Serge sat at the head of the table and relished in the knowledge that his team still had the ambition to do more tasks, and this would mean more money. It was a red-letter day at the Bouchard house. They continued to talk and exchange ideas and, while this was all taking place, they were all finally getting the chance to meet Serge in a completely unique way. He had always been a voice on the phone, Jimmy's boss, but now it was interactive and creating a harmony amongst the group. Suddenly, he seemed like a real person. Except for Scarlet, she still saw Serge as the son of a gun that stripped away her mother's youth and, her dignity. He had violated her mother, and he must pay for what he did. She couldn't let that deed go unpunished. After another hour of camaraderie at the table the men decided to go out on the patio and smoke some exclusive imported cigars that Serge had managed to get his hands on. Scarlet moved herself into the kitchen and chatted with Chloe as she finished tidying up the space and preparing for the following mornings breakfast. She then felt isolated from the group. She peered outside and no longer saw them as colleagues, she now saw all of them as predators. Just another group of arrogant, horny men who really were bad people. "Thou shall not kill," the bible has told us, however; sometimes you just must break the rules.

Scarlet had a tough time sleeping that night. She had planned to be up at the crack of dawn to see what time

Simone and Claude their rounds of the property did, as they did several times a day. The two men walked by the exterior of her room in the guest house at just after 7:00 am. The one thing about these boys is they were consistent. They did their rounds like they did everything, to the letter.

They came into the main house one by one in the morning and Scarlet could see that the boys had stayed up late into the night drinking, smoking, and shooting the breeze. Chloe was in the kitchen ready to make eggs, toast, waffles or whatever else they felt like eating. No surprise to her that they all had a cup of black coffee and slice of toast. With all the heavy drinking the night before they were all a touch hungover. Serge came into the room and announced that he had a few team building exercises that he wanted to do and then they would spend the afternoon playing yard games and chilling out. Chloe had mentioned to Scarlet earlier that morning that for dinner she was preparing Chicken Coco Vin which was one of his favourites and this also meant that Serge had the entire day planned for the team and she assumed that attendance was not an option. When she had finished her coffee and oatmeal, she headed back to her room to change into appropriate attire for the day's schedule and to call her mom and fill her in on all the latest gossip. They made their plans and hung up. She left her room and headed back to the main house to rejoin the others and continue with the day.

Scarlet could not stop looking and listening to every word that Serge spoke trying to attach herself to his mannerism or his style or even his thought process, but she kept drawing a blank. She searched for the connection between them but there was none. It wasn't psychosomatic, if she had any similarities to Serge, it was only the DNA kind. Scarlet didn't understand why she was trying so hard to find a common thread but, she had been raised without a father and her mind knew that this hunk of flesh happened to be her birth father, but he was just another man, like every other man she had passed on the street or had to sanction over her life. He was nothing to her but a disappointment.

At 6:00 am the following morning Scarlet was up donning her jogging attire and out the door scoping out the trails running through and around the massive property. She was looking for the ideal ambush area for this morning's responsibilities. She looked until she found a spot where the two bodyguards would meet and then continue their rounds together until they returned to the main house and continued their duties. She slipped in behind a stand of thick bush and crouched down and waited for the two brutes to walk into her vantage point and she would make her move. She unholstered her weapon and controlled her breathing, slow down, relax, in through the nose, out through the mouth, and then they appeared and started walking towards her. Three, two, one, she stepped out from behind the branches, and it clearly startled the two men, but when they saw it was Scarlet, they both smiled and said, “Good morning.” Before they could react, she aimed the pistol and shot both men and down they went. She instantly walked over to the fallen bodies, took careful aim, and added a bullet into both men’s heads. “One has to be sure in this business,” she thought to herself. She pushed the bodies off the main path with her feet and then covered the two with some sticks and fallen branches she had collected earlier from around the forest floor. Once they were undetectable, she ran back down the driveway to about the halfway point to her car that she had moved there earlier that morning. She started the car and headed off down to the nearby highway.

A couple of hours later Scarlet returned to the house and she parked her car and tried to stay out of sight of the others. She changed from jogging attire to business attire and headed for the main house. She came into the great room and was met with smiles and warmth which made her realize that she actually liked these men and was getting used to being around them in a casual setting, rather than hunkered down some place waiting for the right opportunity to jump out and shoot someone.

“Can I get you anything?” Chloe asked Scarlet. “Something to eat or drink?”

“No thank you Chloe, but many thanks for checking in with me.” Scarlet replied.

Shortly after, Serge came into the great room and began saying his good mornings and interacting with his guests when there was a knock at the front door. Jeanette happened to be walking by the door and swung it open to a stranger. It was an old woman who a clearly fallen and hurt herself and was bleeding from the hands and knees. She had a rub rash on her cheek, and she was weary on her feet.

"Oh, my goodness, are you okay? What happened to you? Chloe inquired.

"I was taking a nature walk and seemed to have gotten lost…again. It seems like every time I go out of the home for a spell, I end up lost or hurt, or both." The old woman explained.

"Come into the kitchen and let's get you cleaned up." Chloe said.

She led the old lady through the foyer and into the kitchen area where she sat down on a counter stool so Chloe could tend to her wounds. Scarlet walked into the kitchen and headed directly over to Chloe and whispered to her, "Leave now. Find Jeanette and leave now." She whispered, staring directly into her eyes and making sure her message was perfectly clear. Chloe put the first aid kit down on the counter and quietly slipped away. Scarlet came around the corner and looked in the room and could see that Serge was sitting on a large, upholstered chair and leaning back and enjoying himself. He noticed that Scarlet had returned to the room and said, "What happened to our visitor? Has she been mended and sent on her way?" Serge asked.

"No Serge. She wanted to come and meet you and thank you for your kindness." Scarlet explained as Marie-Jose turned the corner and entered the room. Nobody on the team had ever met her mother so they all thought she was an old lady wanting to say thank you. She stared at Serge, momentarily frozen in fear, and then asked, "Do you recognize me, Serge? We met when we were much younger?" She continued to stare at him until he said, "Sorry, I am quite sure we have never seen each other before today. I am glad that we were able to provide first aid to you to get you back on your way. Safe travels." He said and went back to looking at his cell phone.

"Actually Serge, I would like you to meet my mother, Miss Marie Jose Larsen, formerly Marie-Jose Cote. Does that name bring any memories back?" Scarlet asked.

The rooms vibes were rapidly changing, and the other guests could feel the tension was rising. Scarlet removed a gun from her pocket and pointed it in the direction of the men and said, "This issue had nothing to do with any of you. I am however, going to ask you all to remain seated and DO NOT make any sudden movements because that could get you killed. My mother just wants to have a conversation with an old friend and, then be on her way. I hope that sounds okay with all of you."

All the men, including Serge, all nodded in agreement. No one moved a muscle. They knew what Scarlet was capable of doing. Serge was searching his memory banks trying to put together the pieces, and then it hit, Marie-Jose, the sock king's daughter. The young woman he raped all those years ago. He looked at her face and it was almost like she was going through a time warp, and she was shape shifting into that pretty little high school girl he knew decades before. Marie-Jose could see the recognition come across his face and she knew he was the right guy. She pulled from her pocket a gun with a silencer attached to it and aimed it directly at Serge's face.

"How could you rape me and leave me for dead Serge? How could you be so cold and callous?" Marie-Jose asked.

Serge was pressing the button on his watch that let Simone know and Claude that he was in a crisis. He continued to press the button until Scarlet said, "They're dead. Claude and Simone are not going to burst through the door and save you. Nothing is going to save you now, you repulsive old bastard."

The group was still. No one was going to move an inch. Scarlet turned to her mother and said, "If you have anything to say to him, now would be the time to get it out." Scarlet added.

She was brandishing her firearm in his face when he looked her in the eye and stammered to her in a harsh and aggressive manner, "You were a stuck-up little bitch when you were growing up and I see you have become a grown up and bitter little bitch now. I apologize for nothing, so go screw yourself."

Thump…thump, thump. Marie-Jose put three rounds into victim. She paused for a moment when Scarlet instructed, "Remember what I told you Mom, a head shot is proof of death. One more please."

Thump. The bullet entered his head through his forehead. Serge was dead.

Jimmy was sitting in a deep comfy chair and feeling vulnerable when he spoke, "So now what happens?"

"Well, you heard Serge, the program is a success, and we all need a new boss. Is there any chance that you may be interested in a new position? I have always respected you Jim, and I have been 100% loyal. This was a complete and total coincidence that I would end up working for the man that ruined my mother life. She had to seek her revenge, and I couldn't stop her from getting it. I know that all of you know that he had it coming. If it wasn't my mom, it was going to be someone else. He didn't deserve to live after what he did. So, Jimmy, what do think about taking over. Let's face facts, you were always the boss of the Ministry. We know our services are needed and as it turns out, we now have the possibility of going offshore to find other opportunities. What do you say Jim, are you in?" Scarlet asked still holding a gun and pointing it in his direction.

"Are you kidding me? You spared my life and I get a promotion. I'm in guys. I have loved working with all of you and if all of you are okay with me moving to the number one chair, I would be honoured to occupy that distinction. And, if this is the case, then I suggest we all get the hell out of here ASAP and reconvene at another time and another place. Leave your phones on and we will talk soon." Jimmy replied.

They left the room, headed to the guest house, and exited the building in a hurry. Within a few minutes the team was racing their cars down the driveway like a group of kids partying when the parents come home, and everyone has to leave in a rush.

Scarlet and her mother pulled the car out onto Hwy 11 and headed south back towards civilization. Scarlet grabbed her purse and handed it to her mother and asked her to open it up. Marie-Jose opens the zipper and looked inside and found the white envelope stuffed in amongst its contents and removed it from the bag. She peeked inside and could see the wads of new bills filling the package, "Where did you get this?" Marie-Jose asked.

"From work. I got a bonus that I would like to give to you and Nana. I can assure you Mom that I have plenty more, so this isn't a hardship. Besides, I think you will be working a lot more in the future. All the times we would talk about travelling the world well, now we can, and we will get paid handsomely for doing it. You're still able to get around and I can show you how to use a gun, mind you, you did make quick work of Serge Bouchard. I have shot lots of bad people in my life but when you disposed of Serge, I could just see the potential. His "Senior Assailant" concept wasn't such a bad idea. I don't know about you Mom, but I need to go pee and get a hot cup of coffee in me." Scarlet said.

"I would love to get a cup of coffee, and to travel the world with my child, rubbing people out. It's the most exciting retirement news I've had in years." She mused as they pulled off the highway into a gas station with a Tim Horton's.

The End

www.ingramcontent.com/pod-product-compliance
Lightning Source LLC
Chambersburg PA
CBHW031138020426
42333CB00013B/434
* 9 7 8 1 9 1 7 0 9 5 1 8 1 *